INTRODUCTIONS
TO
ENGLISH LITERATURE

Edited by
BONAMY DOBRÉE

Volume V

THE PRESENT AGE

THE
PRESENT AGE
FROM 1914

By
EDWIN MUIR

THE CRESSET PRESS
LONDON

First Published 1939

PRINTED IN GUERNSEY, C.I., BRITISH
ISLES, BY THE STAR AND GAZETTE LTD.

NOTE

I HAVE made no attempt in this book to deal with contemporary American literature, or with Irish or Scottish literature. It is true that two of the chief writers in this survey are American, and two more are Irish; but it is impossible to give any idea of the present state of English literature without referring to Eliot and Pound, Yeats and Joyce. On the other hand, there is a vast body of American literature, and a considerable body of Irish and Scottish, which I have not attempted to touch, and which would require a different treatment altogether, since the conditions which have given rise to them are different.

My chapter on poetry is more detailed than any of the others, not because all the poets dealt with are greater than all the novelists or general writers, but because it seems to me that poetry must be treated in some detail or not treated at all.

I wish to acknowledge my great indebtedness to Professor Bonamy Dobrée for his generous help and for many invaluable suggestions.

E.M.

CONTENTS

EDITOR'S PREFACE

IF there is a danger of literature becoming separated from life, and at times the danger becomes actuality, there is a still greater one of the same thing happening in the study of literature. For one thing, it is apt to become that most arid of studies, literary history, in which history is largely, and literature, in any real meaning of the word, entirely ignored. The literature of the past is only of value in so far as it has significance to-day, just as history is only of use if it can throw a light upon the contemporary scene. But in the same way as history becomes illuminating by study, by finding out not only what people did, but why they did it, what circumstances, thoughts and emotions brought them to act, so we enlarge the boundaries within which the literature of the past has value if we gain an insight into the circumstances, thoughts and feelings which produced not only the writers, but also the readers of any particular period.

People of different ages speak different languages; not that the words are necessarily different, but the implications are. We of the twentieth century mean very little when we speak of the "social virtues", whereas to an eighteenth-century writer the phrase implied a whole philosophy of civilisation. For us to understand what Donne meant when he wrote

> On man heavens influence works not so,
> But that it first imprints the ayre,
> Soe soule into the soule may flow. . . .

we have to be at least aware of a whole body of philosophic thought, we might say of philosophic apprehension, to which most of us are likely to be strangers, but which was common at the beginning of the seventeenth century. Thus one of the objects of literary study should be to enable us to translate the language of another day into that of our own, which we can only do if we realise that these divergencies of expression are not merely a question of literary allusion, but of what entered the minds of educated people every day, coloured the spectacles through which they looked at life, and moulded the form in which they uttered their feelings. Thus it is not altogether idle to ponder why Ben Jonson should have written:

> What beckoning ghost besprent with April dew
> Hails me so solemnly to yonder yew
> > (*Elegy on Lady Jane Pawlett*)

while Pope should have preferred:

> What beckoning ghost athwart the moonlit glade
> Invites my steps, and points to yonder shade
> > (*In Memory of an Unfortunate Lady*)

for there is a reason which lies deeper than personal idiosyncrasy.

It has become a platitude to say that an age is reflected in its literature, and like all platitudes the saying has ceased to have any force. Moreover, an age is often much better represented by what is no longer read, than by the works which we still take from our shelves. If, for instance, we try to reconstruct the Restoration period from the plays of the time, we shall get a view which is, to say the least of it, misleading: the age is far better represented by the turgid flood of pamphlets which issued from the inkpots of Penn and Muggleton, Thomas Hicks, John Faldo, and a dozen other forgotten and vituperative sectarians. We tend to read Dryden's plays, or certain of the satires, in preference to his other work, but he is far nearer his age in *Religio Laici* and *The Hind and the Panther* than in his now more popular writings. And if each age brings forth its own recognisable progeny, how is it that Milton and Etherege appeared to-

14

gether? or Thomas Hardy and Max Beerbohm? Each age
has so many facets, that it is difficult to pitch on any as being
its outstanding mirror though each age will have certain
peculiarities not shared by the others. But these peculiarities
are often merely the surface of fashion, accidental rather than
essential, and until we know something of the age, we cannot tell which peculiarity, when explained, can have any
significance for us.

Yet, if it is dangerous to regard literature as the looking-
glass of its time, every age has certain problems which seem to
it to be of major urgency. In the Shakespearian age it was to
incorporate the "new learning" into life; later in the seventeenth century, the politico-religious issue was the important
one; the eighteenth century, again, was lured by a vision of
civilised man. That is to say that each age has its philosophy, its scale of values. But philosophy, which to some extent conditions literature, is itself conditioned, partly by the
way people live, and partly by the influx of thought from
foreign countries, though it is as well to remember that such
thought will only penetrate or take root in a country already
prepared for it. Therefore, the way people live, their social
and political grouping, their economic formation, to some
extent determine the way they write. Much has lately been
made of the influence of economics: too much, for Marx cannot account for Milton, and it is as easy to argue that the
economic development of the eighteenth century was due to
the idea of the universe as defined by Newton as that "Dutch
finance", commercialism, and the expansion of trade, gives a
clue to the philosophy of history which runs through Gibbon's
Decline and Fall. Yet economics have an effect on literature;
we can see it to some extent in *Piers Plowman*, and without the
rise of the middle classes at the end of the seventeenth century
we could not have had Defoe, Steele or Addison; the polite
essayist could not have come into being, quite apart from
whether or not he preached the bourgeois virtues.

The influence of foreign thought is a subject that has
loomed too large, perhaps, in most histories of literature,
mainly because literature has on the whole been treated as

separate from life. The influence of something on somebody has been a favourite subject for theses, and the answers have been as dubious as the theme has been ill-defined. Because Chaucer, having read Dante's

> *Quali i fioretti di noturno gelo*
> *chinati e chiusi, poi che il so gl'imbianca,*
> *si drizzen tutti aperti in loro stelo;*
>
> *tal mi fec' io. . . .*
>
> *(Inferno* II, 127. . . .)

or, more probably, the corresponding lines in the *Filostrato* of Boccaccio, proceeded to sing

> But right as floures, thorugh the colde of night
> Y-closed, stoupen on hir stalkes lowe,
> Redressen hem a-yein the sonne bright,
> And spreden on hir kinde cours by rowe;
> Right so gan. . . .
> . . . .Troilus. . . .
>
> (*Troilus and Criseyde*, II St. 139)

that is not to say that Chaucer was influenced by Dante or by Boccaccio; indeed no prettier contrast to the *Divina Commedia* could be found than *The Canterbury Tales*, though it is clear that there is some connection between them and the *Decameron*. No one really familiar with the comedy of France and England in the seventeenth century, with an understanding of what they were up to, can believe that the English were influenced by the French to more than a superficial degree. Nevertheless, the thought of one country, or of one individual, can very profoundly affect a period, and the scepticism of Montaigne is apparent throughout the seventeenth century from Shakespeare to Halifax. In the same way, German thought obscured the clarity of Coleridge, and puffed the thought and style of Carlyle to an almost intolerable smokiness.

The writer, therefore, is, besides being a unique individual, the product of the forces of his time. However much we may regret it, we have to abandon Shelley's contention that "poets are the unacknowledged legislators of the world", though we need not altogether throw over the position: for though, no doubt, thought does sometimes influence action, it is more usually the successor of deeds, and it will not be denied that Locke is a child of the Revolution just as Hobbes was of the Great Rebellion. It is truer to say with Arnold that poetry is a criticism of life, though not quite true, for literature is, rather, a growth from life itself, a part of life, not its harvest only. We can go further and say that it is so ravelled with life that it can be described also as the soil and the seed. But that a metaphor should lead to such confusion is enough to indicate how closely tangled with life literature is, how complex the relation between them, and how impossible it is to separate one from the other.

.   .   .   .

The object of the Introductions in this series is to give the student some idea of the soil out of which the works of literature grew, so as to be able to grasp with fuller understanding the books mentioned in the Bibliographies. This, then, is not yet another History of English Literature, but rather, to exaggerate a little, a History of England in which not kings, battles, diplomatic or constitutional struggles, nor even economic development, are given pride of place, but literature. As is suitable to our age in which economics have come to be given a high place as determinants not only of our lives, but of our manner of thinking and feeling, and even of our religion, economics will be given more stress than they have hitherto been allowed in books on literature, but not, as some would no doubt wish, to the exclusion of everything else. For instance, though the question of the control of money no doubt played a larger part in the Great Rebellion than we were most of us brought up to believe, it would be absurd to neglect the religious elements in the struggle: indeed, as Professor R. H. Tawney has shown, it was religion itself that largely determined the economic trend of the eighteenth century. The effect of religion on literature is more easily traceable; it begins with Beowulf and runs through the whole, most markedly in the periods where the Church to a large extent stamped the nature of society, or when controversy raged high, as it did from the Reformation—or at least from the time of the *Marprelate Tracts*—to the foundation of the Bank of England. Philosophy also plays an important part, not only as being the matter of much admirable writing, but also in the general attitude towards life exhibited by writers who unconsciously, rather than in full awareness, absorbed the ideas of their time. But philosophy again is affected by economics, for no one can doubt that the individualism of the nineteenth century was largely the result of the Industrial Revolution, and that Carlyle's Cromwell must own as forebears Adam Smith and James Watt. Science also can affect literature, and without Huxley there would probably have been a different Hardy.

Another addition to the view of literature is made in these volumes by giving due place to the sister arts where they rose to any height, or seem to have importance with respect to writing. Thus music had an effect on poetry in the seventeenth century, while painting and architecture affected the poetry, and perhaps the prose, of the eighteenth. Wherever, in short, the literary "movement" of a time seems congruous with that of the other arts, they are included in the survey. Most important of all, however, is the social background, the changes of milieu indicated, say, by the decay of the guilds or the rise of nationalism; for these are the things which most affect the way people live, and therefore what they will most wish to write and to read.

The Bibliographies which form the major part of each volume are designed to give the reader a detailed view of the literature of each period, and being classified and commented will enable him to study or to enjoy either any special branch, or the whole literature of the period. Only the specialist can read everything; but the aim of this series is to enable anyone who so wishes, to get a clear idea of any one period by reading with a certain degree of fervour for a year, a clear notion not only of what was written, but, so to speak, of why and how, from what impulses, with what objects, and in what conditions morally speaking. It is hoped by this method to integrate literature with life, and so give the writings of the past that meaning without which to read is to be baffled, and to miss that greatest of all pleasures, a sense of unity of feeling with the writer of any work. Lacking this, literature is too far separated from living, and can have but little value.

The manner in which English literature has been split up in this series no doubt demands an explanation. There are many ways in which it can be split up. This has been done variously, sometimes rather arbitrarily, by centuries or other irrelevant measuring rods, more often by grouping it around great figures: The Age of Wordsworth and so on: or by literary movements: The Romantic Revival, for instance. These divisions have their uses, but for our purpose here they tend to subordinate life to literature. It is admitted that there is an element of arbitrariness in the present divisions also, but the object is to relate literature to life, disregarding movements, which may only be different aspects of the same thing. The divisions here correspond in the main with social sense; roughly indeed, with what reservations you will, and with contradictions of a rule which cannot be rigid, since human nature refuses to fit into compartments.

In the first period, after the Conquest, you can say with some plausibility (though it is in this period that our structure is weakest) that literature was much more diffused among different classes; it was written for no particular brand of person. Everyone would read *Piers Plowman*, or applaud the miracle plays. There is, it is true, much that is courtly about Chaucer, but there is much that is not. When we get to Spenser, say, we feel that literature is being written for an aristocracy: the drama still maintained its general appeal (though even as early as the moralities and interludes there is a shift away from the people), but it became more and more aristocratic, till under Charles II it was entirely courtly. This period, then, we can describe as the aristocratic period: Donne, Jeremy Taylor, Sir Thomas Browne, Milton, are writers for an aristocracy, and this social sense we may say was established by the Tudors, and exploited by the Stuarts, till it came to an end at the Revolution of 1688. Then, with great suddenness, there appeared a literature written by the middle class, of the middle class, and for the middle class: the pamphleteers, the essayists, and soon Defoe and the novelists. Even the drama changed with startling rapidity, with the anti-aristocratic satire of Farquhar, and the sentimental comedy of Steele.

The ideas of the middle class, with its strong sense, as it then had, of an organised society, gave place in the last century to the idea of individualism, due partly to the French, and partly to the Industrial Revolution. It had been begun by the romantic poets, with their break-away from the idea of "society" so dear to the eighteenth century. It might grieve Shelley to think that he was the forerunner of the excellent Dr. Smiles, but so it is. At all events, individualism dominated literature until the War. But even before that it was breaking down (having somewhat oddly consorted with a blatant imperialism), as can be seen from the plays of Mr. Bernard Shaw, and still more, perhaps, from the novels of Mr. E. M. Forster. The post-War period has its own characteristics; a new twist has been given to our view by the recent investigations into psychology, ethnology, physics, and by the Russian Revolution.

There are, of course, several objections to this sort of division: odd elements appear everywhere: you cannot, for instance, rank Bunyan among aristocratic writers. But some division has to be made along chronological lines. It may be objected that the first period needs at least two volumes: it is so long and so varied. That is true, but the number of works which remain which can be of interest to the general reader are comparatively few, and it was thought better to devote more space to our more recent heritages, as being both fuller of works we are likely to read, and as having a closer influence upon our present-day approach to living.

BONAMY DOBRÉE

20

EDITOR'S NOTE TO VOLUME V

THIS book has not quite the same structure as the other volumes in this series, as it was thought better that a larger proportion should be given to the Introduction, and a smaller to the Bibliography. Since, as Mr. Muir himself suggests, any point of view put forward in this book must be an individual one, unaided by the purgative work of time, it was considered that it would be more illuminating and more stimulating to have a longer discussion of the period than has been given in the earlier volumes.

The bibliography, therefore, is comparatively short, though it contains not only what most of us would consider important, but a considerable amount of what is merely representative. No doubt the omission of certain names will seem to some readers to be a gross oversight, as the inclusion of certain others will appear astonishing: but any writer on his own period must take his own stand; to try to be catholic would be as bad as to have the book compiled by a committee—and good books are not written by committees.

The period is an extremely interesting one, and, at this short distance, richly confused; it is impossible to disentangle action and reaction. The literary scene, naturally, reflects the scene of social and "ideological" disintegration. It has been enlivened by several bright gleams which seemed to presage the opening of doors into better realms—psycho-analysis, ethnology, Marxism, time-philosophies, and new views of the mysterious universe. These developments have certainly influenced our view of life, and have made themselves felt, directly or indirectly, in our literature; but it will take a few decades before their relative values are sifted out. Two literary and critical magazines have been foremost in this period, *The London Mercury* which began under the editorship of Sir John Squire in 1920, and has varied in quality; and *The Criterion*, from 1923, under the editorship of Mr. T. S. Eliot, now becoming more devoted to philoso-phico-theological ideas. A perusal of these, together with *The Times Literary Supplement*, would give a fair view of the literary activity of the period since the War. *New Verse*, the most vivacious of the newer journals, will be invaluable to students of the younger generation of poets.

There are perhaps two distinctive signs in the reading of this period. The first is the popularity of biography, seeming to betoken a new interest in individuals; the second the issue of cheap books of first-rate quality. There have been series of cheap biographies; and as regards books in general, while the old cheap series such as the World's Classics and Everyman have expanded their lists, other series of good contemporary works, at an even lower price, such as the Pelican, have made a wide appeal to the public. These signs are of good augury, and perhaps indicate the formation of a new reading public, larger than the old, though at present less selective, to which authors, at present scarcely knowing for whom they write, will be able to address themselves.

B.D.

THE PRESENT AGE

CHAPTER I

GENERAL BACKGROUND

THREE periods may be distinguished in the history of
the present century. The century began with a belief
in the future, lost that belief and relapsed into a mood of
hopelessness tempered by faith in the past, and has now
returned to a modified belief in the future, coloured by the
intervening disillusionment.

The first period, which lasted almost but not quite to the
outbreak of the War, perpetuated the nineteenth-century
faith in progress. Commerce, industry, knowledge and individual freedom were expanding, and to reformers there did
not seem to be any reason why that expansion should stop
until by a natural process it achieved a perfect society.
Change in itself was supposed to be making for this end,
and the task of the reformer was therefore to destroy every
restriction, so that the good work might be accomplished.
The social criticism of this period was directed mainly at
the institutions which confined development, such as the
church, the marriage laws, traditional morality, and the rights
of property. It was the age of Shaw and Wells. The motor-
car, the aeroplane, wireless and the week-end habit were
all coming in. Capital was being more and more centralised,
and when the process was finished all capital, it was hoped,
would pass painlessly into the hands of the State. But there
was no need for hurry; the development required a little
guidance, but that was all. Certain writers such as Belloc
and Chesterton combated this optimistic view; others, such
as Conrad, stood apart from it; but in the pamphlet, the
novel and the drama it was the prevalent view of the time,

and it reflected the confidence of an era of rapid expansion and of "unexampled prosperity".

After this came the War and a quick contraction of all hopes into the hope that the nation would survive. There was not for the time being, nor for several years afterwards, any question of improving the state of society; nor was there much effective faith in the possibility of improvement: the disillusionment caused by the War was too deep. This disillusionment found expression in novels which tried to show that mankind was not up to much and would never be up to much, or that the fathers of the War generation were to blame for the fate of their sons and daughters. It found expression also in biographies which ironically reduced the great figures of the past to certain irreducible vanities and cupidities, as in the early work of Lytton Strachey, which was not yet vitiated by sentimentality. In poetry it took the form of an absolute rejection of romantic hopes and romantic diction, by virtue of which civilisation became "an old bitch gone in the teeth". In some poetry such as Eliot's it assumed the more reasonable form of a return to tradition; more reasonable, for since the present was chaotic and the future doubtful, the past seemed the one remaining thing which could be depended upon. But Eliot's disillusionment with the modern world had begun before the War, and he had had more time to reflect upon it than the others. D. H. Lawrence was equally discontented with the state of the world and the trend of reform, which meant that he was discontented with the process of history itself; accordingly the only hope he saw was in a return to the primitive. This disillusioned, unreforming literature seemed, to the previous generation brought up on Shaw and Wells, new, disturbing and almost incomprehensible.

The mood of disillusionment crystallised first into a comprehensive scepticism regarding society and the various programmes designed to improve it, a doubt not only of certain conceptions and certain ideals, but of all conceptions and all ideals. The writer was left alone with his reactions, and he felt that he could not trust anything else. In Aldous

Huxley's early stories, the only real things about the characters are their desires and their sensations; their emotions,
on the other hand, are exposed as hypocritical, for emotion
is associated with ideas of human hope, and at the time all
ideas connected with human hope seemed to be presumptuous
and false. There was accordingly a radical distrust and dislike of general ideas, and this was not confined to the few;
it was popular, as can be seen from the early plays of Noel
Coward and the early stories of Beverley Nichols and
Evelyn Waugh. This scepticism was probably inevitable; but
it was also a sort of indulgence which could be had only
at a time when there was no call and no energy for immediate
action, a time when, after the immense effort of the War,
people felt there was nothing to be done. Europe was in
confusion; society was dislocated; private hopes of a kind
were still possible; but there was no common hope.

It was the actual worsening of the state of the world, the
recognition that society might suffer a greater disaster than
it had suffered in the War, which put an end to this phase.
For if disaster came, it would liquidate the private hopes as
well. So something like a belief in the future returned. Yet
the form it took was very different from the form it had
taken before the War. Then everything seemed to be making
for progress, or the chief writers of the time thought so;
there seemed no real alternative to improvement but the
status quo; no one thought that society had more than two
choices—to go forward, or to remain as it was; no one
seriously believed that it could go backwards. But various
events after the War were clearly taking it backwards, and
particularly the rise of Fascism as an international power,
with the consequent stamping out of liberty.

This is the great alternative which has now come into
literature as into politics. It was unknown to the pre-War
world, whose belief in the future was almost untinged with
fear. There is no longer any belief in the future in that
sense; there is at most a belief that the future must be made
secure, otherwise there will be disaster, that society must be
changed, or else go to pieces. This is not a natural faith,

25

but an emergency one; and it is very unlike the early faith of Shaw and Wells.

.   .   .   .

To find the causes of this state of things a prolonged study of history would be necessary, and that cannot be attempted in a brief study such as this. In the previous volume Professor Bonamy Dobrée gives a hint of the problems which were piling up during the Victorian Age. "Our period," he says, "covers the extinction of the country interest and the triumph of industrialism, and it carries us almost as far as the capture of the latter by finance. But apart from this, and in the face of the individualistic spirit of the period, it also covers an almost bewildering development of State, and particularly municipal control, not only in industry, but outside it, in schools, colleges, libraries, trams, swimming baths, communications. It is another of the odd paradoxes of the time. It was the middle class that decreed all this, and at the same time decreed, perhaps, its merging into another class; for our period covers the rise, if not to power, at least to political importance of the workers, of what has come to be called the "proletariat"; and at the same time it covers the expansion to its utmost limit of the Empire from the maintenance of which the working classes would dissociate themselves."

Professor Dobrée continues:

> "Economically the period was in the main one of previously unthinkable progress. There were troubled times until 1848, for some people indescribably cruel times that called out the early revolutionary spirit. Then, until the late seventies, an unparalleled prosperity and an astonishing increase in population carried the nation forward; a profound optimism and complacency seems to have been the dominant sentiment; revolution was dead. The difficulties that arose after that period were overcome, or lived through, but the seed of doubt had been planted. Neither a new prosperity nor the songs of the Imperialists could hide the fact that something

was wrong; it was this that made the middle class critical, or at least dubious of itself, and gave the solid basis to socialistic thought which, characteristic of the Edwardian period, has yet to work itself out".

This period ultimately led in, Professor Dobrée says, "the age in which we struggle and hope with scarcely a trace of complacency left." Another way of putting this is to say that the Victorian Age was an age of enormous development; and free, or what seems to be free, development engenders a mood of hope. In our own day that development has produced a number of results, most of which are problems that the Victorian capitalist system did not solve, problems which have now become a public danger. Yeats, who was not pre-eminently a politically-minded man, said recently:

> Things fall apart, the centre cannot hold,
> Mere anarchy is loosed upon the world,

and the same sentiment may be found repeated in various forms throughout present-day literature, from the obscurest utterances of poetry to the most obvious clap-trap of the newspapers.

To discover when things begin to fall apart, or when a society begins to disintegrate, is a task of inconceivable difficulty; and I shall confine myself to indicating one or two landmarks which must be known to everyone. The Industrial Revolution clearly brought about a great change in society. Before that the workman and the employer had a personal though unequal relation to each other, if only because they worked in the same shop. That relation, both satisfactory and unsatisfactory, was therefore an image of society, and an accurate one. Political and economic entities, that is to say, could still be conceived in human terms. But with the growth of Industrialism came division of labour, the huge factory, the joint stock company, the syndicate, the ring; in that inexorable process master and workman disappeared; and

27

for the personal relation were substituted two impersonal forces, Capital and Labour. In one sense it may be argued that when this happened society began to fall apart, for industrialism cut the immediate ties which had bound men and society together. Society has since become impersonal in a sense which was unthinkable before. Within it there is Capital, on the one hand, following its own laws, regardless, or as regardless as it can be, of Labour, and Labour, on the other, trying to get what it can at the bottom, its essential law that of necessity. There is no over-arching law in which these two laws meet and are reconciled. There is no essential relation between them except that of impersonal interaction. Above them there is only the State, run mainly by the capitalist class. An impersonal society, that is a society constituted by the interaction of mere forces, is a dangerous society, for it runs counter to human instinct, and is founded on a hostile balance which is ultimately self-destructive. It is a system of which the two main functions, working in theoretical dissociation from each other, have no direct bearing upon the whole.

.   .   .   .

This dissociation, which for convenient illustration I have referred to the Industrial Revolution, can of course be pushed much further back. Hermann Broch, the Austrian writer, in his novel *The Sleepwalkers* attributes it to the breakdown of the medieval synthesis. Five hundred years ago, he says, all the arts and sciences were bound to one central idea, whose secular emblem was the Roman Catholic church. At the Renaissance the arts and sciences "freed" themselves and the result was for a time an unexampled burst of discovery and creation. Poetry followed its own laws, the lyric "freed" itself from music, painting from architecture, philosophy from religion, science from philosophy, economics from politics: in extreme cases action from thought. This liberation produced Shakespeare, Beethoven, Rembrandt, Kant, James Watt, Napoleon. It also produced Nationalism, which divided Europe; Capitalism, which divided society; Protestantism, which divided religion; and Imperialism, which hopes to divide, in the most literal sense, the earth itself. The freedom was salutary so long as the framework of society held together round it and there was a common ground on which all arts, all ways of thought, all modes of existence were comprehensible to themselves and to each other. But as it expanded it made society increasingly incoherent, and Broch sees its logical result in a no-society in which every human activity runs parallel to every other one, without meeting: in which business follows a law of its own, militarism a law of its own, religion a law of its own, philosophy a law of its own, science a law of its own, poetry a law of its own, painting a law of its own, so that only the specialist, whether financier or poet or painter, can understand his own work. This, according to Broch, is the stage we reached about twenty years ago. It is a falling apart, and when things fall apart there is an uprush of the irrational. We have seen and are seeing that uprush. This analysis may be in need of modification in detail, but it is the most illuminating one I have been able to find.

The increasing incoherence of society can be clearly enough seen, I think, in the increasing incoherence of feeling and expression in literature during the last century and a half. The looseness of the Victorian style, as compared with the Elizabethan or the Augustan, mirrors an uncertainty of perception which was due to the fact that after the growth of the Industrial system society could no longer be seen or felt as a whole. A wide public could be reached, therefore, only by writing loosely. The looseness was not deliberate, but a symptom of the state of society. The Victorian Age is therefore pre-eminently an age of vague thought and feeling: of vague humanity as in Dickens, vague indignation as in Carlyle, vague religion as in Tennyson and Arnold. The exact writers came from some small isolated part, like Emily Brontë, or were securely rooted in the past, like Newman. But in general the writer could not correlate his life satisfactorily with the life of society; he could not fit into it without a hitch, like Pope; he had to make a sentimental compromise, hoping that somehow good would come of ill, and clinging to honest doubt as a form of faith. In doing this he insensibly became a public figure very like an eminent statesman. Professor Bonamy Dobrée has already noted that the Victorians were not concerned to resolve their private problems. They could not; they were too painfully in doubt about the society in which they lived. For a writer can devote himself to his private problems only in a society which he regards as settled or in a society which he regards as damned. The exception is the mystical writer, who ultimately lives in a changeless world, no matter what the changes in society, or the form of society.

In Victorian times the imaginative writer could be widely popular only by writing loosely. It may be said that to-day he can be widely popular only by writing falsely. Dickens could mingle the rich and the poor and bring them into some relation, no matter how romantic, in his picture of society: the mixture was unconvincing, but it was not incredible. To-day novelists still occasionally attempt to do this; but the result is incredible. Consequently the novel has become typically a picture of the middle and upper middle classes, since most novelists come from one of these. The standpoint of such novels is naturally also middle-class, and the poor come into them as figments of middle-class imagination or adjuncts of middle-class existence: as spectres, domestic servants, porters, taxi-drivers, shop-assistants, charwomen, policemen; not as engineers or boiler-makers. Scott was the last novelist to treat the poor as complete human beings, probably because he lived in a small backward community, and knew an older world than his contemporaries knew. Thackeray was already a full-fledged middle-class novelist. Meredith treated the poor facetiously. Wells began with some admirable pictures of the lower middle classes; but when he tried to reinstate society again his society was a schema, not an actual society such as Fielding described. To Galsworthy the poor were a middle-class problem. Bennett scarcely touched them, for this

essential theme was success; and the cult of success, which
presupposes a sort of cockpit instead of a society, derives
from capitalist ways of thought. The novelists who followed
from Walpole and Compton Mackenzie to Aldous Huxley
were quite definitely middle-class. Lawrence, who was not,
belongs to a different category, the category of those who,
seeing the rottenness of society, tried to create private
worlds of their own.

The retreat of writers into private worlds, which had
begun before the War and was much stimulated by it, was
a natural result of the fact that society could not be seen and
felt coherently. The retreat began in poetry. At the beginning
of the century Yeats turned aside from his time and fixed
upon the peasant and the legends of the peasant as a foundation for his world. Pound went back to medieval Provence
and old China. This return did not have very much in common with the return of Coleridge and Keats to the fairy
tale and the ballad. Yeats and Pound did not go to the
past entirely for its strangeness or its beauty, but for an
actual foundation on which to build a coherent personal
world in a world which had grown incoherent and abstract
to them. They recognised later that this could not be done
and that they must deal with the confused world in which
they lived, and some of its incoherence accordingly came
into their work, in measured doses in Yeats's poetry, in an
overwhelming flood in Pound's. Yet the first archaic foundation they had laid remained; the original structure, Irish
or Provençal, was still there; it is inundated now and then
in Pound's *Cantos*, but in Yeats's poetry it remains high
and dry, for he never dipped more than one foot at a time
into the contemporary muddle. Pound took the plunge,
trusting to Confucius, Homer and Arnaut Daniel to buoy
him up.

Eliot's position was somewhat different, for from the
start he was acutely aware of his time. The world of his
early poetry up to *The Waste Land* is highly contemporary,
the world of Prufrock and Sweeney, not of Cuchulain
or Odysseus. But he was conscious that it was a world

31

where Cuchulain and Odysseus, and figures still more momentous, had once been, and he saw this earlier world as a temporal order, a great though imperfect norm, a tradition. But the order was broken. His early poetry is consequently fragmentary, since he saw the contemporary world as a heap of fragments. Yet he had to impose some coherence upon it, and he did this by accepting the order which was broken, and using it as a sort of measure, just as Yeats had used Irish legend and Pound Provençal and Chinese literature. Or rather, as the order was broken, he used his own reconstruction of it, which, though broadly based, was inevitably personal. This is what makes both his poetry and Pound's difficult to understand. The standards by which experience is judged in this poetry are in an unavoidable sense private, since they are drawn from a specific reading of the past with which the reader is not immediately acquainted, and with which he need not necessarily agree if he grasped it. This does not apply, however, to Eliot's poetry after *The Waste Land*.

That these three poets should turn to the past was perhaps inevitable, for when society is in confusion ages of order and stability acquire a new importance; they have to be examined so that we may discover what a society means. Transitional periods encourage apocalyptic visions, or the historical sense. A man living in an ordered society accepts it without thinking very hard about it; if he is a writer the implications of that society will be present in his work; he will be traditional in spite of himself. But a writer living in a changing society becomes aware that in its development civilisation has vicissitudes as violent as those of human growth and decline; that it has its good and bad phases; its periods of health and sickness; its moods of faith and despair; and that all these accidents are collective and individual at the same time, affecting society as well as the intimate life of the millions of people who compose it. He sees warnings and hopeful omens in past occurrences; events which throw light on his own age; and from all this dissolving yet continuous order imposed by time he tries to educe an order which he can apply to the current confusion: the only extant order, since he can find none in itself. This was perhaps inevitable in the age of Eliot, for the writer could not but regard his age as an abnormal one, which therefore needed to be set in historical proportion. A stable age has little historical sense, for it has no need of it. It does not think in terms of historical periods, but in terms of birth, life and death: the permanent pattern.

Yeats, Eliot and Pound in various degrees then have used history as a standard by which to show the nature of their own time. They have naturally used it with a difference. History is not Yeats's final standard, nor is its Eliot's; from his poetry it may be Pound's. But all three have used it alike in one way; for it is doubtful whether without it they could have done anything with their age; they could not have got the requisite sense of significance which Tennyson and Doughty got before them, perhaps too easily. Tennyson did not need the Arthurian cycle. He was genuinely attracted by it; but once he had chosen his theme he imposed Victorian standards upon it; and he did so because he thought them better than the originals. For he lived in a society which, if not entirely satisfactory, seemed to be broadening down from precedent to precedent, and he felt no need to compare it adversely with previous ones.

The poets with a relatively wide appeal before and after the War wrote mainly of simple uncontroversial things in a fresh way: of trees and birds and rivers, urban quarrels and reconciliations, boat-races, football matches: the few things of which there was still no doubt. The War added an enormous item to this list, and during the War poetry was produced, and also read, in greater volume than it had been for many years before. For English society during the War, with the bulk of the adult population either in the army or engaged on war service, acquired a dreadful coherence, and became overwhelmingly comprehensible; so that the feeling it evoked was both impersonal and personal in the highest degree. Consequently for a time the War was as indisputable a theme as fishing or boat-racing; and it did not ask for or receive the benefit of a private idiom. Yet the War was also a crucial theme; accordingly it produced good poetry which could be generally understood. With the end of the War popular poetry reverted, except for a few post-humous martial echoes, to its former themes. This is one of the most astonishing facts about the period under review.

The Waste Land appeared in 1923. The years since have brought one public crisis after another, and the cracks in society have become more and more apparent. The temper of poetry has accordingly changed, and in one way conspicuously. Near the end of his poem Eliot had this line:

"These fragments I have shored against my ruins,"

by which he implied that he looked back, though without much optimism, on what remained of human tradition, and hoped that it might still be conserved by the effort of a minority, and civilisation thus saved. But society went on falling apart with a fitful and alarming acceleration, and the generation of Auden and Spender could no longer see any choice but to hasten the process and work for a new order. This difference, which is typical of two generations, reflected the worsening dilemma of European society and the increasing violence and alarm within it. When Pound called it "an old bitch gone in the teeth", it was a sort of fond abuse. He has been telling civilisation for a long time that it should be ashamed of itself. Eliot's earlier poetry gives a genuine sense of the tragedy of the passing of civilisation. A little of Auden's does this too: the difference is that he sees it as necessary, and wants it to be accomplished.

This change from a conservative to a revolutionary attitude is the main change in the period covered by this book. It brought another less important change with it. In trying to conserve the remnants of civilisation, in shoring the fragments against his ruins, Eliot necessarily addressed himself to a small audience, for a tradition can be saved only by those who know that it needs to be saved and by those who know what it is. More people may have known what tradition was than Eliot assumed; but whatever their number, they were isolated individuals without effective public power; people with private knowledge which was ignored or derided by the world in general; and so the poem was a sort of confidential communication. Knowledge that society is in a critical stage is no longer private and no longer confined to those who know what tradition is. Accordingly Auden has a public, and not merely a private, audience, for he writes about what a great number of people feel or guess. His audience, it is true, does not represent society however fragmentarily, as Eliot's did; it is a sectional public which frankly believes that society no longer effectively exists, that it does not deserve to exist, and that it must make way for another order. Yet, though sectional, it is a much larger audience than Eliot's was. The period begins, then, with a private attempt to save existing civilisation, and ends with a public attempt to destroy it and create another one.

These three phases can be distinguished fairly clearly in the history of the present century, but behind them there is something whose effects are difficult if not impossible to describe: that is, the fact of the rapidity of social change itself. This speeding up of change has profoundly affected our feelings of Time and led to an unusual insistence on its importance, quite apart from the various time philosophies which have appeared. The difference can be seen more clearly in the novel than in poetry, since the novel is a full-length description of life, in most cases over a considerable period. Generally speaking, the novel is concerned with contemporary life, that is, with time still going on. The classical novelists, such as Fielding, Dickens and Thackeray, leave their heroes and heroines living, in most cases happily, at the end of their stories; these characters are therefore contemporary with the contemporary reader. Now while this posthumous happy survival would give the thoughtful reader to-day a feeling of doubt and insecurity, to the reader of the traditional novel it did not, for Fielding and Jane Austen and Dickens and Thackeray did not think that the

35

world, and time with it, was going to change very much: the characters would go on living in much the same circumstances as in the last chapter. They would grow old and die, but they would do so in the world they were accustomed to. That world might have deplorable abuses, but if the necessary reforms were carried out, society would merely become more like itself than before: no fundamental change was needed or could be expected. This implicit dependence on time, this feeling that characters could be left comfortably settled in the last chapter of stories, continued well into last century, and still continues in the more popular kinds of fiction. To Dickens time was a sort of eight-day clock, or rather eighty-year clock which, if it were wound up now and then, could be completely relied on. We can hear it ticking peacefully away through the posthumous lives of his happy characters.

A great difference has come about in the novel and in people's feelings about time since then, and perhaps the best way to show this is to give a few extracts from the last chapters of novels before and after the change. Before the change first:

> "The wedding was very much like other weddings, where the parties have no taste for finery or parade; and Mrs. Elton, from the particulars detailed by her husband, thought it all extremely shabby, and very inferior to her own. 'Very little white satin, very few lace veils—a most pitiful business!' Selina would stare when she heard of it. But in spite of these deficiencies, the wishes, the hopes, the confidence, the predictions of the small band of true friends who witnessed the ceremony were fully answered in the perfect happiness of the union".

> "Old Edie, the most important man that ever wore a blue-gown, bowls away easily from one friend's house to another, and boasts that he never travels unless on a sunny day. Latterly, indeed, he has given some symptoms of becoming stationary, being frequently found in the corner of a snug cottage between Monkbarns and Knockwinnock, to which

Caxon retreated upon his daughter's marriage, in order to be in the neighbourhood of the three parochial wigs, which he continues to keep in repair, though only for amusement. Edie has been heard to say, 'This is a gey bien place, and it's a comfort to hae sic a corner to sit in in a bad day'. It is thought, as he grows stiffer in the joints, he will finally settle there".

The first of these passages is from Jane Austen's *Emma*, the second from Scott's *Antiquary*.
Now for the contemporary novel:

"Calamy watched them go, watched them till they were out of sight round a bend in the road. A profound melancholy settled down upon him. With them, he felt, had gone all his old familiar life. He was left quite alone with something new and strange. What was to come of this parting?
Or perhaps, he reflected, nothing would come of it. Perhaps he had been a fool.
The cottage was in shadow now. Looking up the slope he could see a clump of trees still glittering as though prepared for a festival above the rising flood of darkness. And at the head of the valley, like an enormous precious stone, glowing with its own inward fire, the limestone crags reached up through the clouds into the pale sky. Perhaps he had been a fool, thought Calamy. But looking at that shining peak, he was somehow reassured".

"April 26. Mother is putting my new second-hand clothes in order. She prays now, she says, that I may learn in my own life and away from home and friends what the heart is and what it feels. Amen. So be it. Welcome, O life! I go to encounter for the millionth time the reality of experience and to forge in the smithy of my soul the uncreated conscience of my race.
April 27. Old father, old artificer, stand me now and ever in good stead."

" 'Aren't they lovely?' said Delia, holding out the flowers. Eleanor started.
'The roses? Yes . . .' she said. But she was watching the

cab. A young man got out; he paid the driver. Then a girl in a tweed travelling suit followed him. He fitted his latch-key in the door. 'There,' Eleanor murmured, as he opened the door and they stood for a moment on the threshold. 'There!' she repeated, as the door shut with a little thud behind them.

Then she turned round into the room, 'And now?' she said, looking at Morris, who was drinking the last drops of a glass of wine. 'And now?' she asked, holding out her hands to him.

The sun had risen, and the sky above the houses wore an air of extraordinary beauty, simplicity and peace.''

The first passage is from Aldous Huxley's *Those Barren Leaves*, the second from James Joyce's *Portrait of the Artist as a Young Man*, and the third from Virginia Woolf's *The Years*.

Taking these five passages, what is bound to strike us is that the first two are genuine endings, so far as any ending not tragic can be genuine, and that the last three are not. The hopes, confidences and predictions of Emma's friends "were fully answered in the perfect happiness of the union". Edie Ochiltree and the other characters in *The Antiquary* are shown going about their business like the figures in a medieval picture: nothing will change that order. But the end of *Those Barren Leaves* is more like a beginning. After describing life as he sees it, Huxley discovers that there is something which he has not included in his description: a different life from the life he knows, which can at best be vaguely suggested. Calamy is left with something new and strange, though what that something is he does not know and Huxley does not know. Stephen Dedalus, again, after living for a novel's length, welcomes life ands sets out to discover the reality of experience, as if experience were something different from the novelist's painstaking representation of it. Eleanor murmurs "And now?" Paul in Lawrence's *Sons and Lovers* clenches his hands and sets out rapidly for the distant lights of the town. We are intended to believe that a profound change of some kind has taken place, and that the succeeding

38

story, which is unwritten, will be different from the written one. In all these endings two things are simultaneously implied: the future, and an unspecified but radical change.

This difference between the classical and the contemporary novel seems to me to cast a light upon the contemporary novel in general and on the age it describes. The sudden discovery of a new way of life at the end of a story is not a satisfactory way of dealing imaginatively with experience. We know that Paul's hands will unclench again, that Calamy will discover whether he is a fool or not, and that Eleanor will not always go on asking "And now?" We know, too, of course, that Edie did not live happily ever after, and that Emma's marriage was not perfect. But the lie involved is a comparatively harmless conventional one. All that it amounts to is that Emma's subsequent life, in Jane Austen's opinion, did not provide matter for an interesting narrative, whereas the circumstances of her courtship did. We are left, therefore, to imagine that life for ourselves. The novelist describes his characters, selecting for his purpose the most interesting things that happened to them: then he leaves them, having shown them as completely as he could. The novelist of the generation of Joyce, Lawrence, Virginia Woolf and Huxley does something else. He follows his characters for a while and then deserts them on the point of an extremely important change, which will presumably turn them into something else, unrecognisable by us. We know that countless people have gone through crises which have altered their lives; the history of religion is filled with such events. But the contemporary novelist never describes the crisis and its outcome: he merely mentions it. In doing this he seems to imply two things: first, that the actions and thoughts of contemporary people, set down no matter how honestly, do not contain a complete meaning; secondly, and as a consequence of this, that life must be changed in some way. In Fielding and Dickens what the characters do and feel makes up the significance of the story, so that the end itself can be largely conventional. But the end of the contemporary story is a hiatus, and into that hiatus something

39

must be flung: an illumination, a question, a wish-fulfilment, a significance. The novelist seems to be saying that experience as he knows it does not have a meaning, but that there is a meaning nevertheless. And as it is not in the story, he has to postpone it to an ever-receding future which is different from the present, and presumably to a society which is different from the existing one.

Many influences have probably combined to bring about this change in the novel; among them the decay of religion, and with that of the belief in immortality; for it may be reasonably argued that any picture of changing events which is painted against a background of changing time can never be complete, can never have an end, and with that a meaning. But that is a controversial theory unsuited for a history of literature, and an approximately adequate explanation of the change may be found, I think, in a change in the life of society itself. To the classical novelist time as it affected the life of society seemed much slower than time as it affected the lives of individual men and women; so slow, indeed, that it could be conveniently considered as stationary. The world was constant; the life of man was all change. Consequently, when the novelist set out to portray life, he painted it on a ground which was constant, and everything stood out in clear relief. Society was not, of course, as dependable as he thought; it was perpetually changing. But the important thing was the feeling of the novelist and of the people who read him. Society was imperfect and needed reform, both would have been willing to admit. But they thought, nevertheless, that society was stable in quite an extraordinary degree, and stable in a way which we can scarcely imagine now.

If we turn to our own time, we find that all this is changed. People still become ten and twenty and thirty and forty at a regular progression: there is no change there. But time as it affects society, instead of remaining stationary or seeming to do so, rushes on at a terrific speed, sweeping away with it the constant ground on which the novelist once painted his picture. The figures in this picture change as they have always done; but the ground changes too. There is not only a development in the old-fashioned sense; there is nothing but development. The frame of the picture dissolves away in spite of every attempt to keep it stationary. In the end we are left with the characters still developing: the presumption being that ultimately, in some place, they will develop into themselves, that is into complete characters. Yet at the same time they cannot be shown completely except in a fixed frame: as the frame changes they have to change with it, and in that ceaseless change the very idea of completeness is lost. To be a character no longer fits this conception of the world; life at most is shown as something feeling, reacting, changing, hoping, becoming. Accordingly Lawrence declared that it was not his business to describe characters. Joyce produced a marvellous comic character in Bloom (comic characters can be produced in any condition of society), but his Stephen is a pure continuum, becoming something at the end of *A Portrait*, and still becoming something at the end of *Ulysses*. Yet the need for coherence continues to exist in the novelist's imagination; and we may therefore interpret the setting out, the illumination, the resolve to meet experience, as a sort of desperate plunge into coherence, an attempt to reach the stage where the process of becoming a character at last ends in the achievement of a character.

All this can be put in another way. In a stable society, or one which is felt to be stable, human relations and human beings along with them have a certain permanence. Every man has a sort of finality, for there is an approximate finality in society itself. A story can be more or less satisfactorily rounded into a whole, for society is a whole. But when society is dissolving and cannot be grasped, the portrait loses its coherence and meaning, and the story ends with a mystical hope that something will happen to put an end to an incurable relativity.

This difficulty has a further consequence. Where the sole remaining hope of the novelist is in development, the novel itself begins to develop: it ceases to be a form and becomes a process. Discovering that society did not provide a structure

41

for a work of imagination, the novelist was driven to modify the shape of the novel, create a structure of his own, and impose a personal, idiosyncratic significance upon his material by manipulating it in various ways. The significance is sometimes traditional, as in *Ulysses*, whose pattern is taken from *The Odyssey:* an indirect admission that life was once coherent but is no longer so. Or the novelist may upset the time order, to see whether it will have more meaning, arranged in a different way. Or he may try to create an impression of simultaneousness, as in *Ulysses* and *Mrs. Dalloway*. The experiments in the form of the novel after the War were countless. The most plausible explanation for them is the increasing confusion of society. In a stable society a novelist has no need to create an impression of simultaneousness: everything he writes about implies everything else: in other words, the complete society in which he lives. Nor would any one think of interfering in such a society with the order of time, for time as it is reflects the social order: to violate it would be almost a subversive act, a sin against society. The classical novelists had no heart-searchings about the sequence of time, nor had they any need to show that while A was living, B and all the others were alive too. This did not become an interesting question until the novelist realised that there was no general picture of society in his mind which included in the same system of relations A and B and all the others. Then the simultaneous existence of these various characters became an absorbing question and the attempt to bring them together in some relation an important task. But he could only bring them together; the actual relation generally resolves itself into an imaginative experiment. The significance which Joyce gives, for instance, to the meeting between Bloom and Stephen at the end of *Ulysses* seems to be deliberately willed; not the description of a reality, but the utterance of a wish.

CHAPTER II

POETRY

THE period under review in this book has been called by Yeats a great age of poetry. I confess that this description surprised me when I read it, for though the last twenty years have produced poetry of a more interesting and a more vital kind than the half-century before them, the quality which it seems to lack, or to show very sparingly, is the quality of incontestable greatness. But "great" is a rhetorical term; it may imply size, or abundance, or elevation, or depth, or nature written larger than nature, or all these together. There is little use in trying to analyse such a word, which seems to be indispensable, since it undoubtedly represents something, and yet cannot be given a strict meaning. That being so, it may be best simply to indicate a poetic quality, often found in great poetry, and generally an ingredient of it, which is rarely met in the poetic production of the last thirty years. This quality is the power to make a natural, immediate and yet overwhelming statement which produces such conviction that we forget the voice that utters it. Statement of this kind always strikes us as being newly forged, without a trace of poetic reminiscence; as being a concrete addition to the utterance of mankind. Shakespeare is full of this kind of statement. But it is to be found in all the periods which we regard as great:

> Than upon him scho kest up baith her Ene,
> And with ane blenk it come into his thocht
> That he sumtime her face befoir had sene. . . .

My race of glory run, and race of shame . . .

43

> My former thoughts return'd: the fear that kills,
> And hope that is unwilling to be fed . . .

Such radical poetic statement without poetic reminiscence is uncommon in the poetry of the last twenty years. We find it occasionally in Eliot's poetry:

> The host with someone indistinct
> Converses at the door apart,
> The nightingales are singing near
> The Convent of the Sacred heart,
>
> And sang within the bloody wood
> When Agamemnon cried aloud,
> And let their liquid siftings fall
> To stain the stiff dishonoured shroud.

We find it too, though less perfectly, in Hopkins, who comes into this period, but wrote in another:

> And every saint of bloody hour
> And breath immortal thronged that show;
> Heaven turned its starlight eyes below
> To the murder of Margaret Clitheroe.

We find it less often in Yeats and hardly at all in Pound.
The distinctive quality of the poetry of our time is shown better in another well-known passage from Eliot's work:

> Phlebas the Phoenician, a fortnight dead,
> Forgot the cry of the gulls, and the deep sea swell
> And the profit and loss.
> A current under sea
> Picked his bones in whispers. As he rose and fell
> He passed the stages of his age and youth
> Entering the whirpool.
> Gentile or Jew

O you who turn the wheel and look to windward,
Consider Phlebas, who was once handsome and tall as you.

That is beautiful, but its quality can easily be distinguished from

      And sang within the bloody wood

or from

      And hope that is unwilling to be fed.

We are farther away here from the object which is being described, and closer to the means which are being used to describe it. The language is manipulated with great skill, but "the deep sea swell and the profit and loss" are verbal entities and do not evoke what they stand for, as the nightingale does. The use of words is at bottom the same, though employed with more skill and seriousness, as in the three lines by the early Yeats which Joyce quoted so often in *Ulysses*:

      And no more turn aside and brood
      Upon love's bitter mystery,
      For Fergus rules the brazen cars,

or indeed as in many a line from Yeats's later poetry, so miraculously skilful in their structure:

      An ancient bankrupt master of this house . . .

      As I would question all, come all who can;
      Come old, necessitous, half-mounted man. . . .

where the mere movement of the verse, the mere arrangement of the words, smoothes away the roughness of reality and puts in its place a beautiful artificiality, in which squalid terms like "bankrupt" and "necessitous" acquire a dignity by virtue of the position which they are given in a line. How splendid these transformations of sordid experience into pure style can be is shown in the same poem, *The Tower*:

> And certain men-at-arms there were
> Whose images, in the Great Memory stored,
> Come with loud cry and panting breast
> To break upon a sleeper's rest
> While their great wooden dice beat on the board.

The poetic vision here is undeniable; but it is a vision of figures from literature and painting flung into violent movement, and it calls up Shakespeare and Breughel, not the Ireland of which Yeats is writing. The use of language is extremely skilful, and perhaps inspired, but it is not the use of language in:

> Light thickens, and the crow
> Makes wings to the rooky wood:
> Good things of the day begin to droop and drowse.

It is not the use of Wordsworth either:

> And hope that is unwilling to be fed.

In the lines from *Macbeth* the words are used to bring nature before us in a certain mood, and the line from Wordsworth expresses directly a fact of human experience. But Yeats's words give the impression of having been steeped for a long time in some solution, until they have lost their ordinary quality and acquired a new specific one. When these words are set in motion, by the passion of the writer, or by inspiration, they do not call up ordinary things, directly and immediately, as Shakespeare and Wordsworth did, but with a difference which is determined by the difference in the new specific gravity and colour of the words; so that what is produced is an artificial effect, which is sometimes however of great beauty, and sometimes deeply moving.

> While their great wooden dice beat on the board

is, compared with the lines I quoted earlier, an arranged and
staged picture of undoubted intensity, but taken from
painting, drama, the ballet, not directly from life. Or, as
there is undoubtedly life in the line, it would be truer to say
that that life had to pass through some preliminary trans-
formation in which it changed its form while keeping much
for its energy, before it could be given the authoritative
ratification of Yeats's style.

To find the appropriate epithets for these two ways of
using language is extremely difficult, and perhaps impossible;
and it is made harder by the current dislike of the word
natural as applied to poetry, a dislike which is excused by
living memory of a kind of poetry which was falsely natural,
and a dislike which I share. But all that I am seeking is a
rough characterisation of the poetry of our age; this can be
achieved only by comparing it with the poetry of other ages,
and it seems to me that there is a sense in which we may call

> My race of glory run, and race of shame

or

> And hope that is unwilling to be fed

highly natural, and

> And no more turn aside and brood
> Upon love's bitter mystery

highly artificial. In all the great ages we have both kinds of
poetry; much of Shakespeare is artificial in the sense in
which I have been speaking, as well as a great deal of Milton,
a great deal of Tennyson, and almost all of Keats, and
artificial in a much more radical sense than Dryden and
Pope, who in comparison are simple and direct. In all the
great ages of poetry there seems to be a balance between

47

these two kinds of poetry, so that neither overweighs the other, and the one goes into the other. The natural poet writes out of his direct experience of life; the artificial poet out of that and his knowledge of poetry. There is a balance so long as his knowledge of poetry illumines and penetrates his experience of life; the balance is lost when poetry, or the mental and emotional habit which his acquaintance with it has produced in him, keeps him from seeing and expressing his experience freely. There is about the work of poets of this kind, even when they are as great as Milton, Keats and Tennyson, an incrustation of poetic self-consciousness which makes it difficult for them to say such things as

My race of glory run, and race of shame,

and at the same time makes us realise how much greater they would have been if they could have said such things more easily. It seems to me that much of the poetry of the present age is artificial in this sense.

The best example to show this is the poetry of T. S. Eliot, who has produced work of both kinds, and as much of the one as of the other. In his poem *Gerontion*, they are to be found in almost equal quantities.

> Think
> Neither fear nor courage saves us. Unnatural vices
> Are fathered by our heroism. Virtues
> Are forced upon us by our impudent crimes.
> These tears are shaken from the wrath-bearing tree,

is as "natural" as could be. This is followed a few lines farther on by

> Think at last
> I have not made this show purposelessly
> And it is not by any concitation
> Of the backward devils,

which is as "artificial" as could be. Or, better still, compare these lines from *Burnt Norton*:

> We move above the moving tree
> In light upon the figured leaf
> And hear upon the sodden floor
> Below, the boarhound and the boar
> Pursue their pattern as before,

with the well-known lines from *The Waste Land*:

> By this, and this only, we have existed
> Which is not to be found in our obituaries
> Or in memories draped by the beneficent spider
> Or under seals broken by the lean solicitor
> In our empty rooms.

The boarhound and the boar are alive, though heraldic; the beneficent spider and the lean solicitor are inanimate, though realistic, evoking more associations with Elizabethan drama and the detective novel, than with the days after death. The two artificial passages are effective, the second particularly: the first somewhat weakens the moving passage into which it comes. No one, I think, can mistake the difference between these two passages and the passages with which I have compared them. Both are equally characteristic of Eliot, and both have a legitimate though not an equally important place in his work. But almost all the poetry of Pound and much of Yeats's is of the second, artificial kind, rising sometimes to magnificence in Yeats, and to an ethereal music in Pound, but not often changing its mode. As it is the artificial Eliot who has been imitated, the same influence can be seen in the younger poets, though Auden, whose poetry is full of influences, more full than Pound's, has now partially escaped from it, and Spender shows only a few traces of it. But for the greater part of the period with which I am dealing it was the prevalent influence.

To appreciate the virtues of this artificial poetry, and the reasons for it, we must consider the state of poetry a few years before the War. The verdict of two men of poetic sensibility who took a chief part in the reaction from it will give the best idea of the impulse of the reaction. "Nineteen-twelve was a bad year," Pound wrote, "we all ran about like puppies with ten tin cans tied to our tails. The tin cans of Swinburnian rhyming, of Browningisms, even . . . of Kiplingisms, a resonant pendant, magniloquent, Miltonic, sonorous." And T. E. Hulme, speaking of the contemporary critics, said: "The dry hardness which you get in the classics is absolutely repugnant to them. Poetry that isn't damp isn't poetry at all . . . Verse to them always means a bringing in of some of the emotions grouped round the word infinite." The romantic vocabulary, in other words, was still being used without the romantic afflatus. A much watered-down "natural" poetry, dealing with simple subjects, and ignoring everything that was not simple, was the rule. A new technique was therefore needed, and the creation of a new technique must lead sooner or later to the study of past techniques.

But it did not do so at once, and the first response to the need for a new way of writing was Imagism, a somewhat naïve theory of the practice of verse-writing for which F. S. Flint, Richard Aldinton and H. D. (Hilda Doolittle) were chiefly responsible. The three main principles of poetic practice were:

"(1) Direct treatment of the 'thing' whether subjective or objective.

(2) To use absolutely no word that does not contribute to the presentation.

(3) As regards rhythm: to compose in the sequence of the musical phrase, not in the sequence of the metronome."

Pound defined an image as "that which presents an intellectual and emotional complex in an instant of time". Imagist poems were produced for a while by the chief supporters of the school, and many of them took up not much more than an instant of time; but Pound held—this was before he had begun the *Cantos*—that "It is better to present one Image in a lifetime than to produce voluminous works." He himself conceived what has become perhaps the most famous imagist poem:

> The apparition of these faces in the crowd;
> Petals on a wet, black bough.

But the theory of Imagism was insufficient, though salutary (it was merely a selected part of the theory of all good poetic writing), while its practice was constricting. And in *A Few Don'ts by an Imagiste* which appeared in 1913, Pound showed that in his opinion it required considerable enlargement. Among these "don'ts" are the following:—

> "Don't imagine that the art of poetry is any simpler than the art of music.
>
> Let the candidate fill his mind with the finest cadences he can discover, preferably in a foreign language, so that the meaning of the words may be less likely to divert his attention from the movement.
>
> Let the neophyte know assonance and alliteration, rhyme immediate and delayed, simple and polyphonic, as a muscian would expect to know harmony and counterpoint and all the minutiae of his craft. No time is too great to give to these matters or any one of them, even if the artist seldom have need of them.
>
> Consider the definiteness of Dante's presentation as compared with Milton's rhetoric. Read as much of Wordsworth as does not seem to be too unutterably dull.
>
> If you want the gist of the matter go to Sappho, Catullus, Villon, Heine when he is in the vein, Gautier when he is not too frigid; or, if you have not the tongues, seek out the leisurely Chaucer. Good prose will do you no harm, and there is good discipline to be had by trying to write it.
>
> Translation is likewise good training.
>
> If you are using a symmetrical form, don't put in what you have to say and then fill up the remaining vacuums with slush."

Here we see the search for a new technique of verse-writing naturally developing into a study of the techniques óf past times. Pound recommends Sappho, Villon, Gautier, not Keats and Tennyson; for the technique of Keats and Tennyson was only too well known and the imperative need of the poet was to get away from it. Eliot tells us that the form in which he began to write in 1908 or 1909 "was directly drawn from the study of Laforgue together with the later Elizabethan drama", and he adds that he does not know of anyone else who started from that point.

The aim of Imagism was really to simplify the art of poetry by removing unnecessary rules and a burdensome mass of dead associations. But the poets, or the best of them, who set out "to compose in the sequence of the musical phrase, not in the sequence of the metronome", soon realised the truth of Eliot's statement that "no vers is *libre* for the man who wants to do a good job". They were consequently forced to undertake an independent study of verse such as had not been made for a long time (except by Hopkins, who at that time was unknown to them), and as a result of that study they saw the various metrical forms afresh and were able to use them in a new way. There is no inherent inconsistency between composing in the sequence of the musical phrase and in the sequence of the metronome; the metronome is a necessary instrument, however much it may be despised; but by insisting on the exclusive importance of the first method the Imagists rendered a service to the art of verse, though not such an essential one as Eliot, who was not connected with the movement at all, or as Pound, who was avuncularly interested in it, rather than identified with it. Eliot has divided modern *vers libre* into three kinds, "my own type of verse, that of Pound, and that of the disciples of Whitman". The first two kinds owe more to the study of past verse forms than to the injunctions of Imagism, and they have also influenced more profoundly the art of poetry. Their influence has been, roughly, to free poetry from a false naturalness, a conventional lyricism, by insisting upon a more exact use of language and a more fundamental conception of form. This gave a new impulse to poetry.

Yeats was already an established poet when these problems

were troubling the generation of Pound and Eliot. His long poem, *The Wanderings of Oisin*, had appeared in 1889. *The Countess Kathleen*, a poetic tragedy, and the first poem which gave promise of his genius, came a year later. After that his poetic production was copious and fairly regular, and from sometime about the beginning of the War, roughlyt he time of the early Pound and Eliot and the Imagists, his poetry became more and more concerned with the contemporary world, a change which is shown in a direct and less conventionally poetic use of language and in a closer rendering of experience. The two volumes in which this change is most apparent are *The Tower* and *The Winding Stair*, the latter of which appeared in 1933, forty-four years after his first published verse.

Yeats's poetry is so voluminous, and describes such an extraordinary development, that only a rough and ready account of it is possible here. The most illuminating criticisms of his development which I have been able to find are in Miss Dorothy H. Hoare's book *The Works of Morris and of Yeats in Relation to Early Saga Literature*, a brilliant and too little known piece of criticism, and in Stephen Spender's *The Destructive Element*. Miss Hoare points out the "lyrical feeling for the delicate and quiet colourings of the Irish scene which is evident in the early poems", and she instances the beautiful first verse of *The Falling of the Leaves*:

> Autumn is over the long leaves that love us
> And over the mice in the barley sheaves;
> Yellow the leaves of the rowan above us,
> And yellow the wet wild-strawberry leaves.

She goes on to say that "unlike Morris, who found reality in the sights and sounds of the English landscape", Yeats was moved by his contemplation of the Irish country-side "to alter his direction as a poet, from the consideration of reality, to the romantic consideration of the past, and to fantasy. . . . Yeats himself expresses this—the mountains, the woods, the waters of his familiar West Country symbolised the greatness

53

of Ireland's history; on the hills he could see in imagination
the figures of Maeve and the gigantic heroes. This secondary
and derived interest in place ousts for him . . . the primary
and simple delight in the scene." She quotes Yeats himself:
"Our legends are always associated with places, and not
merely every mountain and valley but every strange stone
and little coppice has its legend, preserved in written and
unwritten tradition. Our Irish romantic movement has
arisen out of this tradition and should always, even when it
makes new legends about traditional people and things, be
haunted by places."

"This links up," Miss Hoare says, "three important things,
country-side, tradition, and peasant belief," and she stresses
the importance of the last, since it implies a very close connection between the peasantry and tradition. Yeats himself
explicitly declared this: "Ireland can discover, from the beliefs
and the emotions of her common people, the habit of mind
that created the religion of the Muses." This attitude of mind,
Miss Hoare adds, "is one which must inevitably lead, in
poetry, ultimately to the expression of trance."

Trance is a valid description of the mood of Yeats's early
poetry, after he had ceased to take delight in the Irish landscape as a landscape and saw it as the embodiment of legend
and history. But the predisposition to see "every strange
stone and little coppice" in this way must have originally been
there, and it seems to have been powerfully reinforced by
certain contemporary influences. Among these was the
Irish Nationalist Movement, with which Yeats was partly in
sympathy and partly at variance. If Ireland was not a visible
nation, at least "every strange stone and little coppice"
made it an invisible one, or a secret one, and secret knowledge had always allured him. There was also the Irish
Literary Movement, which was in essence traditional. "When
Lionel Johnson and Katherine Tynan (as she was then) and
I myself began to reform Irish poetry," Yeats writes, "we
only thought to keep unbroken the thread running up to
Grattan which John O'Leary had put into our hands, though
it might be our business to explore new paths of the labyrinth.

We sought to make a more subtle rhythm, a more organic form than that of the older Irish poets who wrote in English, but always to remember certain ardent ideas and high attitudes of mind which were the nation itself, to our belief, as far as a nation can be summarised in the intellect." This shows that Yeats was more moved by the idea of Ireland, an idea partly historical and partly legendary, than by the Ireland he saw; or rather that half-historical, half-legendary Ireland was the Ireland he actually came to see, until a little coppice was no longer a little coppice to him, but something more.

There was finally the influence of his contemporaries and friends, whose very considerable effect on him Mr. Spender has pointed out. He had his circle in London in the 'Nineties, composed of poets like Lionel Johnson, Ernest Dowson, and the members of the Rhymers' Club, men who are more important now because they formed a circle than because they wrote poetry. Later he had his circle in Dublin, in which several men of high talents were gathered. In the past of Ireland he was fortunate enough to find a cycle of legend, another circle. And from this theosophical book, *A Vision*, we know that he conceived human history as a circle produced by the action of two diametrically revolving cones upon each other. The circle, then, both actual and symbolical, seems always to have impressed him deeply. As an image it is found in numberless forms in his poetry, as *The Second Coming, The Tower, The Winding Stair.*

But to realise how profoundly his imagination was moved by the priority he allotted to the circle as a symbol of reality, we must turn to certain passages in *A Vision*, a book describing the whole metaphysical construction which, as he says, provided his poetry with metaphors. "One must bear in mind that the Christian Era, like the two thousand years, let us say, that went before it, is an entire wheel, and each half of it an entire wheel, that each half when it comes to its 28th Phase reaches the 15th Phase or the 1st Phase of the entire era. It follows therefore that the 15th Phase of each millennium, to keep the symbolic measure of time, is Phase 8 or Phase 22

55

of the entire era, that Aphrodite rises from a stormy sea, that Helen could not be Helen but for beleagured Troy."

A Vision has been dismissed as a mere fanciful bye-product of Yeats's mind, and as having no relevance to his poetry. But passage after passage could be quoted from it to show how truly he spoke when he said that it provided his poetry with metaphors. Indeed, it provided his poetry with its most striking metaphors. There is a close connection between the explanation of the circle as it is given in *A Vision* and the last verse of *The Second Coming:*

> Surely some revelation is at hand;
> Surely the Second Coming is at hand.
> The Second Coming! Hardly are these words out
> When a vast image out of *Spiritus Mundi*
> Troubles my sight: somewhere in sands of the desert
> A shape with lion body and the head of a man
> Is moving its slow thighs, while all about it
> Reel shadows of the indignant desert birds.
> The darkness drops again; but now I know
> That twenty centuries of stony sleep
> Were vexed to nightmare by a rocking cradle,
> And what rough beast, its hour come round at last,
> Slouches towards Bethlehem to be born?

The twenty centuries which were vexed to nightmare by a rocking cradle were the two thousand years before the Christian Era, mentioned in the passage I have just quoted. Another two thousand years have almost passed since then; so the poem begins:

> Turning and turning in the widening gyre
> The falcon cannot hear the falconer;
> Things fall apart; the centre cannot hold;
> Mere anarchy is loosed upon the world.

But the proof of this did not lie, for Yeats, in the actual falling-apart world as we see it or as the newspapers describe it; the proof lay in the cosmological scheme outlined in *A Vision*, a scheme which was given to him by invisible communicators who spoke to Mrs. Yeats while she was in a state of trance. The passion in the image of

A shape with lion body and the head of a man,

slouching towards Bethlehem to be born, comes from the same source, not from the extraordinary history of our time.

The connection between the abstract scheme and the poetry is just as close in *Leda*, one of Yeats's greatest poems. "I imagine," he says in *A Vision*, "the annunciation that founded Greece as made to Leda, remembering that they showed in a Spartan temple, strung up to the roof as a holy relic, an unhatched egg of hers; and that from one of her eggs came Love and from the other War." And in the poem, after describing that curious annunciation, he repeats his theory in a few lines which imply the circle, and with that a thousand years;

> A shudder in the loins engenders there
> The broken wall, the burning roof and tower
> And Agamemnon dead.

The two poems, *Sailing to Byzantium* and *Byzantium*, are more loosely related to the abstract scheme; but their mysterious impressiveness comes from the fact that Byzantium represented something specific to Yeats, which is not the Byzantium that other people know. "Each age," he says in *A Vision*, "unwinds the thread another age had wound, and it amuses one to remember that before Phidias, and his westward-moving art, Persia fell, and that when full moon came round again, amid eastward-moving thought, and brought Byzantium glory, Rome fell; and that at the outset of our westward-moving Renaissance Byzantium fell; all things dying into each other's life, living in each other's death." The two poems about Byzantium, along with *Leda* and *The Second Coming*, are among the greatest of Yeats's poems, and they are inspired by the thought that time is a great wheel of two thousand years.

I have insisted on this close relation between Yeats's poetry, and especially his later poetry, and his conception of human history as a fixed scheme, because it is sometimes said that he was best as an occasional poet. He wrote some fine occasional poetry, though none of it has the same imaginative intensity as *Leda* or *Byzantium*; but in the best of that poetry the occasion is an occasion within the wheel, an occasion in two thousand years, not in ten or twenty. This gives the fine poem *Coole and Ballylee* its intensity, and allows Yeats, after lines like

> Sound of a stick upon the floor, a sound
> From somebody that toils from chair to chair,

to end up with

> But all is changed, that high horse riderless
> Though mounted in that saddle Homer rode
> Where the swan drifts upon a darkening flood.

The house and the lake described in the poem exist in the great wheel as well as in the late nineteenth century or the early twentieth. Again *A Dialogue of Self and Soul* in *The Winding Stair* can be regarded as an argument either between two selves of Yeats, or between the two gyring cones whose interaction produces the wheel: it is both highly personal and quite impersonal:

> I am content to live it all again
> And yet again, if it be life to pitch
> Into the frog-spawn of a blind man's ditch,
> A blind man battering blind men . . .

This effect of millennial time is one of the most extraordinary qualities of Yeats's later poetry, whether it is expressed in direct mythical images of a

58

rough beast, its hour come round at last

slouching towards Bethlehem to be born, or of

The broken wall, the burning roof and tower

engendered in Leda's loins by the touch of the swan; or whether it merely gives an added meaning and impressiveness to common things, such as the house at Coole, or to Yeats's argument with himself, by setting them all in a frame of two thousand years. That frame, in which the generations are woven into a pattern, and along with them a Platonic image of human life, certainly excited his imagination more deeply than the events of his own lifetime: so that it is not too much to claim that when he said

Things fall apart; the centre cannot hold,

he was not thinking of the actual disruption of society happening under his eyes, but of the approaching end of his millennium.

To say this is not to impugn his poetry. A poet must write about whatever theme inspires him; and what seems to have inspired Yeats is this image of the wheel of time, vast and inhuman compared with the little revolution of the single individual life, yet an impersonal extension and development of that; for the wheel is the wheel of human fate: it may not be ruled by humanity, but it is made up of it.

Using the image of the circle, the development of Yeats's poetry may be described by saying that at the beginning there was only one somewhat vague twilight circle for him, and that afterwards it separated into two. One half of it extended and hardened to take in Troy and Bethlehem and Byzantium, while the other contracted and hardened to the Ireland of the last two hundred years, and finally to the Ireland of the old Irish families whose life Yeats could remember. "In the early symbolist poems," Stephen Spender says, "in *The Wind Among the Reeds*, the symbolism, the magic

59

and the twilight are all interwoven, and the symbols therefore lose power because they are not sufficiently isolated."
This is not true of the later poems; there we have the symbolical frame on the one hand, the wheel of time or fate, and
on the other the Ireland Yeats once knew; and the one is set
against the other. To see life within a self-contained circle has
obvious disadvantages. Yeats's imaginative speculation had
an unusual range, but the sphere of his human sympathies
was narrow. It was aesthetic at first, and after he turned
his mind to politics and contemporary things it became
aristocratic, which is perhaps another way of saying that it
was still aesthetic.

> And may her bridegroom bring her to a house
> Where all's accustomed, ceremonious;
> For arrogance and hatred are the wares
> Peddled in the thoroughfares.
> How but in custom and in ceremony
> Are innocence and beauty born?
> Ceremony's a name for the rich horn
> And custom for the spreading laurel tree.

If this attitude is aristocratic, it is clearly an offshoot of an
aesthetic view of life as well. The fifth and sixth lines are fine
examples of Yeats's authoritative style when it is not really
saying much, or saying anything true, and yet goes on
"impressing" us. These lines sound false when they are put
beside the poetry of *Byzantium*, and they irrelevantly remind
us that Yeats was a member of an old Irish family. When he
wrote of Leda and Bethlehem he did not think so much of
custom and ceremony. Even his conception of the wheel is
more aesthetic than religious; and his very idea of immortality is somewhat exclusive, though in a different way from
Calvin's; a way which the Rhymers' Club would have liked.
Mr. Spender may be right when he says that "Yeats's poetry
is devoid of any unifying moral subject." But when his
imagination is inspired by the wheel Yeats can create, as
no other poet of our time, a vision of archetypal human fate.

His direct criticism of life is not that of great poetry: there is a lack of moral immediacy in it, concealed by his high, dignified, authoritative style, with its touch of the brogue:

> The innocent and the beautiful
> Have no enemy but time;
> Arise and bid me strike a match
> And strike another till time catch;
> Should the conflagration climb,
> Run till all the sages know.

There is a certain triviality and a certain picturesqueness in these lines, and the triviality comes from the picturesqueness. The moral subject of which Spender speaks is lacking, as it is not in Marvell's famous lines. But the moral subject is present when Yeats writes of the wheel with a full sense of its inevitable revolution, as in *Leda* and *Byzantium*. Then his imagination is not only solid, but rises to an extraordinary splendour.

In the poetry of Ezra Pound a development roughly similar to Yeats's can be seen; that is, a movement from the shadowy and the "poetic" towards the hard and the clear. In his earlier poetry, as in that of Yeats, all the qualities are interwoven, to use Spender's term, and the qualities accordingly "lose power because they are not sufficiently isolated". Many of the qualities in the early poems are influences; the influence of Provençal poetry, of Browning, of Swinburne, of Yeats, and of the poets who influenced Yeats. Perhaps the work of no other poet shows more strikingly the benefit and the dangers which can be extracted from the close study and imitation of poetic models. This seems to have been a deliberate discipline to Pound, by which he perfected his own style. In the early poems the imitation is sometimes very close.

> In vain have I striven
> to teach my heart to bow;

In vain have I said to him
  "There be many singers greater than thou",

is almost Swinburne, as this is almost Browning:

You grabbed at the gold sure; had no need to pack cents
Into your versicles.
                      Clear sight's elector.

But this imitation led to *Altaforte*, in which, while there is still something both of Browning and Swinburne, there is also something which is not to be found in either:

Damn it all! all this our South stinks peace.
You whoreson dog, Papiols, come! Let's to music!
I have no life save when the swords clash.
But ah! when I see the standards gold, vair, purple, opposing
And the broad fields beneath them turn crimson,
Then howls my heart nigh mad with rejoicing.

That is not Pound at his best, for the voice is neither quite his, nor quite that of the imaginary monologist, Bertrand de Born. But as a piece of poetic craftmanship in the medieval sense it is extraordinarily skilful. The poetry which it resembles most is the poetry of the Scottish Makars, and particularly that of Dunbar, the interest of whose verse does not consist in originality of thought or even of imaginative treatment, but in the skill of the actual verbal and metrical working. Dunbar's integrity as a poet resided mainly in that, and Pound's integrity is more strictly confined to that than is usual in our time. He is more concerned than any other contemporary poet with the actual material with which he works: that is with words and the skilful use of them. He translated Guido Cavalcanti to rid himself of "the crust of dead English". He welcomed Imagism because it gave him an opportunity to continue the process. Honest material and skill; these were the medieval artist's requirements, and these are probably Pound's too. Eliot in dedicating *The Waste*

Land to him called him "il miglior fabbro"; and he is a *Maker* in much the same sense as Dunbar; indisputably, in any case, the most honest, skilful master of *verse* of his time. His skill is not the barren, correct skill which turns everything into the same perfect pattern; it is endlessly creative; it has invented new modes for poetry; and in this it is once more medieval. Skill of this kind is highly specialised. "Don't imagine," Pound said in *A Few Don'ts by an Imagiste*, "that the art of poetry is any simpler than the art of music." Skill of this kind tends also to dwarf the importance of the subject and even of the imaginative treatment. The poet is so confident of his technical mastery that he feels he can say anything; and so he takes it wherever he finds it, equally pleased with a situation out of his experience and with someone's transcription of experience.

It seems to me, on the other hand, that Pound is not a poet of great imaginative power, any more than Dunbar was. He prefers to transpose themes already imagined by other poets. Or rather he enters into the imagination of these poets, and here probably no other writer has excelled him. He has accordingly been called a translator, but this title takes away from him the credit for the very thing which he can do with such skill: that is to create new things by virtue of his mere mastery of language. To call a poet a translator is to attribute part of his excellence to the writer whom he is translating; and to give the credit for the poetic virtue of *Homage to Propertius* to Propertius seems to me absurd, and equally absurd to apply the same judgment to the poetry in *Cathay*. Such skill in language as Pound's is creative; and Eliot's claim that "Chinese poetry as we know it to-day is something invented by Ezra Pound," is true. The poetry is a fact; but there seems to be some idea that it is due to Mei Sheng or Rihaku. It is due to Pound's skill as a poet.

The early poems are filled with reminiscences, and some of the lines read like a pastiche:

Strange spars of knowledge and dimmed wares of price.

63

But in this delightful, highly-coloured poetry there are also countless evocative passages which are both medieval and Pound, lines such as:

> Rest brother, for lo! the dawn is without!
> The yellow flame paleth
> And the wax runs low.

or

> and we knew all that stream,
> And our two horses had traced out the valleys;
> Knew the low flooded lands squared out with poplars,
> In the young days when the deep sky befriended.

About Pound's Provençal and early Italian poetry Mr. Eliot seems to me to have said the last word, and there is nothing I can add to it:

> "It is almost too platitudinous to say that one is not modern by writing about chimney-pots, or archaic by writing about oriflammes. It is true that most people who write of oriflammes are merely collecting old coins, as most people who write about chimney-pots are merely forging new ones. If one can really penetrate the life of another age, one is penetrating the life of one's own. . . . The people who tire of Pound's Provence and Pound's Italy are those who cannot see Provence and medieval Italy except as museum pieces, which is not how Pound sees them, or how he makes others see them. . . . He does see them as contemporary with himself; that is to say, he has grasped certain things in Provence and Italy which are permanent in human nature. He is much more modern, in my opinion, when he deals with Italy and Provence, than when he deals with modern life. His Bertrand de Born is much more living than his Mr. Hecatomb Styrax (*Moeurs Contemporains*). When he deals with antiquities, he extracts the essentially living; when he deals with contemporaries, he sometimes notes only the accidental."

The student of Pound should begin with this Provençal and

early Italian Poetry; it is the most obviously delightful work that he has written, and the most easy to understand; it is, in any case, necessary to an understanding of his later work.

From his Provençal phase Pound passed by way of his rendering of the Anglo-Saxon poem, *The Wayfarer*, to the Chinese poems in *Cathay*. He is still dealing in these with a medieval or at least a pre-Renaissance world. In *Lustra*, which appeared in 1915, there are some poems concerned with his own time. And in a longish poem, *Hugh Selwyn Mauberley*, which was published in 1920, he turned his full attention on the world around him.

Hugh Selwyn Mauberley has been more highly praised, perhaps, than any other poem of Pound, and it has had a considerable influence on modern poetry. "This seems to me a great poem," says Eliot.

"On the one hand, I perceive that the versification is more accomplished than that of any other poems in this book[1] and more varied. I only pretend to know as much about versifying as my carpenter knows about woodwork, or my painter knows about distemper. But I know very well that the apparent roughness and *naïveté* of the verse and rhyming of *Mauberley* are inevitably the result of many years of hard work: if you cannot appreciate the dexterity of *Alaforte* you cannot appreciate the simplicity of *Mauberley*. On the other side, the poem seems to me, when you have marked the sophistication and the great variety of the verse, verse of a man who knows his way about, to be a positive document of sensibility. It is compact of the experience of a certain man in a certain place at a certain time; and it is also a document of an epoch; it is genuine tragedy and comedy; and it is, in the best sense of Arnold's worn phrase, a 'criticism of life'."

Other writers have also praised this poem very highly, but I am unable to agree with them. I admit that the versification is more accomplished than that of Pound's earlier poetry, accomplished as that was; it is an extremely

[1] *Selected Poems of Ezra Pound.*

E

skilful, deliberately *crippled* versification, admirably adapted
to its purpose, the description of a crippled world. I admit,
too, that the poem is compact of the experience of a certain
man in a certain place at a certain time, and that it is a
document of an epoch. And I admit, finally, that

> For three years, out of tune with his time,
> He strove to resuscitate the dead art
> Of poetry; to maintain "the sublime"
> In the old sense. Wrong from the start—

is more genuine utterance, and therefore better poetry, than

> In vain have I striven
>   to teach my heart to bow;
> In vain have I said to him
>   "There be many singers greater than thou".

But I cannot admit that the poem is genuine tragedy, or a
criticism of life in the best sense. It has an impressive indignation.

> Died some, pro patria,
>   non "dulce" non "et decor" . . .

> walked eye-deep in hell
> believing in old men's lies, then unbelieving
> came home, home to a lie,
> home to many deceits,
> home to old lies and new infamy;
> usury age-old and age-thick
> and liars in public places.

> Daring as never before, wastage as never before.
> Young blood and high blood,
> fair cheeks, and fine bodies;

> fortitude as never before

66

frankness as never before,
disillusions as never told in the old days,
hysterias, trench confessions,
laughter out of dead bellies.

But what Eliot said of Pound's Hell in the *Cantos* can also
be said of this poetry: that it is a poetry directed at *other
people*, as indignation always is: at old men's lies, usury age-
old and age-thick, and liars in public places. These lines
are moving because of their passion and their sincerity;
but even while we are moved by them, we are conscious
of their inadequacy as a poetic response to their subject,
which was the War: they are certainly not tragic. Nor is
the poem a criticism of life in the best sense:

There died a myriad,
And of the best, among them,
For an old bitch gone in the teeth,
    For a botched civilization,

Charm, smiling at the good mouth,
Quick eyes gone under earth's lid,

For two gross of broken statues,
For a few thousand battered books.

This is the comment of a craftsman. In the Middle Ages
the judgment of a craftsman had a general bearing, for the
craftsman had a recognised function in society; the over-
ruling idea which governed the whole social structure, both
religious and political, applied to him too; so that the conclusions which he came to in following his vocation were
applicable to the other vocations and ranks of society, and
not merely to a generality, "an old bitch gone in the teeth",
with which he was neither acquainted nor concerned. The
craftsman now has no recognised function in society, and his
position is exactly enough described in another passage in
the same poem:

Beneath the sagging roof
The stylist has taken shelter,
Unpaid, uncelebrated,
At last from the world's welter

Nature receives him;
With a placid and uneducated mistress
He exercises his talents
And the soil meets his distress.

The haven from sophistications and contentions
Leaks through its thatch;
He offers succulent cooking;
The door has a creaking latch.

This is a conventional Bohemian portrait of the position of
the artist in the modern world as Pound saw it; and it is all
the better, in one way, for being conventional; for it defines
the centre from which the criticism of life in the poem
comes. *Mauberley* has a number of incontestable and even
lofty virtues: honesty, seriousness, indignation, and sometimes an exquisite sense of comedy. But it seems to me
strikingly inadequate as tragedy, as a criticism of life,
and as a criticism of Pound's age.

There is an allegorical aphorism by Franz Kafka which
is peculiarly applicable to the age of Pound and Eliot, to
which Kafka himself belonged. "He was once part of a
monumental group," says Kafka. "Round some raised figure
in the centre there stood in significant order effigies of the
military class, the arts, the sciences, the handicrafts. He
was once one of those countless figures. But the group has
long since been dissolved, or at least he has left it and takes
his way through life alone. He does not have even his old
occupation any longer; indeed he has actually forgotten
what he once represented." This forgetting of what he once
was, Kafka goes on to say, causes a certain melancholy, uncertainty, unrest, a longing for vanished ages which troubles
the present. But at the same time that longing is a vital
element in the energy of the man who suffers from it.

This aphorism seems to me to apply strikingly to Pound and Eliot, who both look back to the group, and whose inspiration is that looking back. But it applies to Pound with this difference, that he does remember what he represented: so that what he looks back at is not the group but the place, now empty, which the arts occupied in it. His qualities as a poet are the qualities immemorially adapted to the occupation of that vacant place; they go with it; they do not go with a world where the group is dispersed. Pound is the archetypal poet, or the mere poet, who rises to greatness in an age of faith when men's conception of life is given to them complete, objectively, and all that the poet has to do is to say it out. But in a sceptical age where the poet has both to shape his conception of life and say it out, these virtues cannot come to fulfilment; they fight against the times, and the times against them.

In *Mauberley* Pound criticised society from the standpoint of the poet. In the *Cantos*, of which we have now had roughly a half, that is fifty-one, he recognised that something more was needed; and that more was, of all things, Social Credit. I have no quarrel with Social Credit, but it is not a substitute for a genuine criticism of life, any more than Dialectical Materialism is. In the *Cantos* it has certainly inspired some eloquent passages:

With usury has no man a good house
made of stone, no paradise on his church wall
With usury the stone cutter is kept from his stone
the weaver is kept from his loom by usury
Wool does not come to market
the peasant does not eat his own grain
The girl's needle goes blunt in her hand
The looms are hushed one after another
ten thousand after ten thousand . . .
Usury destroys the craftsman; destroying craft
Azure is caught with cancer. Emerald comes to no Memling
Usury kills the child in the womb
And breaks short the young man's courting

Usury brings age into youth; it lies between the bride
and the bridegroom
Usury is against Nature's increase.

In this passage there are many of Pound's virtues both as
a poet and a thinker, and all of them medieval: the direct
apprehension of simple good and simple evil, not quite the
ordinary man's good and evil; the use of words as they
were originally meant to be used; the respect for skill and
honesty in all work; the feeling that false work is not only
contemptible but iniquitous. There are in the *Cantos* fine
passages in this style, and fine passages in the descriptive
style, among them the Hell cantos, which I think have been
unjustly depreciated. But in spite of what both Yeats and
Eliot have written about the *Cantos*, I feel that their meaning
is lost under a mass of detail, presented without order, or
in an order which is unknown to the reader, and that their
meaning, even without this encumbrance, would not be
of the first importance, partly because Pound's judgments
of life are the specialised judgments of the artist and the
reformer, and partly because his world, as Eliot said of his
Hell, is a world "*for other people*, the people we read about in
the newspapers, not for oneself and one's friends".

Yeats once described the plan of the *Cantos* as he gathered
it from Pound in 1928.

> "It will, when the hundredth Canto is finished, display a
> structure like that of a Bach fugue. There will be no plot, no
> chronicle of events, no logic of discourse, but the two themes,
> the descent into Hades from Homer, a metamorphosis from
> Ovid, and mixed with these medieval or modern historical
> characters. He has tried to produce that picture Porteous
> recommended to Nicholas Poussin in *Le Chef d'Oeuvre In-
> connu* where everything rounds and thrusts itself without
> edges, without contours—conventions of the intellect—from
> a splash of tints and shades, to achieve a work as characteris-
> tic of the art of our times as the painting of Cezanne, avowedly
> suggested by Porteous, as *Ulysses* and its dream association
> of words and images, a poem in which there is nothing that

can be taken out and reasoned over, nothing that is not part of the poem itself. He has scribbled on the back of an envelope certain sets of letters that represent emotions or archetypal events—I cannot find any adequate definition—A B C D and then J K L M, and then each set of letters repeated, and then A B C D inverted and this repeated, and then a new element X Y Z, then certain letters that never recur, and then all sorts of combinations of X Y Z and J K L M and A B C D and D C B A, and all set whirling together. He has shown me upon the wall a photograph of a Cosimo Tura decoration in three compartments, in the upper the Triumph of Love and the Triumph of Chastity, in the middle Zodiacal signs, and in the lower certain events in Cosimo Tura's day. The Descent and the Metamorphosis—A B C D and J K L M— his fixed elements, took the place of the Zodiac, the arche- typal persons—X Y Z—that of the Triumphs, and certain modern events—his letters that do not recur—that of those events in Cosimo Tura's day."

I find this explanation almost as difficult as the poem itself, and I do not know how much of it to attribute to Yeats and how much to Pound. If in the *Cantos* the Zodiac in Cosimo Tura's picture is represented by the Descent and the Metamorphosis, the Triumphs by the archetypal per- sons, and the contemporary figures by figures of our own time, it is clear, of course, that these can be inverted and even sent all whirling together: it is an exciting idea. But to excite us, it is necessary that we should know the principle on which they are sent whirling, and here Yeats leaves us as uncertain as Pound himself does. To set them whirling is not in itself meritorious; if there is not an order in the whirling, it will merely confuse us. As I cannot discover an order, it seems to me that Pound in his manipulation of these elements often inverts and combines them at hazard, under a momentary impulse, not in obedience to a firm and governing plan; and the result is not a pattern, but a confusion of the legendary, the historical and the contem- porary in a featureless present. A featureless present has something of the quality of a Day of Judgment, for it effaces temporal differences and with that what Nietzsche calls the pathos of distance. In the *Cantos* the seventeenth century is as close as the present, Greece and China as near as Paris or London: or rather nearer, for they were generally more real. The endless day, then, is there; but one may remain doubtful of the judgment; for the crowd is one undistinguished crowd: the trumpet, by some oversight, has not blown. Before listening to Pound's explanation of the *Cantos*, Yeats said that he had "often found there brightly printed kings, queens, knaves", but had "never discovered why all the suits could not be dealt out in some quite different order". This, I think, is not an uncommon and perhaps a legitimate feeling, but the brightly printed kings, queens and knaves remain, and much beside them; a music unparalleled in contemporary poetry and passages of concrete strangeness, as in the description of the metamorphosis in the second canto:

> And where was gunwale, there now was vine-trunk,
> And tenthril where cordage had been,
>> grape-leaves on the rowlocks,
> Heavy grape on the oarshafts,
> And, out of nothing, a breathing,
>> hot breath on my ankles,
> Beasts like shadows in glass,
>> a furred tail upon nothingness,
> Lynx-purr, and the heathery smell of beasts,
>> where tar smell had been,
> Sniff and pad-foot of beasts,
>> eye-glitter out of black air . . .
> And the ship like a keel in ship-yard,
>> slung like an ox in smith's sling,
> Ribs stuck fast in the ways,
>> grape-cluster over pin-rack,
>> void air taking pelt.
> Lifeless air become sinewed,
>> feline leisure of panthers,
> Leopards sniffing the grape shoots by scupper-hole,
> Crouched panthers by fore-hatch,

72

> And the sea blue-deep about us,
> green-ruddy in shadows . . .

There is in the *Cantos*, along with a mass of jumbled knowledge divulged in obscure hints, a great volume of various
kinds of poetry. But a poem without a significant order
cannot be a good poem; and it seems to me that the *Cantos*
is not so much a masterpiece as a monument of Pound's
faults. Pound is in one way the most creative poet
of his time; he has invented more new poetic modes
than anyone else, and influenced poetry more than anyone
else. But the *Cantos* give the impression of being inventive
without a plan, or with an insufficient one: this is perhaps
a summary judgment, but summary judgments cannot be
avoided in a book such as this.

More has probably been written about Eliot than about
any other modern poet. The two best explanatory studies
of him which I know are *The Poetry of T. S. Eliot*, by Hugh
Ross Williamson, a simple exposition, and *The Achievement
of T. S. Eliot*, by F. O. Matthiessen, a critical work of considerable interest, which insists on the unity of Eliot's work
in poetry and prose. To anyone who wishes to understand in
detail Eliot's poetry, these books will be useful. But this is
an introduction, not an explanation; it merely tries to give a
first impression, and to prepare the reader for the immediate
quality which he may expect to find in the particular poet.
In writing about a poet who has been so much discussed as
Eliot, it is not easy to disentangle the first impression from
the others. And when I try to find an epithet to distinguish
him from Yeats and Pound, his chief contemporaries in
poetry, the one that comes to my mind is one on which he
himself has cast something amounting to an aspersion:
that is, originality.

In the Introduction to his selection of Pound's poem
(the best approach to Pound, incidentally) Eliot conveniently summarises his ideas on originality.

"Poets may be divided into those who develop technique,

73

those who imitate technique, and those who invent technique. When I say 'invent', I should use inverted commas, for invention would be irreproachable if it were possible. 'Invention' is wrong only because it is impossible. I mean that the difference between the 'development' and the 'sport' is, in poetry, a capital one. There are two kinds of 'sports' in poetry, in the floricultural sense. One is the imitation of development, and the other is the imitation of some idea of originality. The former is commonplace, a waste product of civilization. The latter is contrary to life. The poem which is absolutely original is absolutely bad; it is, in the bad sense, 'subjective', with no relation to the world to which it appeals.

Originality, in other words, is by no means a simple idea in the criticism of poetry. True originality is merely development; and if it is right development it may appear in the end so *inevitable* that we almost come to the point of view of denying all 'original' virtue to the poet. He simply did the right thing."

This analysis seems admirable to me, except for the fact that in the second paragraph it is vitiated by two adverbs which, I think, show a certain partisanship, as if Eliot were arguing with an invisible, immature opponent. Originality is *merely* development; the poet *simply* did the right thing. The implied assumption seems to be that it is a great feat to start something, and a comparatively easy and natural business to improve and change that thing by developing it. James Watt did the right thing when he drew his conclusion from the behaviour of the kettle. The development of Beethoven's music was the right development, or at least there is nobody who can say that it was not. But the thing was not obvious, and the development was not easy. About the beginning of things we know almost nothing, and can say almost nothing; but some beginnings seem to have been almost as fortuitous as the discovery of roast pork as fancifully described in Lamb's essay: such discoveries as that wood will float, and that a wheel will roll. From the wheel came so many things that it would be hopeless to try to enumerate them. From the piece of wood came the rowing

74

boat, then the sailing ship, then the steamship; and between the steamship and the piece of wood there is a great distance, for into each of these phases something new entered, and new in the same way as the original discovery that a piece of wood will float. The development, then, was not *merely* development; it was at every stage an addition which changed what it was added to, thus creating, or at least bringing about, something new. There are not many examples in poetry or in the arts of development on this scale; but all genuine development, on whatever scale, has this double character, and is at once derivative and independent; and this in reality is what people generally mean by the word original. It is in this sense that I think Eliot is the most original poet of his time. He has brought to poetry an independent mind and an independent consciousness; a mind and a consciousness, it seems to me, more independent than either Yeats's or Pound's. He has never been in a movement, even the one which has started from his work.

His originality was shown from the start, though the form in which be began to write, in 1908 or 1909, he tells us, "was directly drawn from the study of Laforgue together with the later Elizabethan drama". These influences can be seen clearly enough in his first work, the influence of Laforgue most clearly in *Prufrock*, and that of the later Elizabethan drama most clearly in *Gerontion*, but there is nothing "derivative" in the result, nothing of the same kind as Pound's

> For I was a gaunt, grave councillor,
> Being in all things wise, and very old,

or as Yeats's
> And no more turn aside and brood
> Upon love's bitter mystery.

Even when Eliot took Laforgue's line "Simple et sans foi comme un bonjour" and made it "Simple and faithless as a smile and shake of the hand", he did not compromise his

75

style; the words were a simple and open borrowing of something that he wanted, nothing more. What gave his first
poetry its essential effect was not that its form was directly
drawn from the study of Laforgue and the later Elizabethan
drama, but that it came from an original vision of life; and
Eliot tells us something more important about it when he
confesses that he hated the "cheerfulness, optimism, and
hopefulness" of the nineteenth century so much that he
acquired "the prejudice that poetry not only must be found
only *through* suffering but can find its material only *in*
suffering", a prejudice so strong that for many years it kept
him from appreciating the *Paradiso*. He tells us a great deal
too when he says that the first thing for the poet "is not to
have a beautiful world with which to deal: it is to be able to
see beneath both beauty and ugliness; to see the boredom,
and the horror, and the glory". Yeats's poetry and Pound's
poetry, like so much of the poetry of the nineteenth century,
began by dealing with a beautiful world, or a beautified
world. Eliot's did not, he saw through the beauty and the
ugliness to the boredom and the horror; not so much, it
must be admitted, to the glory, though there must be some
perception of the glory before the boredom and the horror
can be seen at all.

The attribution of "cheerfulness, optimism, and hopefulness" to the whole nineteenth century is one of those rash
judgments, two-thirds true, to which Eliot commits himself
when he feels deeply; he obviously did not think of *Resolution
and Independence* or *The Trials of Margaret* or *Death's Jest Book*,
but rather of the attitude implied in "Joy in widest com-
monalty spread," and law broadening down from precedent
to precedent. The "cheerfulness, optimism, and hopefulness",
in any case, were consonant with a poetry which dealt with a
beautiful world; it was not consonant with a poetry which
saw beneath the beauty and the ugliness to the boredom, the
horror, and the glory. The later Elizabethan drama, on the
other hand, and Laforgue in a lesser degree, were consonant
with such poetry. So that while Eliot says that he drew the
form of his first poetry from these sources, it is clear that he

was first drawn to them by his own way of seeing the world, and drawn to them, too, in an age which was even more hopeful and optimistic than the Victorian one, for he began to write in 1908 or 1909.

Eliot is a poet whose quality is felt at once, no matter what poem one may take; the reader does not have to go, or to be led to, his later work, as in the case of Pound and Yeats, to find the essential poetry. He is as unquestionably himself in *Ash Wednesday*, which appeared in 1930, as in *Prufrock and other Observations*, which appeared in 1917. This is worth insisting upon, for there is an interpretation of Eliot which implies that he wrote one kind of poetry before, roughly, *The Waste Land*, and another kind of poetry after it: the later poetry generally being considered by critics who make this distinction as inferior to the earlier. The only difference in spirit which I can find between Eliot's early poetry and his later poetry is that doubt predominates in the one and faith in the other. The view of life as it is lived in this world is the same in his poetry all through, before his acceptance of Anglo-Catholicism and after it. The way in which he looks at life in *Gerontion* and *Sweeney Erect* is the foundation for the way in which he sees life in *Ash Wednesday*. *Gerontion*, a soliloquy of "an old man in a dry month", raises such questions as:

After such knowledge, what forgiveness? Think now
History has many cunning passages, contrived corridors
And issues, deceives us with whispering ambitions,
Guides us by vanities. Think now
She gives when our attention is distracted
And what she gives, gives with such supple confusions
That the giving famishes the craving. Gives too late
What's not believed in, or if still believed,
In memory only, reconsidered passion. Gives too soon
Into weak hands, what's thought can be dispensed with
Till the refusal propagates a fear.

In *Ash Wednesday*, a poem of tentative hope, Eliot has not

77

forgotten the questions asked here, or the conception of life which goes with them, but he sees them from a different point of vantage, praying that he may forget

> These matters that with myself I too much discuss
> Too much explain,

and going on to say

> Because these wings are no longer wings to fly
> But merely vans to beat the air
> The air which is now thoroughly small and dry
> Smaller and dryer than the will
> Teach us to care and not to care
> Teach us to sit still.

I think that anyone who agrees with Eliot's definition of originality as development will admit that this is at least the *next* thing. Or rather not merely the next thing, for the poem describes an intense spiritual effort. In *Gerontion* it may be said that Eliot keeps going round in a circle, and in *Ash Wednesday* that he climbs an ascending circle, typified by the stair with its different stages. There was a foreshadowing of this effort, or rather a recognition of its necessity, in the last part of *The Waste Land*, with its disguised exhortation to "give, sympathise, control"; but *Ash Wednesday* is concerned with the effort itself, and it is real in a different way, because it is the next step, not merely an admission that a next step is required. It is worth insisting upon this, for disapproval and astonishment have been expressed at Eliot's development as a poet. His development seems to me far less astonishing than that of Donne, between whose secular and religious poetry there is a really surprising difference. The astonishment, therefore, I imagine, is not at Eliot's development as a poet, but at the idea that anyone now can accept the Christian religion; and to be surprised at that implies an attitude which retains some of the "cheerfulness, optimism, and hopefulness" which Eliot hated so much, and of which there is no trace either in his early or his later poetry. In *Ash Wednesday* there is no invocation of these qualities, but rather of

> strength beyond hope and despair
> climbing the third stair.

And the impulse of these lines comes as necessarily from a perception of the horror, the boredom and the glory of human life, as the cheerfulness, optimism, and hopefulness came from a perception of the beauty of life.

Eliot was from the first acutely aware of the contemporary world, and had in a very high degree what is called the social sense. This awareness is so strong that he keeps it even when he is alone with a natural scene. In *Burnt Norton* there is a beautiful passage describing a garden, and the beauty comes mainly from human associations:

> Go, said the bird, for the leaves were full of children,
> Hidden excitedly, containing laughter.

Again when he wrote a short poem on *Rannoch, by Glencoe* what struck him first was

> Here the crow starves, here the patient stag
> Breeds for the rifle.

Even in a decorative verse such as

> Gloomy Orion and the Dog
> Are veiled; and hushed the shrunken seas;
> The person in the Spanish Cape
> Tries to sit on Sweeney's knees,

there is not only a contrast, but a bringing together as well: it is a grotesque landscape with human figures. A finer example comes near the end of *Gerontion*:

> De Bailhache, Fresca, Mrs. Cammel, whirled

79

> Beyond the circuit of the shuddering Bear
> In fractured atoms.

There is certainly no communion with Nature here, in Wordsworth's sense; the world is a scene set for the drama of human life, and it is filled to the last nook with associations of human life:

> And the bird called, in response to
> The unheard music hidden in the shrubbery,
> And the unseen eyebeams crossed, for the roses
> Had the look of flowers that are looked at.

This is closer in spirit to Pope, on the one hand, and to the medieval view of the world, on the other, than to Wordsworth.

> The silence that is in the starry sky,
> The sleep that is among the lonely hills

does not exist in Eliot's world. The starry sky there is something which has been looked at for thousands of years by human eyes, and the lonely hills have been crossed by human feet. Also the patient stag breeds for the rifle, and behind the rifle there is a social class with all that it stands for, and behind that class there is society itself, and behind that is history, which made society what it is, and in and through history there is tradition. In a brilliant essay Heine said that the romantic poet sang his hymns to the Almighty alone; preferably in suitable natural surroundings. There is no trace in Eliot's poetry of this attitude; he is always conscious of society and of social values, and even when he addresses the Almighty, it is a social as well as a personal act, and involves participation in a church. No poet since the Romantic Movement has possessed so strongly this imaginative knowledge of the reality and the ubiquity of the ties which bind the individual to society, and society together; and that knowledge is founded in the last resort on a perception of

man's weakness. Part of the impulse of the romantic poets
came from a sense of unexpressed powers latent in man, as
in Wordsworth's lines;

> Enough if something from our hands have power
> To live, and act, and serve the future hour;
> And if, as toward the silent tomb we go,
> Through love, through hope and faith's transcendent
>   dower,
> We feel that we are greater than we know.

This is an attitude, essentially religious, which might well
prompt the poet to sing his hymns to the Almighty alone; for
it insists on the power, not on the weakness, of the human
soul. To be aware of the soul's strength is to be aware of the
individual at his highest potentiality; but to be aware of the
soul's weakness is to be aware of the whole human complex.

I think that three stages can be roughly discerned in
Eliot's poetry, corresponding to his growing realisation of the
nature of human society. In *Prufrock and other Observations* he
is concerned with contemporary society as it is, and its
environment. The mood of these poems is perfectly
represented by the first verse of *The Love Song of J. Alfred
Prufrock*:

> Let us go then, you and I,
> When the evening is spread out against the sky
> Like a patient etherised upon a table;
> Let us go, through certain half-deserted streets,
> The muttering retreats
> Of restless nights in one-night cheap hotels
> And sawdust restaurants with oyster-shells:
> Streets that follow like a tedious argument
> Of insidious intent
> To lead you to an overwhelming question . . .
> Oh, do not ask, "What is it?"
> Let us go and make our visit.

This gives an idea of Eliot's picture of contemporary society
with its touch of nightmare in the evening spread out like a
patient etherised upon a table, its occasional grimy pathos:

> Shall I say, I have gone at dusk through narrow streets
> And watched the smoke that rises from the pipes
> Of lonely men in shirt-sleeves, leaning out of windows?

Its occasional desperation:

> I should have been a pair of ragged claws
> Scuttling across the floors of silent seas.

Its recognition of ignominious weakness:

And indeed there will be time
To wonder, "Do I dare?" and, "Do I dare?"
Time to turn back and descend the stair,
With a bald spot in the middle of my hair—
(They will say: "How his hair is growing thin!")
My morning coat, my collar mounting firmly to the chin,
My necktie rich and modest, but asserted by a simple pin—
(They will say; "But his arms and legs are thin!")
Do I dare
Disturb the universe?
In a minute there is time
For decisions and revisions which a minute will reverse.

Of opportunity missed:

But though I have wept and fasted, wept and prayed,
Though I have seen my head (grown slightly bald) brought
        in upon a platter,
I am no prophet— and here's no great matter;
I have seen the moment of my greatness flicker,
I have seen the eternal Footman hold my coat, and snicker,
And in short, I was afraid.

The scene is absolutely contemporary, the spirit quite disillusioned, as in the other poems in the same volume. But in a volume which appeared in 1920, three years later, history and history's ruins begin to appear behind the foreground of society in a series of poems of which *Burbank with a Baedeker: Bleinstein with a Cigar* is an example:

> A lustreless protrusive eye
> Stares from the protozoic slime
> At a perspective of Canaletto
> The smoky candle end of time
>
> Declines. On the Rialto once.
> The rats are underneath the piles. . . .

The poem ends:

> Who clipped the lion's wings
> And flea'd his rump and pared his claws?
> Thought Burbank, meditating on
> Time's ruins, and the seven laws.

The real or imagined past is employed here as a deliberate foil to the present. This method was used with much more ingenuity and imaginative force in *The Waste Land*, which appeared in 1922. There is no space here to give an analysis of that extremely complicated poem; and if the reader wants one, I must refer him to Mr. Hugh Ross Williamson and Mr. F. O. Matthiessen. I am doubtful of the use or importance of such analyses of poetry; but the poem is difficult at a first reading, and requires some elucidation. The main clue to its structure is to be found in Miss Jessie L. Weston's book on the Grail legend, *From Ritual to Romance*, mentioned in one of the notes at the end of the poem. In this volume Miss Weston relates how the mystery of death and rebirth is often symbolised in mythology by a kingdom where, when the reign has been weakened or destroyed by sickness, old age or war, "the land becomes Waste, and the task of the hero is that of

83

restoration", not by seeking personal power but the salvation of his country. The second clue to the poem is given by Eliot himself in the notes:

> "Tiresias, although a mere spectator and not indeed a 'character', is yet the most important personage in the poem, uniting all the rest. . . . What Tiresias *sees*, in fact, is the substance of the poem."

Probably another clue may be found in one of Eliot's essays, in which he says that the mature poet is

> "one who not merely restores a tradition which has been in abeyance, but one who in his poetry retwines as many straying strands of tradition as possible".

There is perhaps a too deliberate retwining of the straying strands of tradition in *The Waste Land*, and it is this that made most of the notes necessary. The strands had in some cases to be identified, and the knots explained, and when we know how a knot is tied we can untie it again. But the poem is an extremely complicated one, and never, I think, perversely complicated, and some licence was not only permissible, but necessary.

The poem is on the one hand a description of the contemporary world, which is a land become waste because the reign has been weakened or destroyed. On the other, it is a vision of society or rather of humanity seen historically, through the eyes of Tiresias, "old man with wrinkled dugs", both male and female:

> I who have sat by Thebes below the wall
> And walked among the lowest of the dead.

The historical background of civilised man is suggested in all sorts of ingenious ways, with a skilful unexpectedness, and the poem sets up a number of complex reverberations, which roll back through time until the contemporary scene finds its original in one that happened long ago, giving the feeling that we are contemplating the prototypes of human conduct. The effect is above all an effect of depth.

It may be this constant reference back of contemporary actions which makes Stephen Spender say that there is no scene in *The Waste Land* taken from life; that they are all spun out of Eliot's mind. Spender quotes some lines of Wilfred Owen to illustrate the distinction: the well-known lines in which a living soldier meets his dead enemy:

"Strange friend," I said, "here is no cause to mourn."
"None," said the other, "save the undone years,
The hopelessness. Whatever hope is yours,
Was my life also; I went hunting wild
After the wildest beauty in the world,
Which lies not calm in eyes, or braided hair,
But mocks the steady running of the hour,
And if it grieves, grieves richlier than here.
For by my glee might many men have laughed,
And of my weeping something had been left,
Which must die now. I mean the truth untold,
The pity of War, the pity war distilled.
Now men will go content with what we spoiled.
Or, discontent, boil bloody, and be spilled.
They will be swift with swiftness of the tigress,
None will break ranks, though nations trek from progress.
Courage was mine, and I had mystery,
Wisdom was mine, and I had mastery;
To miss the march of this retreating world
Into vain citadels that are not walled.

The immediacy of these lines, their direct concentration on the reality as it is, make them intensely moving and give them a high moral force. They certainly confront the horror of life more patiently than Eliot does when he writes:

But at my back in a cold blast I hear
The rattle of the bones, and chuckle spread from ear to ear.
A rat crept softly through the vegetation

Dragging its slimy belly on the bank
While I was fishing in the dull canal
On a winter evening round behind the gashouse
Musing upon the king my brother's wreck
And on the king my father's death before him.

To anyone concerned with the objective evils of society, with
war, poverty, tyranny and injustice in all its forms, it may
appear a perverse occupation to fish in the dull canal and
muse upon a prince's wreck and a king's death. Even as the
symbol of past glory, now vanished, the lines will seem too
curious, too personal. Yet it is by means such as this that
Eliot gives depth to the poem. The depth is sometimes more
apparent than real, as in the last three lines of the scene in the
pub, when the customers are leaving:

Goonight Bill. Goonight Lou. Goonight May. Goonight.
Ta ta. Goonight. Goonight.
Good night, ladies, good night, sweet ladies, good night,
    good night.

These lines show one of the weaknesses of the poem, which
is a tendency to conceive the past as beautiful and noble and
the present as ugly and low. Here one has an unmistakable
feeling that the two contrasting scenes are mainly in Eliot's
mind, as Mr. Spender says. But this is true only in part. The
depth remains, and it is a depth which cannot be found in
Owen's poetry. *The Waste Land* has been called a tragic poem;
it is perhaps tragic in the sense that it expresses a communion
between the living and the dead, and sees all that can be
done bound up with all that has been done; but the dead in
the poem sometimes strike one as being perversely idealised
at the expense of the living. *The Waste Land* is in any case a
poem of great poetic force.

In *Ash Wednesday* Eliot passes from a historical conception
of society to a religious one, or rather to that society within
society in which he sees man's sole hope of salvation. A church
is the only kind of institution in which the individual can

86

hold communion not only with the living, (the ideal of the Socialist and the Communist) but with the dead as well; and so membership of a church was perfectly consonant with Eliot's view of life and his development as a poet. *Ash Wednesday* is one of the most moving poems he has written, and perhaps the most perfect. It contains, I think, his most essential poetry, and, whether one agrees with his religious views or not (and I belong to no church), it is his most satisfactory comment on human life, the comment, at any rate, to which, after his other work, he was bound to come. It is a poem of great austerity, great integrity, and in reading it one is often reminded of an aphorism of Frank Kafka's: "There is a point after which there is no turning back. That is the point to be reached." All the poetry which Eliot has written since illustrates this saying.

Pound and Eliot have influenced modern poetry more than any other two writers. But in 1918 appeared the work of another poet who has since had an almost comparable influence: Gerard Manley Hopkins. Born in 1844, Hopkins was converted to the Roman Catholic Church in 1866 and ordained to the priesthood in 1877. He died in 1889. His poems were not published until twenty-nine years later, under the editorship of the late Robert Bridges, who had corresponded with him for many years before his death. A second edition, including some additional poems, appeared in 1930, with a critical introduction by Mr. Charles Williams.

Hopkins was first of all a poet of natural genius, with a purely sensuous apprehension of words such as many greater poets have not had, and an astonishing capacity to render by means of them the palpable shape, colour and feeling of the objects they described. This is perhaps Hopkins's most extraordinary single gift, and it came straight from his genius, for his letters and note-books show the passionate interest the physical world, with all its forms, colours and sounds, had for him. *The Windhover*, so well known now that it need hardly be quoted, is perhaps his most consummate achievement in this line, with its opening:

I caught this morning morning's minion, kingdom of daylight's dauphin, dapple-dawn-drawn Falcon, in
      his riding
Of the rolling level underneath him steady air,

where the order of the words in the third line seems to give a
primitive substantiality to the air itself, and make it into a
sort of transparent floor. Hopkins can write simply and get
this effect:

Degged with dew, dappled with dew,
Are the groins of the braes that the brook treads through,
Wiry heathpacks, flitches of fern,
And the beadbonny ash that sits over the burn.

Or splendidly and rhetorically:

How far from then forethought of, all thy more boisterous
    years,
When thou at the random grim forge, powerful amidst peers,
Didst fettle for the great grey drayhorse his bright and
    battering sandal.

Or vaguely and obscurely:

Even strains to be times vast, /womb-of-all, home-of-all,
    hearse-of-all night.
Her fond yellow hornlight wound to the west, /her wild
    hollow hoarlight hung to the height
Waste; her earliest stars, eárl-stars, /stárs principal, overbend
    us,
Fire-featuring heaven.

There seems nothing that he cannot do in this style;
one cannot keep feeling something exceptional in this talent.
He was as much an exception to his age as Beddoes, a poet
who had also an enormous verbal genius, shown in such
lines as

A wild old wicked island in the sea,

and

A craggy-throated, fat-cheeked trumpeter,
A barker, a moon-howler, who could sing
Thus, as I heard the snaky mermaids sing
In Phlegethon, that hydrophobic river,
One May-morning in Hell.

The imagination of these two poets is of course quite different in quality, as well as their use of language; but Beddoes is probably the most original user of words (though not of course the greatest poet) between Hopkins and Milton, and like Hopkins he found little appreciation from his contemporaries.

The other side of Hopkins's genius, the dark side, is religious, and deals with the torturing doubt which frequently goes with a genuine faith. In two sonnets, *Carrion Comfort* and *No worst, there is none*, the words follow the very convulsions of mental torment, and to find a parallel we must go back to the Jacobeans. In the second of these sonnets particularly, there are lines of a peculiar size and hugeness which recall the great lines of tragic poetry:

My cries heave, herds-long; huddle in a main, a chief
Woe, world sorrow . . .

O the mind, mind has mountains; cliffs of fall
Frightful, sheer, no-man-fathomed.

It is in lines like these that Hopkins is most incontestably a great poet. There is nothing for weight and volume in the poetry of his time to set beside them, except perhaps some lines of Browning.

What is most striking at first in Hopkins's poetry is the freshness and originality of his use of language. This came from the nature of his genius. "The terrible sincerity of the process of Hopkins's thought," says Herbert Read, "inevitably led him to an originality of expression which rejected the readymade counters of contemporary poetics." His letters, his note-books, and his religious poetry in particular show the genuineness of that "terrible sincerity". It determined his use of language; it also led him to make a metrical innovation which he called Sprung Rhythm, as distinct from the rhythm in contemporary use, which he called Running Rhythm. In Running Rhythm the metrical foot has usually two, and at most three, syllables. In Sprung Rhythm it may have any number from one to four, and in exceptional cases even more than that. To anyone who reads poetry with the eye merely, this is bound to be confusing; but Hopkins held that if the poetry were read out this difficulty would disappear, as it generally does, but not always. Whether anyone else will use this measure as successfully as Hopkins did without his "terrible sincerity" is a different question. The attempts to imitate him since his poems appeared have been disastrous. This book is not the place to discuss whether Sprung Rhythm is really the natural rhythm of the English language, as it has been claimed to be, and Running Rhythm merely a bastard form; whether

Christ minds; Christ's interest, what to avow or amend
There, éyes them, heart wánts, care háunts, foot fóllows
   kínd,
Their ránsom, théir rescue, ánd first, fást, last friénd,

is unforced, and

      O were my love yon lilac fair
      That hangs upon the castle wa',

is forced. No rhythm is unnatural if the poet uses it naturally; no rhythm natural if the poet uses it unnaturally. That Hopkins forced rhythm sometimes, as in the above lines, is undeniable. That he used Sprung Rhythm with great effectiveness is equally undeniable. His innovation may have a delayed effect on the metre of English poetry, as free rhythm has had. But there is no sign that it will replace what he called Running Rhythm. And Mr. Williams, in his introduction to the second edition of the poems, points out that "his poetic tricks, his mannerisms, his explorations of the technique of verse, are not in the earlier poems and they are disappearing from the later". They are disappearing, but not without having left their effect on the poetry into which they disappear. The magnificent fragment, *Margaret Clitheroe*, is undated, but by internal evidence it must have been late. The metre is fairly regular, but it has a vigour and inevitability which, it seems to me, Hopkins never equalled elsewhere. The poem is one of the most "morbid" that he ever wrote, with a detailed, passionate lingering on physical suffering; but it rises at once to great majesty:

> God's counsel cólumnar-severe
> But chaptered in the chief of bliss
> Had always doomed her down to this—
> *Pressed to death*. He plants the year;
> The weighty weeks without hands grow,
> Heaved drum on drum; but hands also
> Must deal with Margaret Clitheroe.

The fourth, unfinished verse is magnificent:

> Great Thecla, the plumed passion flower,
> Next Mary; mother of maid and nun
> .   .   .   .   .   .
> And every saint of bloody hour
> And breath immortal thronged that show;
> Heaven turned its starlight eyes below
> To the murder of Margaret Clitheroe.

This is followed by a verse of pure horror:

> Fawning fawning crocodiles

91

Days and days came round about
With tears to put her candle out;
They wound their winch of wicked smiles
To take her.

The regularity of the metre here seems to go with a greater intensity of imagination than we find in his other poems; it is as if the short-cut his mind took to the reality with which it was dealing pulled in the *slack* which he liked to leave in his metrical feet. The effect is of a ruthless lopping of inessentials.

It is difficult to estimate yet how great a poet Hopkins was. He has probably been overestimated because of his extraordinary mastery of the technique of verse and his genius for language. Almost all his good poetry, as Herbert Read says, belongs to two kinds; poetry inspired by a "vital awareness of the objective beauty of the world", and "poetry which is not so much the expression of belief in any strict sense but more precisely of doubt". In nature Hopkins saw the glory of God, and in himself he felt the terror of God. There is little in his poetry between these two extremes, little objective concern with ordinary human life. In poems like *Harry Ploughman*, Harry is merely a section of the physical universe:

He leans to it, Harry bends, look. Back, elbow, and liquid waist
In him, all quail to the wallowing o' the plough: 's cheek crimsons; curls
Wag or crossbridle, in a wind lifted, windlaced—
See his wind-lilylocks-laced.

Harry, one feels here, is a part of the glory of God because he is a part of nature. *Felix Randal* begins:

Felix Randal the farrier, O is he dead then? my duty all ended

92

Who have watched his mould of man, big-boned and hardy-
    handsome
Pining, pining.

The pathos is the pathos of "his mould of man", of natural
decay like that of a tree. Hopkins clearly knew very little
about Harry Ploughman and Felix Randal as human beings,
except on this plane, and perhaps cared to know very little
about them. His letters show that he could make the most
acute common-sense judgments on other people; but his
imagination was never animated by them. He has been
called the greatest poet of his age, greater than Browning
and Tennyson; but as a poet he had nothing to say about a
province of experience on which Tennyson said much, and
Browning much more: that is the life of ordinary human
beings. One has the feeling that his religion was the complement of his sensuality, not of a conviction of Original Sin,
which in a religious man is the key to understanding of
human nature, as distinct from nature. Nature and God,
and God in Nature, are Hopkins's themes. But on human
life he had astonishingly little to say, perhaps because he
was cut off from his age, and simultaneously from the
world. He was a great poet, but he has probably been judged
to be greater than he was.

Another poet who has had some influence, particularly
on the newer generation of poets, is Wilfred Owen, who
while still young was killed in the War. I have already
quoted from one of his best poems, *Strange Meeting*, in
which, as Mr. Blunden says, the employment of assonance
creates again and again "remoteness, darkness, emptiness,
shock, echo, the last word".

In his preface to them Owen wrote: "My subject is War,
and the pity of War. The poetry is in the pity." The quality
of the pity is immediate and sensuous, and at its best
is pointed by a close comparison between love and
violent death, as in the curious and terrible poem, *Greater
Love*:

Red lips are not so red
As the stained stones kissed by the English dead.
Kindness of wooed and wooer
Seems shame to their love pure.
O love, your eyes lose lure
When I behold eyes blinded in my stead! . . .

Heart, you were never hot,
Nor large, nor full like hearts made great with shot;
And though your hand be pale,
Paler are all which trail
Your cross through flame and hail:
Weep, you may weep, for you may touch them not.

In saying that the poetry was in the pity, Owen defined
the character of his work. The pity seems to enclose the
horror, storing it away, saving it up for some future purpose.
It does not find the immediate release of indignation, which
comes from pure repudiation of the horror. The astonishing
thing about this poetry is that Owen could suffer and reflect
so deeply while he was suffering; that he could see what
was unendurable, and yet stop and weigh it. Perhaps the
impressiveness of his poetry comes finally from this moral
quality. He seems to have been strengthened in it by his deep
sense of solidarity with all the others who were in the same
trap:

Happy the soldier home, with not a notion
How somewhere, every dawn, some men attack,
And many sighs are drained.
Happy the lad whose mind was never trained:
His days are worth forgetting more than not.
He sings along the march
While we march taciturn, because of dusk,
The long, forlorn, relentless trend
From larger day to huger night.

We wise, who with a thought besmirch

94

Blood over all our soul,
How should we see our task
But through his blunt and lashless eyes?
Alive, he is not vital overmuch;
Dying, not mortal overmuch;
Nor sad, nor proud,
Nor curious at all.
He cannot tell
Old men's placidity from his.

But cursed are dullards whom no cannon stuns,
That they should be as stones.
Wretched are they, and mean
With paucity that never was simplicity.
By choice they made themselves immune
To pity and whatever mourns in man
Before the last sea and the hapless stars;
Whatever mourns when many leave these shores;
Whatever shares
The eternal reciprocity of tears.

This is poetry which was written to be remembered when
"nations trek from progress".

I would have poured my spirit without stint
But not through wounds; not on the cess of war,

the dead enemy soldier says in *Strange Meeting*. There
is a depth in Owen's poetry even when it is making the
most simple statement, an apprehension, no matter what
he is dealing with, of

pity and whatever mourns in man
Before the last sea and the hapless stars,

and this makes his poetry memorable.

Isaac Rosenberg was another poet of great promise who

died in the War. He wrote only a few War poems, and
they are among his best:

> The darkness crumbles away—
> It is the same old druid Time as ever.

But his real ambition was to be a dramatic poet, and his
development, had he lived, would probably have been in
that direction. His short dramatic poem, *Moses*, has
occasional passages of fine energy:

> Ah! I will ride the dizzy beast of the world
> My road—my way.

This recalls Beddoes, and this does too:

> So many crazed shadows puffed away,
> And conscious cheats with such an ache for fame
> They'd make a bonfire of themselves to be
> Mouthed in the squares, broad in the public eye.

There is also an excessive striving for hugeness, again
as in Beddoes; an extravagant display of muscle. Yet this
poem is a remarkable feat for a young poet not much over
twenty. Mr. Siegfried Sassoon describes Rosenberg's use of
language finely by saying that "often he saw things in terms
of sculpture, but he did not carve or chisel; he *modelled*
words with fierce energy and aspiration . . . his poetic
visions are mostly in sombre colours and looming sculptural
masses, molten and amply wrought". He gives above all a
feeling of power which is not yet certain of itself, which
is sometimes tripped up by its own force. If he had lived
he would have been a major poet or nothing. There is not
very much, perhaps, in his published work that is perfectly
crystallised, except one or two War poems, and certain
passages in *Moses*. There is a great deal of verse such as
this:

> O wilderness of heaven,

Whose profound spaces like some God's blank eyes
Roll in a milky terror, move and move,
While our fears make vague shuddering imprints there
And character such chained-up forms of sorrow
That a breath can unloose; in its white depths
Dream unnamed gulfs of sudden traps for men.

That is half-realised poetry; but one can feel how wonderful
it would have been, realised.

I have been dealing thus far with poets who have influenced the development of modern poetry, and I have
accordingly treated them at some length. But as Professor
Dobrée noted in the foregoing volume, there was a general
revival of poetry during the four years before the War. This
revival produced a number of poets of great interest, some
of whom have developed very greatly since, some of whom
have remained the same, and some of whom have ceased to
write poetry. Among them were W. H. Davies, Walter de la
Mare, D. H. Lawrence, Harold Monro, W. J. Turner,
Lascelles Abercrombie, Sturge Moore, Gordon Bottomley,
J. C. (now Sir John) Squire, John Freeman, John Drinkwater, Edward Shanks, Edmund Blunden, Robert Graves,
Herbert Read, and Edith, Osbert and Sacheverell Sitwell.
It is impossible to deal at any length with more than a
few of them.

The most publicly influential school of poets just before
the War was inspired largely by the counsel and the practice
of J. C. Squire. Squire wrote a common-sense kind of poetry
deliberately toned down. What Professor Dobrée says of a
number of the poets of this time may be said with particular
justice of him: that his work "was lyrical, it was disciplined,
and sometimes the impulse behind it was thoughtful". But
the thought was rarely intense, or the lyricism overmaster-
ing, or the discipline severe. The temper of Squire's poetry,
as of Shanks's and Drinkwater's, and to a lesser extent of
Freeman's, was urbane, liberal, comfortable, and on the
whole anti-romantic. Squire is best in rare poems of nightmare speculation, like *Meditation in Lamplight*. But in most

of his poetry, and still more in Drinkwater's, there is a feeling that experience has gone slightly flat, and that in his comfortable enjoyment of the flatness, the poet has very little curiosity regarding its origin. It was the poetry of an age when it seemed to be the permanent, not unenviable fate of the middle-class intellectual to work in town all week and go to the country for the week-end. Everything seemed to be settled, not perfectly, but on the whole pleasantly; and this pleasant and not quite perfect permanence produced a certain sense of staleness, a certain incuriosity, a preference for simple views, and therefore for themes which were not controversial. The resulting poetry was a blinkered poetry; but gazing between their blinkers at the nascent power age, the poets set down soberly and honestly enough what they saw. That happened to be what a considerable body of other people saw at the time: affable meliorists in the Fabian Society, steady subscribers to the *New Statesman*, intellectual commuters in Surrey who supported cricket in the hope that by playing it they might become Tom, Dick or Harry, at that time three almost holy names. Drinkwater was particularly strong on simplicity. This poetry has already a period air; it belongs to its time, the four years before the War, in the same way as the fashions of dress belonged to these four years, and to no other four. Freeman, who was associated with this group, must be partly exempted from this generalisation; he was a good minor poet with an apprehension of the pathos of life. Lascelles Abercrombie must also be exempted by virtue of his intellectual imagination, slightly dry but at its best powerful. *The Sale of St. Thomas* is a poem of considerable intellectual interest.

Of the older poets of that time, two require longer treatment. W. H. Davies is an inimitable poet in the naïve style; he has without thinking, or with only a little thought, the simplicity for which Drinkwater strained so hard. His poetry is so natural, and is written so consistently within its natural limitations, that there is very little to say about it. Its quality is purely delightful, but sometimes it moves into a

98

strange realm of the imagination, as in the beautiful last four lines of his short poem, *The Villain*:

> While every bird enjoyed his song,
> Without one thought of harm or wrong—
> I turned my head and saw the wind,
> Not far from where I stood,
> Dragging the corn by her golden hair
> Into a dark and lonely wood.

Walter de la Mare has an imagination equally capable of touching extreme delight and terror. Whether his poetry can be called mystical is a matter for doubt, but his imagination seems to draw from the same source as mystical poetry. It has also this in common with mystical poetry, that it is not essentially conditioned by the time in which he lives. It belongs to an ageless tradition of which *Tom o' Bedlam's Song* is one of the most wonderful achievements; perhaps there is also in it something of Lewis Carroll. It has the ethereal fragility and yet firmness of shape which is found only in poetry which deals with the ever-recurring and ever-escaping fancies which hover half-way between the human and the fabulous world. It is filled with a sense of that direct, hidden connection between natural things and human life which we find in Scott's *Proud Maisie*, as for instance in *The Song of the Mad Prince*:

> Who said "Peacock Pie?"
>   The old King to the sparrow:
> Who said, "Crops are ripe?"
>   Rust to the harrow:
> Who said, "Where sleeps she now?
>   Where rests she now her head,
> Bathed in eve's loveliness?"—
>   That's what I said.
>
> Who said, "Ay, mum's the word?"
>   Sexton to willow:

Who said, "Green dusk for dreams,
    Moss for a pillow?"
Who said, "All Time's delight
    Hath she for narrow bed;
Life's troubled bubble broken?"
    That's what I said.

That is Mr. de la Mare's world, or rather part of it, and the rarer part, where terror and delight come together. Here he has no equal, either in delicacy of perception or of artistry. Sometimes the artistry seems actually to create the thing that is perceived, shaping a

    Miracle, bird or gold handiwork,
    More miracle than bird or handiwork.

Mr. de la Mare's stories show more clearly than his poetry the nature of the world from which these miracles are wrested. It is at its roots a terrifying world; not a world of "escape", to use the cliché which is more and more being applied to all literature that does not deal with the facts which are reported in the newspapers. It is rather a world from which there is no final escape, for it haunts us. For a poet like de la Mare to turn from it to the facts reported in the newspapers would be the real escape. In his own sphere of imagination, which is concerned with hidden experience, or experience faintly guessed at by most of us, he has an integrity as unquestionable as the integrity of the writer who insists on coming to terms with the world his mind and his senses present to him. We take more seriously now than we did at the beginning of the century the kind of experience with which de la Mare's poetry deals, simply because certain discoveries in the science of psychology have drawn our attention to it.

De la Mare's artistry has probably been over-praised at the expense of his imagination. Sometimes the music and vowel arrangement of his verse produce a perfect harmony, as in *The Song of the Shadows*:

Sweep the faint strings, Musician,
  With thy long lean hand;
Downward the starry tapers burn,
  Sinks soft the waning sand;
The old hound whimpers couched in sleep,
  The embers smoulder low;
Across the wall the shadows
  Come and go.

But *The Moth*, which has been so much praised, seems to me to be spoiled by an excessively, and romantically, coloured vocabulary. One of the most curious effects of his poetry is a sense of displacement and rearrangement, where the smallest and most trifling object, a snowdrop or a shadow of a weed on a stone, assumes an altered relation to the other objects which together make up the world, altering them too. Perhaps this comes from his apprehension of hidden entities:

Eyes in the green, in the shade,
  In the motionless brake,
Voices that said what I said,
  For mockery's sake.

But from whatever cause this effect may come, the world of de la Mare's imagination is one in which everything is related to everything else with a peculiar logic; it is complete and consistent.

As Edith Sitwell is also a poet of strange quality, she may be considered here, little as her poetry has in common with de la Mare's. She is not concerned with the border-line where the human fades into the supernatural, but rather with a world resembling that of the Russian Ballet, in which human life hardens into certain fixed artificial modes. Nature itself becomes artificial,

Beneath the flat and paper sky,

which is a stage sky.

> The market-square with spire and bell
> Clanged out the hour in Hell.

The spire is a wooden spire on a stage, and Hell a hell filled with ballerinas and clowns, not the place evoked in Beddoes's lines, where he heard

> the snaky mermaids sing
> In Phlegethon, that hydrophobic river,
> One May morning . . .

The suggestion of paint and powder is persistent:

> And shuddering at the noonday light
> The dust lay dead and white

> As powder on a mummy's face,
> Or fawned with simian grace
> Round booths with many a hard bright toy
> And wooden brittle joy.

In the same poem, *Clowns' Houses*, one of Miss Sitwell's best, the stage properties come on one after another:

> The cap and bells of Time the Clown. . . .

> Upon the sharp-set grass, shrill green,
> Tall trees like rattles lean. . . .

> Blind are those houses, paper-thin:
> Old shadows hid therein,
> With sly and crazy movements creep
> Like marionettes, and weep.

This artificiality, especially in the earlier poems is consistent and comes from an original vision of life. The girls have "sheepskin locks", the "green wooden leaves clap light away", and

> In among the plains of corn
> Each tower seems a unicorn.

In her later poetry this vision of the world becomes a formula, producing a certain hard monotony and a repetition of identical images for different objects which gives an effect of arbitrary simplification. In her earlier poetry cheeks were like painted wood or round, hard fruits, and the shift of vision was illuminating; but when cheeks actually become painted wood, and their original texture is lost, they lose their original meaning as well. The transposition of the senses which characterises Miss Sitwell's poetry was also effective at the beginning, for there was often an imaginative excuse for it; but when the visible can be translated into the audible and the audible into the visible at random, there seems no point in the translation. Miss Sitwell's technical dexterity has, I think, been over-rated; but her wit is delicious, and her best poetry has always a tincture of wit; her worst poetry is her serious poetry. This may be said as well of the poetry of her brother, Osbert Sitwell.

Sacheverell Sitwell is also a poet who sees human life in terms of art, and of a different art from that of poetry. The ballet is a sort of concordance of the arts of music, painting and the dance. Sacheverell Sitwell has written poetry inspired by all three modes in turn, and as he is encumbered with only one at a time his poetry is closer to ordinary experience than that of his sister. His early work has sometimes a spontaneous grace and sweetness:

> Full is each river to the brim,
> Running so fast, its glass is dim,
> Those rocks that burn in summer sun
> Bow down to let the waters run.

The same poem, *Variations on a Theme by Alexander Pope*, contains one of the best and strangest verses he ever wrote:

Far down in the myrtle grove
Wander the youths who died of love;
And the hero's arméd shade
Glitters down the gloomy glade.

That, however, is not typical of his poetry, the great virtue of which is spontaneous grace, and the main fault lack of intensity. His most considerable work is *Canons of Giant Art: Twenty Torsos in Heroic Landscapes*, in which he deals with such themes as an antique siege "in the manner of Mantegna", Aeneas hunting stags upon the coast of Libya "from the painting of Claude at Brussels", Agamemnon's tomb, and Bacchus in India. All these poems are inspired by an imaginative passion for the fabulous world of art, and they are unlike any other poetry of their time. They stress the contrast between the little provisional heaven of art and the unhemmed onset of mortality. The poem about Agamemnon's tomb, with its picture of the bees murmuring in the burial place, and its ending:

You are dead, you are dead, and all the dead are nothing
    to us,
There's nothing, nothing, nothing, not a breath beyond,

is perhaps his best. Mr. Sitwell's world of imagination is fabulous in the sense that it seems to animate the static shapes of painting, while leaving them in their original frame. We feel we are watching figures walking about in a picture, but never walking out of it. There is a peculiar pleasure in entering this world, which is an idealised or magical reflection of the actual world. But it is a cold pleasure, for it does not allow a single touch of nature.

A poet of more immediate interest is Robert Graves, for though he has a curiously speculative mind, his imagination sticks close to nature and is fed by first-hand observation.

This quality is to be found in his early as in his later poetry and perhaps at its best in the short poem *Lost Love*:

> His eyes are quickened so with grief,
> He can watch a grass or leaf
> Every instant grow: he can
> Clearly through a flint wall see,
> Or watch the started spirit flee
> From the throat of a dead man.
>
> Across two counties he can hear,
> And catch your words before you speak.
> The woodlouse or the maggot's weak
> Clamour rings in his sad ear. . . .

These lines contain most of the qualities which make him an original poet: intellectual fantasy perpetually brought back to the test of ordinary things, a speculation qualified by humour, an individual consideration of experience, whether ordinary or extraordinary, a distrust of the simple lyrical emotion, and an unusual perfection of form.

These qualities seem to have their source in the very temper of Graves's poetry, which is speculative, but speculative with an eye on practice, on a definite way of life. In his early poetry this speculation sometimes took the form of pure fancy, partly playful, partly macabre. In a note prefaced to *Whipperginny*, which appeared in 1923, Mr. Graves remarks "evidence of greater detachment in the poet and the appearance of a new series of problems in religion, psychology and philosophy, no less exacting than their predecessors, but, it may be said, of less emotional intensity". In that volume there is a good deal of speculation which seems to be mere speculation, without an eye to a definite end; but in his later poetry his concern with the end, and the means for reaching it, is more and more apparent, as for instance in the poem beginning:

> He is quick, thinking in clear images;
> I am slow, thinking in broken images.

> He becomes dull, trusting to his clear images;
> I become sharp, mistrusting my broken images.

There are other signs in his later poetry that he has set
himself a deliberate discipline, and some of the poetry is
obviously a part of the discipline. In certain poems he
achieves a fine economy and abstraction, a pure statement
of relations without sensuous content, yet of great emotional
force:

> To whom else other than,
> To whom else not of man
> Yet in human state,
> Standing neither in stead
> Of self or idle godhead,
> Should I, man in man bounded,
> Myself dedicate? . .

> To whom else momently,
> To whom else endlessly,
> But to you, I?
> To you who only,
> To you who mercilessly,
> To you who lovingly,
> Plucked out the lie?

This is poetry of extreme impersonality and at the same time
of great intensity. The "you" and the "I" are stripped of
almost every human attribute; it does not matter for the
poetry who they are, or who we suppose they are. In Mr.
Graves's later poetry there are not many poems of this perfection, and much of it recalls his lines about broken images:

> He continues quick and dull in his clear images;
> I continue slow and sharp in my broken images,

> He in a new confusion of his understanding;
> I in a new understanding of my confusion.

But in all of it there is the working of a vigorous intellectual imagination.

Laura Riding is a still more impersonal poet, the movement of whose verse often resembles the thesis, antithesis and synthesis of logic. She has a conception of poetry which insists particularly on its value as the revelation of truth. "A poem," she says, "is an uncovering of truth of so fundamental and general a kind that no other name besides poetry is adequate except truth. Knowledge implies specialised fields of exploration and discovery; it would be inexact to call poetry a kind of knowledge. It is even inexact to call it a kind of truth, since in truth there are no kinds. Truth is the result when reality as a whole is uncovered by those faculties which apprehend in terms of entirety, rather than in terms merely of parts". This is a generalisation which, like many alternative generalisations, could be applied to poetry with illuminating effect; it may be said that poetry discovers truth of a fundamental and general kind, and that it tries to apprehend reality in its entirety. But it does not necessarily uncover truth by making a series of true statements, and it does not necessarily reach general truth by dealing with the general. This passage really applies much more appositely to Miss Riding's poetry than to poetry as a whole. For she writes a poetry consisting mainly of true statements, or of statements intended to take her by the shortest road to a true statement. In the poem *Benedictory*, she begins:

> I have done all, you have done all,
> That I, that you, that you, that we,
> As I was, you were, we were,
> Could have done as doing was.

The rest of the poem is a statement of the contradictions of existence, developed in a series of antitheses, from the standpoint of one who has been freed from these contradictions by death. The form of the development is intellectual, but it is animated by genuine passion:

You would see, and made a mystery to see.
The cause of the mystery was that you saw.
The cause of the mystery was that you would see.
The cause of the mystery was that you did not see.

I cannot follow this poem through its antithetical statements
to the end;

For the live things grow dead.
And the dead thing is not.
Such was your likeness to me.
Such is the joining.

And a blessing on us all,
That we may all be joined,
A blessing on us all lest it seem not so
By the end of a false friendship.

Therefore close all our eyes on us.
And in such slow voiding do you wait.
For into such slow voiding shall I bring
Quickly the indivisible.

I do not claim to grasp the reconciliation expressed in these
last verses, or to decide whether Miss Riding means actual
death, or a sort of death to the illusions of the senses, when
she prays that all our eyes should be closed on us. But it is
clear from this poem, as from her other poems, what she
means when she says that poetry should uncover a general
truth for which no name is adequate except poetry or truth,
and that it should uncover truth in terms of entirety. Much
of her poetry consists of question and answer, by means of
which a series of statements converge towards a final statement, in which something of a riddle remains. Some of it is
pure statement, with the beauty of pure statement:

Whatever is before goes behind.

Each makes room for the next of kind.
The unborn beggars cry "Unfed"
Until all are born and dead.
Death is the crumb
To which they come;
God the division of it,
The nothing and no more of it
When the procreative doom
Stops making room—
The name of charity
By which to be is not to be.

There is intellectual power in this poetry; there is also a philosophy, the expression of that intellectual power, with which, so far as I understand it, I do not agree; Miss Riding's entirety is not my entirety. It seems to me that this philosophy sometimes gives a twist to the poetic truth, damaging its general character, and detracting from the validity on which she insists. Poetry which claims to be truth must be judged by what it says, or rather by the reader's sense of what is true in it. Miss Riding's poetry does apprehend reality in terms of entirety, but that is a different thing from apprehending reality, or part of it, in its entirety, which requires a more concrete method, and the perception of the general in the particular. At the same time, what she says has sometimes that truth which she claims for poetry, and sometimes considerable poetic beauty. What gives her poetry its unique quality is the direct way in which she sets out for the fundamental and general truth, ignoring everything else. It may be doubted whether this is poetry, but it is a remarkable kind of utterance.

Herbert Read is also a poet concerned, though not by such a direct road, with fundamental and general truths. The method of his poem, *The Analysis of Love*, is not dialectical, a direct movement from stage to stage to an end, but rather contemplative. He takes up one aspect of experience after another, considering each in turn, and the truth does not lie in the final statement, but in the sum of the parts, which is a

passionate reverie in the poet's mind. The "truths" are sometimes general and sometimes particular:

> The measuring mind can appraise
>   An earthen grace;
> The idiot's chatter
>   Analyses into experience. . . .
>
> Nature has perpetual tears
>   In drooping boughs,
> And everywhere inanimate death
>   Is immemorial.
>
> But I have naught that will express
>   The grief I feel
> When men and moods combine to show
>   The end of this—
>
> This mental ecstasy all spent
>   In disuniting death;
> And the years that spread
>   Oblivion on our zest.

The truth of the poem does not depend on any of these
statements, taken separately, but on its truth to experience,
and on the relation of its parts. In all Mr. Read's poetry
there is a concern with general truth and at the same time
this closeness to the poet's thought and emotion as he seeks
that truth, thought and emotion felt as one thing, one experience. His poetry follows intimately the fluctuations of this
experience, in which emotion and thought do not co-exist in
a perpetual balance, but rather in constant oscillation, and
this may account for the sometimes disconcerting movement
of his verse. His poetry probably shows less sign of outward
influence than any other poetry of his time; it has always
rested upon this interest in the mind at the moment of its
apprehension of experience, and is concerned not merely
with the human response, but with the validity of the human

response. It is a kind of poetry which can never be popular, for the problem with which it deals is, even to many poets, an abstruse one.

Lawrence was a fine poet, but the qualities of his poetry are so like those of his prose, that a longer consideration of them belongs more fitly to the next chapter. *Beasts, Birds and Flowers* contains some of his best poetry, and the repetition which is so maddening in his prose there sometimes becomes an actual virtue, because it is embodied in writing of a different rhythmical cast. The rhythm of these poems is irregular and seems to follow no perceptible law; it belongs neither to Eliot's nor to Pound's kind of free verse, yet it is not like Whitman's either: the only alternative that Eliot admitted is a sentence I have already quoted. The beautiful poem, *Bavarian Gentians*, gives the best idea of his rhythm, with its combined rapidity and fullness:

Not every man has gentians in his house
In Soft September, at slow, Sad Michaelmas.

Bavarian gentians, big and dark, only dark
darkening the day-time torch-like with the smoking blueness
                    of Pluto's gloom,
ribbed and torch-like, with their blaze of darkness spread
                    blue,
down flattening into points, flattened under the sweep of
                    white day
torch-flower of the blue-smoking darkness, Pluto's dark-blue
                    daze,
black lamps from the halls of Dis, burning dark blue,
giving off darkness, blue darkness, as Demeter's pale lamps
                    give off light,
lead me then, lead me the way.

This is a poetry which has intensity but no concentration, falling easily into professional prose phrases, "Bavarian gentians, big and dark", but with an impetuous flow which Lawrence's prose never equalled. The direct exhortation

is often heard in this poetry, and is a more questionable
virtue:

Lead me then, lead me the way.

The poem mounts to a splendid close:

And Persephone herself is but a voice
or a darkness invisible enfolded in the deeper dark
of the arms Plutonic, and pierced with the passion of dense
        gloom,
among the splendour of torches of darkness, shedding darkness
        on the lost bride and her groom.

Poetry seems to have been chosen by Lawrence for a more
direct communion with the powers in nature and himself
which is the theme of his novels; but there is a smaller
difference between his poetry and his prose than in the case
of almost any other writer; there is sometimes a close resemblance in the very rhythm, which is rapid and repetitive
at the same time: an unusual combination, the rhythm of a
man in a furious hurry, or in a furious temper: a wasteful
rhythm.

    Three other poets of the same generation must be men-
tioned. Siegfried Sassoon's War poems are eloquent documents; they are more economically fitted to their purpose
than any other contemporary poetry; and their indignation
is subdued to exact social criticism. They are effective
because of the moderation they observe in the midst of
furious indignation and pity. They are not personal, like
Owen's poems; their force lies in their impersonality, which
sets down with indignant economy the shame and horror of
war.

    Somewhat apart from his generation is W. J. Turner, an
uneven poet who has been unjustly depreciated because of
his unevenness. The best of his poetry has a visionary quality
which is obscured by a striving for huge effects and by a
Pantheistic philosophy. He sometimes expresses with great

force the fleeting and trancelike nature of existence, as in his poem, *In the Caves of Auvergne.*

> The stars flew by the cave's wide door,
> The clouds' wild trumpets blew,
> Trees rose in wild dreams from the floor,
> Flowers with dream faces grew
> Up to the sky, and softly hung
> Golden and white and blue. . . .
>
> The red deer of the forests dark,
> Whose antlers cut the sky,
> That vanishes into the mirk
> And like a dream flits by,
> And by an arrow slain at last
> Is but the wind's dark body.

There is an extravagant expenditure of emotional words like "dream" and "wild" in these verses; the effect is achieved too easily. But Mr. Turner is nevertheless a poet of imaginative power, whose later verse is disfigured by intellectual irascibility.

Edward Thomas, who was killed in the War just after he had begun to write verse, in his thirties, at the encouragement of the American poet Robert Frost, is in a way the opposite of Mr. Turner, for his poetry is founded on close observation yet has sometimes a curious *plain* visionary quality achieved by almost imperceptible means. The best example of this quality is picked out by Mr. Aldous Huxley in his essay on Thomas in *On the Margin,* and as it is one of the most beautiful passages in modern verse, I make no apology for quoting it again:

> It seems I have no tears left. They should have fallen—
> Their ghosts, if tears have ghosts, did fall—that day
> When twenty hounds streamed by me, not yet combed out
> But still all equals in their age of gladness
> Upon the scent, made one, like a great dragon

In Blooming Meadow that bends towards the sun
And once bore hops: and on that other day
When I stepped out from the double-shadowed Tower
Into an April morning, stirring and sweet
And warm. Strange solitude was there and silence.
A mightier charm than any in the Tower
Possessed the courtyard. They were changing guard,
Soldiers in line, young English countrymen,
Fair-haired and ruddy, in white tunics. Drums
And fifes were playing "The British Grenadiers".
The men, the music piercing that solitude
And silence, told me truths I had not dreamed,
And have forgotten since their beauty passed.

The beauty of the lines about the hounds, ending in the
image,
like a great dragon
   In Blooming Meadow.

seems to me unlike anything else in English poetry, though I
feel there must be parallels to it in Celtic poetry. It is strange
and yet the result of close observation. The hounds are
ordinary hounds, though as they run together they are like
a great dragon; and the pleasure the image gives us comes
from a simultaneous realisation of appearance as actual and
fabulous. The beauty is partly in the mood, which Mr.
Huxley defines as a "nameless emotion of quiet happiness
shot with melancholy", an emotion which he finds in almost
all Thomas's poetry. Thomas was only realising his genius
when he was killed.

Like Thomas, Edmund Blunden is also a "nature" poet
with a gift for close observation; but his best poetry has a
visionary quality somewhat resembling Thomas's, though
never quite equalling it. The last verse of the short poem,
Familiarity, contains one of those sudden surprises:

   Sprawl not so monster-like, blind mist;
     I know not "seems";

> I am too old a realist
> To take sea-dreams
> From you, or think a great white Whale
> Floats through our hawthorn-scented vale—
> This foam-cold vale.

The second verse of the short poem, *Masks of Time*, is another example of this bursting out of a different kind of imagination from Mr. Blunden's usual workaday imagination:

> Now is haste returned; the striding fury flings
> That mad mantle abroad, and foots both Pole and path;
> Swarming grasses hiss; pursue wild beaks and wings;
> The clods roll their brown heads, all Golgotha in wrath.

That is violent and extreme, almost melodramatic, because it is an *unwilling* outburst of the imagination, not entirely approved by the poet, who is "too old a realist", preferring to remain on the level of

> So there's my year, the twelvemonth duly told.

Mr. Blunden has these two kinds of imagination, and in his best poetry they come together, somewhat reluctantly, under the eye of the too old realist, and then

> a great white Whale
> Floats through our hawthorn-scented vale.

Two poets of the same generation, one a Scotsman and the other a South African, stand somewhat apart from those I have been dealing with by virtue of their abounding crude energy and a journalistic quality which foreshadows Auden and recalls Byron, the great headliner of verse: that is, Hugh McDiarmid and Roy Campbell. Technically Campbell is by far the more accomplished poet, but McDiarmid excels him in intelligence and in a grotesque, satirical fancy, half philosophical, half comic. Campbell's abounding energy can be felt in the vigorous movement of his verse, but the energy is somewhat commonplace; the roll of the lines is hollow. His conception of life is picturesque: his poetry calls up an image of the elemental forces of nature, and man posed against them in the attitude of Ajax defying the lightning. Mc Diarmid's energy is not often commonplace, and *A Drunk Man Looks at the Thistle* is a continuously interesting and ingeniously varied poem. It is written in Scots, a particular Scots of McDiarmid's own invention; but it can easily enough be read by any English reader who will take the trouble. It is a mixture of everything: Rabelaisian humour, metaphysical speculation, parody, translation, satire, and mere nonsense. Technically it is uneven and often careless, but it contains brilliant passages, it is seldom flat, and it is the work of an interesting mind. McDiarmid's later poetry, much of it Communistic, is poor by comparison and often dull. His poetry shows as many influences as Auden's, some of them digested and some not; but the turn which he gives them is often unexpected. He is concerned more with the potential than the actual; with things which may be true than with things which are true. This gives his work a high degree of suggestiveness, but also robs it of final conviction.

An original poet always has, at his first appearance, a violent aspect, as if he came from some hitherto unknown country whose laws and customs are different from all recognised ones. In an age when change is rapid, each generation is born into a different world and seems to grow up in it in a sort of predestined isolation from the generation which preceded it and produced it. When it comes of age it presents the appearance to the already adult of an invasion by a strange race, armed with knowledge drawn from sources accessible only to itself. The War generation had this knowledge, and the generation of W. H. Auden has grown up in a period filled with thoughts and fears of war; its knowledge is conditioned by these thoughts and fears. That poets brought up in such a time should think and feel politically, should be concerned with the state of society, is not so much a virtue as a necessity. That they should face that precarious world in a positive rather than a despairing temper is greatly to their credit, though again there is something of necessity in the choice. For when they arrived at manhood people had begun to realise that civilisation could not be relied upon to develop peacefully towards perfection, but must actually be fought for. Also they had begun to doubt whether there was any valid justification for literature, poetry and the arts as such, if these activities did not help in the fight.

In his autobiography, *Blasting and Bombardiering*, Mr. Wyndham Lewis has an interesting chapter on the generation which included himself, Joyce, Pound and Eliot; and it ends with a glance at the succeeding generation. Mr. Lewis, listening to memory, may have involuntarily idealised the days of his early triumphs; but he is a highly independent observer, and he cannot be accused of sentimentality. He describes "the men of 1914" as "a haughty and proud generation", quoting a phrase of Mr. Ford Madox Ford. After discussing the reasons for their pride, he continues:

"I have said, 'the men of 1914'. But we were not the only people with something to be proud about at that time. Europe was full of titanic stirrings and snortings—a new art coming to flower to celebrate or to announce a 'new age'.

In retrospect already one experiences a mild surprise. In future this surprise will increase, year by year. What will become of those stern and grandly plastic glimpses of a novel universe, which first saw the light in the Western capitals immediately before the War, it is impossible to say. . . . To the English eye—and I am of course speaking here of how these things are seen from London—the period of *Blast*, of *Ulysses*, of *The Waste Land* will appear an island of incomprehensible bliss, dwelt in by strange shapes labelled 'Pound', 'Joyce', 'Weaver', 'Hulme'. . . .

I do not mean to say that all the masterpieces of this school have yet been penned, painted, or planned. But what I do say is that whatever happens in the world during the next century or so, there will be no society present upon the globe to think, live, and speculate in a manner conducive to the production of such works as *Bouvard and Pecuchet*, *Ulysses*, *The Hollow Men*, *The Ambassadors*, *The Portrait of Carlyle*, to name a few of the sort of productions that I mean, and to mix my times and arts a little too. The last society likely to do anything of that sort vanished with the War. It is a case of goodbye to all that, and for good. And one has to be no great prophet to foresee that whichever of the forces confronted upon the political stage to-day may get the upper hand, the Red or the Black, any detached artistic effort, on the grand scale, will be quasi-impossible. There will not be present the will, the psychological incentive, the time, or *the peace*, that are requisite for that. This applies to Germany as much as to Russia, to America as much as to Japan. Martial law conditions have come to stop. The gentler things of life are at an end.

We are not only 'the last men of an epoch' (as Mr. Edmund Wilson and others have said): we are more than that, or we are that in a different way to what is most often asserted. *We are the first men of a Future that has not materialised.* We belong to a 'great age' that has not 'come off'. We moved too quickly for the world. We set too sharp a pace. And, more and more exhausted by War, Slump, and Revolution, the world has *fallen back*."

This passage is interesting because it is a description of the feelings of the 1914 generation by one who shared those feelings, and because, whether the picture is true or not, the younger generation seem to accept it. They look back upon the time when Eliot was shoring fragments against his ruins as a comparatively happy and comfortable time. They seem to agree with Mr. Lewis, too, that in the struggle between Fascism and Communism, "any detached artistic effort, on the grand scale, will be quasi-impossible". Indeed they regard detachment as irrelevant, since the struggle involves them on the one side or the other. The case for detached artistic effort rests on the recognition that art has its own peculiar characteristic effect, an effect different from the

118

effect of political ideas or movements, whose end is practical, organised, common action. That art has such an effect is obviously true. But in a period when the struggle has begun its truth is not effective; it is true much in the same way as the statement is true, in times of war, that peace is good. So that the poetry of Auden's generation is inextricably involved with propaganda. It has something also of the character of a *fait accompli*, not for the moment to be argued with. It is the poetry of a state of emergency; there is an echo in it of the martial law of which Mr. Lewis speaks. Yet that poetry itself, and all the other arts, are necessary to civilisation and a good life, that poetry loses its unique power when it has to serve the ends of propaganda, that, to quote Mr. Lewis once more, when we "put aside our books and pictures", we always "take them up again, when the dark age is over, with less assurance and with less of genius", seems to me to be self-evident. Capitalism is the greatest existing danger to civilisation; yet to let poetry and other arts lapse even into propaganda against Capitalism, to rob them of their integrity even with the best intentions, is also a danger to civilisation. But in a state of emergency there is a rush to combat the chief danger, and every weapon is snatched up as a weapon of war, no matter what its original purpose may have been, or how ineffective it is for its new one. That is the present situation. General truth and "detached artistic effort" have gone by the board, comprehensibly, inevitably, and almost virtuously. This is a danger which the situation itself keeps us from seeing. That does not make it less but more of a danger.

W. H. Auden is the most original poet since Eliot, and also the most derivative. His work shows more influences even than Pound's: the influence of Eliot, of Hopkins, of Yeats, of Anglo-Saxon poetry, of the Icelandic saga, of Marx, Freud, the newspaper, the music hall, the detective story, the public school magazine, the Boy Scout's handbook, the popular broadsheet, the adventure story, the private joke and the private cliché. He is indiscriminately derivative, that is to say, not by choice, like Pound. But he is also actively derivative: he turns everything into poetry, some of it good, some bad, some indifferent. In doing this he assumes, like Pound, various masks, but they are modern. He is the up-to-date Bogey Man when he wants to make the flesh of the bourgeois creep; the mystic Harley Street healer; the popular preacher; the lone scout; the captain of the team; the pioneer; the practical joker; so that a good deal of his poetry comes out of a private myth. One of his favourite parts is that of the mystifier; some of the poems in his first published collection, according to his friend Christopher Isherwood, were made up of the best lines from a number of other poems, irrespective of coherence. The best of his poetry, it seems to me, comes from none of those mythical personalities. How bad it can be when it does is shown in the opening scene of *The Ascent of F6*, by the lone scout, with its Wild West sentimentality.

What makes Auden a remarkable poet is this susceptibility to all kinds of experience, combined with an unusual ability to organise it imaginatively into an unexpected shape. His imagination is mainly grotesque, or what is now called surrealistic, and it borrows largely and sometimes directly from books on psychoanalysis. It is his greatest single endowment; and it is reinforced by wit, a satirical social sense, moral passion and humour. His social sense is more discriminating than his moral passion, and that in turn more discriminating than his humour, which comes last, a good distance behind his other qualities. There are times when all these gifts, the humour excepted, come together, and then he writes poetry of a peculiarly condensed and direct kind, which owes hardly anything to poetic association. His humour is probably an expression of his irresponsible side; the complement to his sentimentality; a facetious but ineffectual warder, always panting along well behind the patient. Morally, Auden can sometimes be resoundingly shallow, as on the much quoted sonnet beginning

Sir, no man's enemy, forgiving all
But will his negative inversion, be prodigal,

in which it is hard to tell whether the person addressed is
the Head of the universe or of the school:

> Send to us power and light, a sovereign touch
> Curing the intolerable neural itch,
> The exhaustion of weaning, the liar's quinsy,
> And the distortions of ingrown virginity. . . .
> Harrow the house of the dead; look shining at
> New styles of architecture, a change of heart.

There is something exasperatingly unreal about this Harley
Street selection of exhortations; they imply an appalling,
and an appallingly complacent view of human life, the
view of the team resolved to stand no more nonsense, but
to be up and at the good life at once, having discovered
and jotted down in their diaries

> each healer that in city lives
> Or country houses at the end of drives.

This treatment of moral questions in terms of clichés
(probably derived from psychoanalysis) sometimes influences
Auden's approach to nature as well, which is drenched in
moral associations:

> Taller to-day, we remember similar evenings,
> Walking together in the windless orchard
> Where the brook runs over the gravel, far from the
> glacier.

> Again in the room with the sofa hiding the grate,
> Look down to the river when the rain is over,
> See him turn to the window, hearing our last
> Of Captain Ferguson.

The glacier here is not a glacier to Auden, any more than
a little coppice is a little coppice to Yeats. It is a cliché
for one of a comparatively simple set of virtues, and is
probably associated with mountain-climbing, like Captain

Ferguson. This simple, up-to-date view of morality is fairly common among the other poets of Auden's generation; there are many Captain Fergusons under other names in the work of Day Lewis, and he comes in as

alone, on a tall stone, stood Grant,

in a poem by Charles Madge. He has something of Livingstone, more of Stanley, and a little of Red Indian children's game. He is what happens when writers who have attended public schools idealise them instead of seeing them satirically, for it is not a distortion but a development of the moral sense which makes adults see public schools satirically.

Auden's later poetry is far less vitiated by this moral simplification, and as a consequence less hortatory and more human. In *The Ascent of F6*, a poetic drama which he wrote with Christopher Isherwood, he sees round it, in spite of the excelsior symbolism. But he does not quite get rid of it. The tragic conception of morality in that play is embodied in a sentimentally idealised figure, Ransom, the leader of the expedition. It is not, that is to say, a conception for everyone, for Auden's readers, let us say, or for Auden himself, but for a possible figure who does not exist, yet ideally should exist. Auden's morality, like Pound's Hell, is for other people. It is at best for a sort of "We", which is selective but not coherent; perhaps, in the last resort, Auden's generation, but only as a whole, not as individuals. It suggests a crowd so eager to be a team that every member is busy pulling up his neighbour's socks and has no time to attend to his own. In Auden's last volume of poetry, *Look Stranger*, this easy conception of morality has almost disappeared, with the result that the poetry, while appearing to have less direction, has much greater depth.

Auden's best poetry comes from his grotesque imagination and his alert social sense, inspired by his moral passion when it is in actual working order:

The earth turns over, our side feels the cold,
And life sinks choking in the wells of trees;

The ticking heart comes to a standstill, killed,
The icing on the pond waits for the boys.
Among the holly and the gifts I move,
The carols on the piano, the glowing hearth,
All our traditional sympathy with birth,
Put by your challenge to the shifts of love.

Your portrait hangs before me on the wall
And there that view I wish for, I shall find,
The wooded or the stony—though not all
The painter's gifts can make its flatness round—
Through the blue irises the heaven of failures,
The mirror world where logic is reversed,
Where age becomes the handsome child at last,
The glass sea parted for the country sailors.

The poem from which these lines are taken moves convincingly from the existent world of illusion and fantasy to the wished-for one of simple truth:

Gale of desire may blow
Sailor and ship past the illusive reef,
And I yet land to celebrate with you
Birth of a natural order and of love;
With you enjoy the untransfigured scene. . . .

The wit of the poem rises from its union of social observation and grotesque fancy, its concrete perception of the actual scene side by side with potentialities inherent in it. Auden's susceptibility to trifling and journalistic aspects of life gives fullness to his poetry when it moves on this level of grotesque imagination; susceptibility then becomes one of his virtues. It is impossible to judge him yet as a poet, because most of his work is still probably to be written. As far as his development has gone, it seems to have moved from a relatively optimistic to a tragic view of life. He is an excessively unequal poet, but his power cannot be gainsaid.

Day Lewis has considerable verbal talent, a great deal of moral passion, a social sense much less acute than Auden's, and, it seems to me, hardly any imagination at all. The verbal beauty of his poetry is, with some modification to fit the contemporary idiom, orthodox and romantic:

> Do not expect again a phoenix hour,
> The triple-towered sky, the dove complaining,
> Sudden the rain of gold and heart's first ease
> Tranced under trees by the eldritch light of sundown.

That is skilful verse, but it is essentially cold, except for a faint adolescent glow. The poem ends:

> Draw up the dew. Swell with pacific violence.
> Take shape in silence. Grow as the crowds grew.
> Beautiful brood the cornlands, and you are heavy;
> Leafy the boughs—they also hide big fruit.

This is the same moral approach to nature which appears in a disguised form in Auden's poetry. It is extremely simple, a Wordsworthian emotion without Wordsworth's experience: not very far removed from the edifying maxim. Day Lewis is probably best in his poems of fancy:

> Now the full-throated daffodils,
> Our trumpeters in gold,
> Call resurrection from the ground
> And bid the year be bold.

The imaginative coldness of his poetry, which is perfectly consonant with moral ardour, is shown most clearly in the lack of evocative imagery. His characteristic images are descriptive or decorative; they do not add anything to the object; they are simple correspondences or ornaments:

> But think of passion and pain,
> Those absolute dictators will enchain

The low, exile the princely parts:
They close a door between the closest hearts:
Their verdict stands in steel,
From whose blank rigour kings may not appeal.

This is a description, which uses the absolute dictators
merely as an illustration. The other fault of Day Lewis's
poetry is a too insistent and too easy hope. It is not a poet's
business after describing any situation, however desperate,
to affix a hope to the end of it. One may sympathise with the
spirit which leads Day Lewis to do this, and also with the
moral effort embodied in his poetry; but the poetry itself
is vitiated by the complementary defects which go with
these virtues.

Stephen Spender is a poet of genuine traditional quality.
His work shows less sign of external influence than that of
any other poet of his time, except for the unavoidable
influence of the contemporary world. His moral sense is
deeper and accordingly less hortatory than that of Auden
and Day Lewis; he could not have perpetrated Auden's
sonnet to the Head. His fault is perhaps a too ready recourse
to pity, as in the last verse of *The Prisoners*:

No, no, no,
It is too late for anger,
Nothing prevails
But pity for the grief they cannot feel.

The peculiar virtue of his imagination, as of his verse, is
lucidity, which is shown both in the imagery itself with its
delight in tracery on a white surface, and in his insistence
on presenting everything in a clear, shadowless light, the
light invisibly suggested by a line-drawing. He says of the
beggars in the railway halls:

No, I shall weave no tracery of pen-ornament
To make them birds upon my singing-tree,

125

and the image returns again, no longer merely decorative, but filled with experience and imagination, in a passage in *Trial of a Judge* describing the sufferings of poor refugees:

The mournful telegraph wires which watched our travelling
From town to town have never worn birds
To sing our harvest in.

In his earlier poetry the imagery, though delightful in itself, often strikes one as being too decorative for its purpose:

The architectural gold-leaved flower
From people ordered like a single mind,

and

Eye, gazelle, delicate wanderer,
Drinker of horizon's fluid line.

The immediate appeal of the poetry is distinct from such images, and gives the impression, indeed, of being secured too directly, and in spite of them. This applies chiefly to his early poetry. There is still a good deal of decorative imagery in *Trial of a Judge*, by far his most striking work up to now; but it is employed in a different way and sometimes with the most moving effect, as in the lines I have quoted. As I shall have to speak of this play in a later chapter, I shall not say anything of it here except that what makes it more impressive than any of the other plays of Spender's generation is the depth of his moral sense, his grasp of the reality of the moral struggle, both in society and in the individual. He seizes it not merely on the level of exhortation, like Day Lewis, or of analytical speculation, like Auden, but on the level of imagination; not as something in itself, desirable and distinct from ordinary human life, but as inextricably involved with human life, inescapable whether it is obeyed or disobeyed. All his poetry is coloured with this sense of morality, which probably required a dramatic theme before it could find adequate expression.

Louis MacNeice is a poet of unusual technical skill who, while having much in common with the Communist poets, does not share their attitudes. He is a sceptic coquetting with a faith which he knows beforehand he cannot accept, and he is consequently fond of the poetic dialogue, which is a statement of his own and no doubt of other people's difficulties. The outcome of this argument is a "somehow" when he is optimistic, a stoical statement when he is not. *An Eclogue for Christmas* ends, after mentioning the saxaphones and the xylophones and "the miles of canvas in the galleries" and yachts' sails, with the hope:

> Let all these so ephemeral things
> Be somehow permanent like the swallow's tangent wings:
> Goodbye to you, this day remember is Christmas, this morn
> They say, interpret it in your own way, Christ is born.

That is an almost perfect example of the mood of his poetry, with its idiosyncratic turn, its qualification of emotion, its consciousness of the reader as a possible collaborator in the argument, though not in the conclusion, which is a foregone one, and what may be called its sincere cleverness. This poetry is very close to the reader and very close to conversation; temptingly pitched only a little above the prose level, attractively tentative, almost gossipy: the poetry of a man who will never go farther than he feels he can legitimately go, and who is never swept off his feet. It has accordingly the virtues and faults of character poetry; every line is in character, and so we cannot get away from the character, who is MacNeice himself, except in simple, general statement:

> The sunlight in the garden
> Hardens and grows cold,
> We cannot cage the minute
> Within its nets of gold;
> When all is told
> We cannot beg for pardon.

His poetry is like a game of chess played with himself, in which at every turn he puts himself in check. It is fascinating, but what its ultimate value is, apart from the complications of the game, I cannot say.

Among the poets still younger than Spender and Mac-Neice, there are two of extraordinary endowment: George Barker and Dylan Thomas. They have remarkable powers of visionary imagination, as yet unformed. Their poetry has much waste matter in it, or matter imperfectly transformed. Some of Barker's poetry, and most of Thomas's, is rationally incomprehensible to me. It would be of little use, therefore, at their present stage of development, for me to attempt any estimate of them.

CHAPTER III

FICTION

SOME of the changes in the novel during the present century have been treated by Professor Dobrée in the previous volume: he has pointed out the influence of foreign models on Moore and Conrad, of imperialism on Kipling, and of socialist ideas on Wells. A writer he did not deal with may be mentioned here. Barrie, though a novelist of excessive sensibility, remained quite impervious to any of these influences. This was partly, no doubt, because he was a safe, canny man, but also because he possessed that peculiar kind of sensibility which is really an armour against unpleasant shocks. To be humorous or pathetic exclusively about things which are by prescriptive right humorous or pathetic is to take the safe line. Consequently Barrie did not question the workings of the heart or of the world outside him, though his books show that these things sometimes troubled him. He encased himself so comfortably in the traditional response, which in him was indistinguishable from the parochial response, that the outside world could not touch him. On the traditional emotions he dealt with he showed a wonderful versatility; and in his treatment of children, as in *Sentimental Tommy*, there is a sort of mawkish cruelty which rises to genius. But his softness was really a kind of toughness, and the most deplorable fault of his work is not sensibility run to seed, but obduracy. He crept into his Kirriemuir heart and was safe there, no matter how loudly the world knocked at it. He began with great gifts and evaded them one by one.

Professor Dobrée has already dealt with the work of Mr. H. G. Wells. The two names which were generally mentioned along with his before the War were those of Arnold Bennett and John Galsworthy. Bennett was a man of immense vitality, or at least a man with an immense appreciation of vitality. He modelled himself on Balzac, both as a personality and a novelist; he possessed and in his stories glorified expensive tastes; worked like a slave; and had Balzac's obsequiously knowing attitude to women, half male attendant and half illicit lover. He was a conscientious craftsman, in the sense that he knew all the tricks of his trade. He prided himself on his knowledge of life, but the knowledge was of the circumstances of people's lives rather than of their hearts. By far his best novel is *The Old Wives' Tale*, in which there is a profoundly realised sense of the passing of time. His idea of the greatness of life was bound up with his worship of success, and was accordingly meretricious. He enjoyed, in every sense, a greater reputation than he deserved; but *The Old Wives' Tale* is still worth reading.

Like Bennett, Galsworthy formed his art on foreign models, and perhaps chiefly on Turgenyev. He did not have Bennett's vigour, but his view of life was a more serious one, if only because he saw the other face of success and was not taken in. *The Man of Property* and *The Country House* have a sort of reluctant cruelty in their presentation of class egoism and the suffering it brings about, which is peculiar to Galsworthy alone. He was probably the most completely honest novelist of his time, so honest that he kept his sensibility on a short lead, and in consequence often seems tongue-tied. His passion for justice gives these two novels an unusually balanced form. His work was in essence a criticism of contemporary society, and particularly of its workings in the upper middle class. In his later work that criticism became blunted; he came to like the people he had exposed; or it may be that his pity, which had once been confined to their victims, grew to embrace them as victims too, though comfortable ones: a comprehensible development, since his criticism of them from the first was based on a humanitarian view of life. He was not a great writer, but, especially in his early work, he performed a valuable task for his generation, without fear and without rancour.

Henry Handel Richardson is a younger writer but by her conception of the novel belongs rather to this generation than to the succeeding one. Her first novel, *Maurice Guest*, seems to me superior to any other novel of the time. It shows perhaps too clearly the influence of the Russians, and of Dostoevsky in particular; but it has an impressive dramatic power, and a profound grasp of character. It contains half a dozen figures moulded on a scale slightly larger than the human, yet with intimate truth. Her later trilogy, *The Fortunes of Richard Mahony*, contains some unforgettable scenes but has not the sustained intensity of her first novel. *Maurice Guest* is probably the last great novel in the traditional style which has appeared in English, and it remains as astonishing to-day as when it was first published.

A writer of considerably less imaginative power, but of immense competence, also belongs properly to this generation. Somerset Maughan has written a great number of stories, none of which falls below a respectable level or relapses into sentimentality. One is tempted to describe his work in negatives: the only way in which to describe efficiency. He rarely illumines experience, but he hardly ever falsifies it. He does not have the faults of Wells and Bennett and Galsworthy; he is never soft; but he does not have their understanding either. He sees clearly but not very far. His view of life is conspicuously neat, but though he recognises some of the things which do not seem to fit into it, he does not allow for them. He has an admirable grasp of the obvious content of a situation and of such facts as that men are men and women are women, that life in the tropics is different from life in the temperate zones, and that men in the colonial civil service must observe certain conventions not required from a coster or a chorus girl. *Of Human Bondage*, in which he deals with a simple, isolated moral problem, is perhaps his best novel.

In the three or four years before the War a new generation of novelists appeared, who had learned a number of things about the novel from George Moore, Henry James and the Russians, and were seriously concerned with the art of fiction.

Among them were Hugh (now Sir Hugh) Walpole, Compton Mackenzie, J. D. Beresford, May Sinclair, Gilbert Cannan, and Frank Swinnerton. Of this group Walpole and Mackenzie had by far the greatest talent. Walpole's novel, *Mr. Perrin and Mr. Traill*, which appeared in 1911, has sustained imagination, an almost perfect structure, and an economy which its author has never equalled since. Sir Hugh's later work is vitiated by a pervasive sentimentality, but is partly redeemed by his genius for the macabre, his most authentic gift. Apart from this specialised talent, however, which does not colour his delineation of ordinary character, his later work presents a mixture of susceptibility to experience immediately qualified by optimism about experience which confuses and softens the picture. As a result he sometimes gives the impression of being simultaneously concerned for his age and blind to his age, since his optimism keeps him from believing that any current danger is a real danger, and not something which can be subsumed in a larger hope. He is a writer of talent, with a touch of macabre genius; but his pervasive, inaccurate optimism has gradually weakened his criticism of life.

Compton Mackenzie's long novel, *Sinister Street*, appeared in 1913 and 1914. It is the most serious and the most sustained story he has ever written, and contains a brilliant description of Oxford life and an unusually honest account of a religious conversion. Since then, for some reason, the energy seems to have gone out of his work, except when he is portraying odd or comic characters, as in *Poor Relations*, *Vestal Fires* and *Extraordinary Women*. Except for its comic scenes, his work is spoiled by an arbitrary romanticism which has something of the same effect on the portraiture as Walpole's optimism.

Of the other members of the group to which Walpole and Mackenzie belonged, Professor Dobrée says that they "wrote of the things which were occupying men's minds at the time, with no special lucidity of vision or originality of style, but as good craftsmen doing their job honestly and well". This description is so just that there is nothing I can add to it.

In the same generation appeared a writer of far greater

endowment: D. H. Lawrence. So much has been written about him since his death, that it is already hard to see him clearly: he has become a prophet and a teacher, and he has been compared to Christ. He was certainly a man of genius; he said wise and penetrating things on human life, love, education, society, and a host of other subjects; but as a prophet he was as honestly bogus as Nietzsche: the leader of a forlorn hope into a false paradise; and his teaching, if it is taken as a whole, is a mass of contradictory absurdities. His attitude to sex was certainly pathological, though sometimes he said penetrating things about that too. When he generalised about life he left out, again like Nietzsche, most of what normally constitutes life. His philosophy, as time went on, more and more distorted his immediate perceptions, which were profound and true, and fitted them into a construction inferior to them in every way. His great gift was direct insight into nature and human experience where it is closest to nature, that is in its subterranean workings, its instinctive life. *Sons and Lovers* is a marvellous description of the relations between a mother and a son, a description not in the least falsified by preconceived ideas, as almost all that he said in his later novels was. *The Rainbow* is astonishing in its intimate treatment of the relations between man and woman, though it is quite without objectivity and sometimes farcically absurd; the hero's bones "melt" a countless number of times, until we accept it as an ordinary occurrence. There is hardly a memorable character in all Lawrence's novels, except for one or two satirical sketches. He had a sharp satirical eye, but not sufficient patience or steady animosity to exercise it for long; exasperation or pique soon ruined the picture. He himself admitted that he was not interested in character. It represented the "fixed" as distinguished from the "fluid" element in human life, which was to him the really vital and creative part. He saw this fluid element being dammed, obstructed and poisoned by all sorts of fixed things; institutions, ideas drawn from the "head", money-making, industrialism, the "artificial" life which civilised people live. This is obviously a simple and one-sided view,

inadequate to the complexity of history. But where he touches
these things directly with his imagination he is a penetrating
critic of society and of the life we all live. He probably saw
deeper than any other writer of his time, and he saw what
no one else saw. But the vision was not clear, or he had not
the patience to let it clarify itself. Accordingly his prose is
filled with repetition; it was as if he thought that by battering
at his vision for long enough with the same collocation of
words he might break through to it. In his later novels, such
as *Kangaroo* and *The Plumed Serpent*, one is conscious of a vast
dispersion of energy illumined by splendid crystallisations.
His most condensed imagination is probably to be found in
his short stories. *The Fox*, a long short story in the volume
entitled *The Ladybird*, is a masterpiece. The essential quality
of his work was illumination; he darkened and circumscribed
his light by a self-made philosophy; but he was probably
the greatest *genius* of his time.

James Joyce is in some ways the obverse of Lawrence. He
too has a peculiar knowledge of the subterranean workings
of the mind and the feelings; but what Lawrence saw as good
he sees as evil, or ridiculous, or comic. Like Lawrence, he has
the Puritan's tortured obsession with sex; but while Lawrence
glorified sex, he subjects it to a relentless inquisition in
which he exposes every sordid, or undignified, or ludicrous
aspect with a theologian's animosity. Unlike Lawrence, he
has no interest in general questions or in society itself,
except as its delineator. He is a moralist, but a traditional
one, not concerned with forms of society, or with modes of life
which might become possible if a great number of people
were to live differently, but with the individual; and *A
Portrait of the Artist as a Young Man* has, in addition to its other
virtues, a high moral force. That book and *Ulysses* are the
most striking examples of "detached artistic effort" in fiction
which our time has produced. The detachment, however, is
troubled by all sorts of undercurrents, the chief of them
being a need for personal confession, from which Lawrence
was comparatively free. One feels, in reading Joyce, that he
is frank with an eye on himself and his own salvation, while

Lawrence was frank with an eye on the object. But while Lawrence inspired, cursed, bullied and lectured his age, it can at least be said for Joyce that he tried to set it down.

Ulysses is a work of such genius and scope, and contains such a wealth of imaginative material, such a burden of horror, both hidden and expressed, that it is still difficult to judge. Its central weakness is the figure of Stephen Dedalus, which is merely the direct embodiment of Joyce's need for confession—the obverse side of his need for inquisition, which, when it is turned upon an objectively conceived character like Simon Bloom, becomes the main strength of his imagination, forcing him to discover everything that can be known about his subject, however curious or morbid or trivial. Bloom is a character on the grand scale, but he has no counterpart in the book. A corollary of his isolation is the absence of personal relations between the characters in general; there is no friendship and no love; at best the impersonal good-fellowship of pub-drinkers and the physical contact of sex. Dublin is solidly evoked, and the swarming population of Dublin, and there is an unstinted amount of brilliant talk; but it is all social, almost impersonal, without a vestige of the "flow" between one human being and another which mattered so much to Lawrence. All the characters live within themselves or on the social plane; and when something resembling a personal relation is established between Bloom and Stephen at the end, it is pathetically inadequate. The power of the book lies in its evocation of the terrifying depths which yawn beneath this social life, and in its vision of the minute residual squalor of ordinary daily existence, caused by the bodily functions. The power of this vision is enhanced by all the resources of Joyce's style, the most wonderful literary instrument which has been fashioned in our time, equal to almost any form of expression except simple utterance. His mastery of language is greater than Pound's, and like Pound's is a specialised gift, not completely subservient to his thought and his imagination, but with a partially independent life of its own. He has said that as a young man he was more deeply moved by certain words than by the objects for which they stood, and words apprehended with this intensity, in dissociation, can be used to evoke a different world from the natural world, as certain passages in *Ulysses* show. They can also produce a false, synthetic beauty which depends on their mere musical collocation, not on the image produced by that collocation; and *Ulysses* demonstrates this too. Joyce's imagery is often trite and pretty. But his control of language is prodigious, and in his *Work in Progress* it has taken him into places where I cannot follow him or distinguish what spell he is casting at the centre of his polyglot jungle.

What influence *Ulysses* has had on the practice of contemporary prose fiction it would be hard to say. Its use of free association has certainly been duplicated in many other novels, giving the novelist a verbal and in some cases an imaginative freedom which he did not have before. Joyce's use of the legend of Odysseus as a framework for the action of the story obviously resembles Eliot's employment of the mythical theme in *The Waste Land* and Pound's employment of his archetypes and other elements in the *Cantos*. In each case the imaginative plan is a recognition of an order which once existed and no longer exists. There is no evidence that Eliot was influenced in this matter, or indeed in any other, by Joyce. The fact that, working separately, they should produce two works structurally so peculiar, so new, and so alike is altogether striking. There are other close resemblances not merely in the temper but in the form of their work; the use of the past, for instance, and the literary forms of the past, to throw the present into relief, and the passionate yet learned approach to experience. Joyce's imitation and caricature of archaic literary modes serves the same purpose as Eliot's literary allusions, and has something in common with Pound's use of translation. All three writers were busy after the War shoring fragments against their ruins, or ruins against their fragments. In Joyce's work this is the sole indication that something was wrong with society: the most indirect of indirect criticisms. His view of human nature, being a vision

of man as an individual, is really timeless. But the pressure
of his age imposed upon him, when he wrote *Ulysses*, a
structure which was fanatically new, and his genius for
language made him work it out with medieval consistency.
The influence of a book like *Ulysses* cannot be estimated, for
when it is obvious it is not genuine, and when it is genuine it
is not obvious; but there is no doubt that the book has had a
considerable influence, both on the style and the temper of
the novel.

The remaining major representative of the great age which
did not "come off" is Wyndham Lewis. He is in some ways
what he holds himself to be: the antidote to the other
writers of his generation, the hair of the dog that bit Lawrence and Joyce. He has written the best negative criticism
of *Ulysses* that exists; and he is inveterately opposed to the
"flow", whether he finds it in Bergson and the various "time
philosophies", or in Lawrence and the worshippers of the
unconscious. He has put a reasoned case against these
tendencies in a very interesting book, *Time and Western Man*;
and he has refuted and caricatured them in several volumes,
and in a periodical called *The Enemy* which came to a pre-
mature end. His attack on the kind of art which deals with
the "inside" of life, the inchoate unconscious, may have
helped indirectly to prepare the way for the political art of
the next generation, which he detests just as violently. His
standpoint is that of the "detached" artist, and it conditions
his treatment of politics, as of every other question: *The Art
of being Ruled* is, in spite of its personal prejudices, the most
"detached" consideration of politics which has appeared in
our time. Lewis knows a good deal from experience about
the "Time flux" and the other things against which he
writes, for he has himself flowed under several bridges. His
detachment is therefore the hostile detachment which
follows a difference: a "no" to the enemy's "yes"; and so his
answer to the claim that art has to do with the "inside" of life
is the blunt negative that it has solely to do with the "outside". The "outside" here must obviously be interpreted in a
wide sense, and the argument is a practical one, applicable

to the contemporary situation alone. It is probably another way of saying that by their fruits ye shall know them. And in an age when vast and cloudy hopes are associated with the passing of time and the operations of the unconscious, "By their fruits ye shall know them" becomes a satirical statement. In his novels Lewis may not be concerned with the "inside" of life, but it is always in the background, or in the "inside", and the implied contrast between it and the "outside" gives his work much of its satirical force.

His imaginative work is too direct a "no" to the "Time flux" and all that it stands for to be an adequate criticism; it is also, like Joyce's inquisition into experience, though in a different way, troubled by all sorts of undercurrents: the chief of them being the need for self-justification. *Tarr*, Lewis's first novel, is also his best, since it is least tinged by this fault; apart from Bloom, Kreisler, its main figure, is probably the most powerfully conceived imaginative figure in contemporary fiction. *The Apes of God*, a satire on contemporary writers, has the fault of Pound's Hell, that it is about other people; a fault superfluously pointed by the postulation in the background of a godlike figure, an image of the satirist himself, who is both exempt from fault and "misunderstood". Satire is perhaps by its nature about "other people"; but the satirist is at perfect liberty, as an artist, to put himself, as a man, among these other people, as Swift did; for the subject of Swift's satire was not any special class but mankind, which he hated impartially, beginning with the representative of it he knew best, himself. There is a complacency in Lewis's satire which, while it does not vitiate the particular force of the satire, damages its general application; for at its centre there is himself, the injured man magically exempt from injury, the winner of a consolation prize for ever beyond the reach of the straightest or the trickiest runner. But in one way his satire has universality: that is, in its vision of the surface of life, which turns human beings into monstrous comics, "apes of God" in a genial nightmare. His grotesque imagination has a visual exactitude beyond the reach of any other contemporary writer: the final expression of his hostile detachment. His novels are distorted by all sorts of specialised antipathies, against the worship of children, the pseudo-artist, the revolutionary ramp and so on; they are all "against" something, and something not of the first importance. But on the level of grotesque imagination he is unsurpassed.

Katherine Mansfield's art showed a steady advance in sensibility and technique to her early death. Her first volume, *In a German Pension*, had a raw and exquisite cruelty, a young girl's ruthless eye for pretence, pomposity and affectation. On one side the advance in her art was an advance towards humanity, and it was for a time slightly involved with sentimentality, perhaps an inevitable adjunct of such a development. She was influenced by the Russians, Chekhov in particular, more fundamentally and less obviously than the other novelists of her time. There are stories in *The Garden Party* and *Bliss* which are as good as Chekhov's best stories, and at the same time quite unlike them, though she certainly derived her way of feeling life, or rather of feeling into it, from Chekhov. Her note-books, published after her death by Mr. J. Middleton Murry, show the high moral conception which she held of the function of the artist. Although the form which she used was a restricted one, she had a deeper apprehension of life on its various levels, and a juster eye, than any other woman writer of her generation. She shows a grasp of the massive outlines of experience and of its light and shade at the same time. Some of her work is still as new as when it appeared first.

Virginia Woolf has an equally sensitive apprehension of the wavering surface of experience, but beneath that one feels there is no solid outline, or at most a conventional out-line derived from certain intellectual conceptions of last century, mostly liberal and agnostic. She writes about the ordinary passions of men and women as if she had been told about them by someone who regarded them as interesting but unreasonable and therefore, like Pound's Hell, "for other people". There is, accordingly, a baffling remoteness in her attitude to what Yeats contemptuously calls "the root facts of life". But in catching the fleeting impressions which play over them she is probably unrivalled. Her art has gradually developed into a perfect vehicle for expressing this fleeting sensibility. Her first novels were more or less traditional and dealt with "the root facts of life". In *Jacob's Room*, *Mrs. Dalloway*, *To the Lighthouse* and *The Waves* she becomes more and more skilful in catching ambiguous surface effects, until in the last-named book characterisation has almost completely disappeared. *Mrs Dalloway* is a delightful work. *To the Lighthouse* and *The Waves* embody, sometimes very movingly, what seems to be Mrs. Woolf's strongest emotion as a writer: her sense of the passing of time. The middle section of *To the Lighthouse*, describing the decay of an empty house in the Hebrides, is striking both as a piece of sustained imagination and as a piece of fine writing. She is a scrupulous and ingenious artist surprised by life, and so fascinated by her surprise that life remains always at one remove away. The sense of beauty in her novels comes from this continuous reflection of the surprising lights of life; but apart from these, life itself is ordinary and uninteresting: the dissociated life of sceptical, enlightened people.

A very different idea of middle class and upper middle class life is given in the novels of Stephen Hudson, which centre round a single character, Richard Kurt. The strength of these novels does not lie in their sensibility, though they have an acute sensibility, but in their grasp of the human passions and appetites and the weakness of the individual caught in them. Richard Kurt is one of the most completely described characters in modern fiction, and the series of novels in which he appears, the best three of which are collected in *A True Story*, are a scrupulous criticism of human motives. They are more French than English in their logical selection of detail for a specific end, their exact definition, and a moral temper drawn from experience and governed by intelligence. The basis of the criticism is circumscribed, but it is always coherent and serious, and *A True Story* has a place of its own in contemporary fiction, by virtue of its objectivity, its high moral temper, and an art which conceals art.

A writer who stood somewhat apart from her age, and yet was a penetrating critic of it, was the late Stella Benson. Her novels have a quality which is very difficult to describe, at once sweet and bitter, ironical and pathetic, ruthless and shrinking. Her wit carries her over the farcical horrors of life which she describes so pitilessly. The mood of her work is comedy, the substance tragedy. This attitude is achieved by a piece of intellectual jugglery which is perfectly serious. The surface of her work is delightful, but it is so transparent that it never conceals the horrible passions which move about, quite without supervision, beneath it. Her wit comes from the contrast between the surface and what it conceals.

The first novels of Aldous Huxley appeared shortly after the War, and reflected the disillusionment of that time. They showed on the one hand a cruel perception of human hypocrisy, and on the other a fascination with ideas, quite apart from their credibility or their use, as curious foibles of the human mind. *Antic Hay*, one of Mr. Huxley's best novels, is concerned almost exclusively with petty lusts, vanities, betrayals, and the physiological. In *Those Barren Leaves*, his next novel, there appeared one of those characters who grow larger and larger in his later stories, and who embody his increasing concern with morality and the good life. In *Eyeless at Gaza*, his latest novel, his ideas have crystallised into a theory of non-resistance as the sole hope of mankind. The intellectual or moral thesis of a work of imagination may be right or wrong without greatly affecting its value; so long as the criticism of life which follows from it is illuminating, it justifies itself; and the criticism of life in *Eyeless at Gaza* does throw light upon the problem of conduct. The problem is simplified, but it is stated with lucidity, and it does not falsify the picture except in one crucial detail: the figure of the main representative of non-resistance himself, who is sentimental. All Huxley's imaginative work has been in essence an exposure of hypocrisy. In his early books the hypocrisy was presented as a thing in itself, covering a moral vacuum, an absence of attributes; and being universal it became meaningless, the expression of a mood which was the mood of a considerable number of people after the War. It was a perpetual improvisation, and the result is that a novel like *Antic Hay* reads as if it also were an improvisation. Huxley is not primarily a novelist, nor a satirist, but a writer interested in moral ideas. The ideas in his later work no longer play round the circumstances of life, but try to deal seriously with it.

The generation of Huxley produced such a number of talented novelists, writers who turned out intelligent and skilful work, that it is impossible to consider them separately without turning this book into a meaningless catalogue. They included Rebecca West, Rose Macaulay, E. M. Delafield, F. Tennyson Jesse, Kate O'Brien, and, most notably, on account of her higher poetic tension, Storm Jameson, all five of them delightful novelists, with wit and sensibility, who contributed to the social criticism of their time. Contemporary with them came the War novelists, R. H. Mottram, A. P. Herbert, and a little later Frederic Manning, whose book *Her Privates We* is probably the best War novel of these years. Evelyn Waugh's novels, *Decline and Fall* and *Vile Bodies*, provided a sort of popularisation of Huxley's disillusionment. The best social criticism came from the women.

One woman novelist, Miss I. Compton Burnett, stands out from the others by virtue of her striking originality and the perfection of her art. She might be put among the comic writers if it were not that the final effect of her work suggests tragedy rather than comedy. Her novels consist almost entirely of conversation, and the conversation is a textually exact analysis of human motives, exposing a frightening world where, beneath the conventions of everyday life in comfortable English houses, a deadly battle for power is waged between the young and the old. The subject of all Miss Compton Burnett's novels is tyranny, and particularly domestic tyranny in all its forms: the struggle for domination and the struggle to escape domination. Her work is social criticism in its most incisive form, but it also goes beyond social criticism; for her conception of human life has more in common with Emily Brontë's than Jane Austen's, and it rests upon an ultimate idea of freedom which gives her a deadly perception of the small shifts of social life. She has an exquisite comic gift, an almost pedantic discrimination between shades of implication, a firm grasp of motive, a superb mastery of dialogue, and perfect nicety and precision of style. She is one of the most original and accomplished writers of her time; and she has treated her chosen subject, middle-class English family life, with an efficiency which no other writer has approached. Beside her novels, Samuel Butler's *The Way of all Flesh* seems vague and harmless.

Among the younger generation there are half a dozen novelists who carry on with great ability the tradition of the age before them, and are at the same time original artists; writers such as H. E. Bates, Neil Gunn, Sean O'Faolain and Eric Linklater. They are novelists of original endowment, and they deserve more detailed mention than they can be given here; but this book is concerned with history rather than with criticism.

Glancing over the development of the novel from the early years of the century, one is struck by its resemblance to the development of poetry at the same time. Before 1910 we find in both vague hopes and loose technique. There are exceptions to this, Conrad for instance; but to the intelligent public before the War the novel meant roughly Wells, Bennett and Galsworthy. After this phase we find doubts and despairs accompanied by all sorts of refinements of technique, whose aim was precision. The mind of the novelist was turned in upon himself or outside on the world with a close scrutiny in which he saw the elements of experience in separation, without being able to grasp any central unity: exactitude seemed at war with wholeness. This made the writer turn to the past for a pattern of life, as Joyce did in *Ulysses*, or retire into a world of "effects", like Virginia Woolf. In either case it was a private world, and the writer withdrew into it to snatch a private salvation from a society where the hope of general security had disappeared. The best fiction of this period is fiction for the "elect" by virtue both of its style and of its attitude to life, which was monastic without being ascetic. Imaginative writing became what Hermann Broch asserted it was bound to become: a form of expression which could be fully understood only by a writer or a potential writer. Art was judged by severely technical standards. The ordinary world, the world as Dickens or even as Bennett had seen it, remained outside, a waste with which the novelist had as little to do as the monk had to do with the world of the dark ages. This aloofness engendered a wonderfully subtle sensibility which, when it was turned upon the world, that distant entity, saw its disorders with dreamlike clearness, as the monk saw the dark ages. In their retreat to their fastnesses, the writers of the time nourished a hope of salvation, but of a particular salvation which was never formulated clearly: embodied in an aspiration at the end of a last chapter, or vicariously laid upon a symbolic hero.

This tension was released in poetry by the *public* emergence of the hero, in the work of Auden and Day Lewis, as an engineer, a lone scout, an explorer, a holder of forlorn posts, and several other things. The novel is a more realistic art than poetry, and it cannot score these symbolic victories. The most that can be said is that in the work of a few young writers it has turned away from the private and abstruse problems of a few people to the life of society. The attempt has shown few striking successes thus far. The proletarian novel has come into existence: that is, the novel dealing with working-class life from a working-class point of view or from a Communist point of view. A number of the resulting novels are competent, a number are not; hardly one has literary merit or shows sensibility, though sensibility is not a prerogative of the middle and upper classes. One "proletarian" novelist of very considerable original endowment we do have: James Hanley. But it would be misleading to call him a "proletarian" novelist; he is simply a born delineator of life, a man of powerful imagination. His work is uneven, but he has the rare gift of being able to deal with any kind of experience which comes his way, of "digesting" life on a large scale. A steady development can be seen in his novels, and the last of them, *Hollow Sea*, a description of the voyage of an army transport ship during the War, rises to impressive heights of imaginative horror.

Apart from the proletarians there is Ralph Bates, a Left writer of great talent, with a wide curiosity about all forms of social life which makes him a real painter of society. There is also William Plomer, who has both sensibility and intelligence, and the same wide interest, the same gift for plastic description. And there is Christopher Isherwood. His subject is the middle classes, but his approach to them is very different from Galsworthy's; it is both more disrespectful and more alive to the place which they occupy in society as a whole. There is always the assumption in his portrayal of them that they are passing away, and that, beguilingly human as they are, they should pass away. He sees them as a demoralised class, but he has an affection for demoralised human beings not unlike Chekhov's; he sees their comic weaknesses and their illusions about the world, and yet likes them. He is one of the most humane novelists alive, yet at the same time clear-sighted, with a ruthless indulgence which is more deadly than condemnation, and a conviction that nothing will help these people. His work has the peculiar neatness which sometimes goes with a conviction that the world is hopelessly confused, as it did, for instance, in Chekhov.

Graham Greene, a Catholic writer of the same generation, is as convinced of the rottenness of society, but sees the rottenness with the minimum of indulgence. The fault of his work is an excessive emphasis; everything is shown up in a harsh light and casts fantastic shadows; and the play of these shadows sometimes produces an effect of melodrama. His stories are logically rather than imaginatively constructed, and give the impression that the characters are working out their fates with more incisiveness than experience, unmanipulated, would have given them the chance to do. This produces an effect of lucidity and of simplification at the same time. The main strength of Greene's novels is in their apprehension of evil.

An extremely interesting "Marxian" work of imagination is Edward Upward's *Journey to the Border*. It is both realistic and symbolic, owing something on both counts to the work of Franz Kafka, a German writer whose stories, *The Castle* and *The Trial*, have had a considerable indirect influence in England. Kafka belonged to the generation of Joyce and Proust and the interior dialogue, and the form he perfected, the psychological allegory, was perhaps the most economical possible for rendering the problems of that time. He is in his way as brilliant a psychologist as Proust and as deep an explorer of the unconscious as Joyce. The concrete allegory of *The Castle* is a means to penetrate into the fastnesses of the mind; it is completely of its age. Upward uses the same method for a different purpose. He starts with a single symbolical hero, like Kafka. The unresolved hopes and fears of the hero produce an allegorical vision of the world, which becomes in turn what he hopes and what he fears it to be; with the disappearance of these hopes and fears, or rather with his knowledge of what they mean, he is in the actual world and sets himself the problem of how to act concretely there. The problem and the conception of life are far simpler than Kafka's; for the resolution of the hero's difficulties is merely that he should cast in his lot with the revolutionary working classes. Nevertheless *Journey to the Border* is a work of genuine imagination; the fantasies in the hero's mind are an accurate and profound criticism of society; and the whole book has an admirable solidity. It is perhaps the most convincing single work of imagination which has been written from a Left point of view by a young writer, and certainly the most original.

I have had to use the word "Left" several times in this chapter, though it is inaccurate and absurd and by now has become almost a cant term. Mr. Wyndham Lewis may be right when he says that almost all writers are "Left" at present. If this is so, obviously the word has very little meaning. But its sudden emergence into general use a few years ago was significant as a popular recognition that society and civilisation were in danger, and that the political as-

This point is worth bringing up, for it seems to me that there is a deeper realisation of the disease of civilisation in certain contemporary work which is avowedly non-political, such as that of Henry Miller. The work of this writer is not easily accessible in England; it employs too frank a vocabulary to be published in London. Miller has something in common both with Lawrence and Joyce; in his detestation of the abstract, depersonalised life of his time he is on the side of Lawrence, and he is like Joyce in that all his work is a confession. But it is undertaken in a very different temper from Joyce's; it completely dispenses with dignity and is all the better for it; for nothing strikes one more in the end about *Ulysses* than Stephen Dedalus's straight back; his head, often bloody but always unbowed; the conspicuous absence of the suggested genuflection. There is nothing of this kind in Miller's work. In *Black Spring* he says: "What is not in the open street is false, derived, that is to say, *literature*." He pours out everything, getting over his shame by a sort of braggadocio, as Rabelais did; not so completely as Rabelais, but more completely than Joyce. He is like Rabelais in one way: that his confessions are not personal merely; that he seems to be confessing for a whole multitude. *Tropic of Cancer* is a shocking book; but in certain scenes it pierces deeper into the disease of our existence than any other book that I know. It is a work of genius, terrifying and comic, alternating between an exasperating jauntiness and an absolute sincerity of purpose. The philosophy implicit in it is not unlike Lawrence's, though more adequate to the complexity of experience. I do not agree with it, but it is at least a philosophy with the courage to show the diseased natural man in all his monstrosity.

A feeling of the corruption of the time where it is most highly developed, that is among the cosmopolitan intelligentsia, is evoked still more powerfully, though with more restraint, in Djuna Barnes's *Nightwood*. Miss Barnes is one of those few writers whose thought and expression become more felicitous, the more painful the theme she is dealing with; here she resembles Webster and Baudelaire. There is no trace of a hopeful or even a hope-inspiring philosophy in her book: her vision is purely tragic, with that leavening of sardonic wit which comes from long familiarity with tragedy: the almost professional note which one also finds in Webster and Baudelaire, but which, though a source of pleasure in itself, does not alleviate in the least the force of the tragic emotion. Miss Barnes's prose is the only prose by a living writer which can be compared with that of Joyce, and in one point it is superior to his: in its richness in exact and vivid imagery entirely without that prettiness which so readily creeps into an Irish style. There is not in her use of language, as there is in Joyce's, the faint suggestion of a possible distinction between the thing said and the way in which it is said, the feeling that one could have said it in another way if one had liked. A style which is inevitable and inventive at the same time is the most powerful of all styles; for it both removes our opposition to it and takes us with its novelty. Miss Barnes has this gift of style. Her imagination is sensuous and intellectual; drawn from hidden, and reinforced by worldly knowledge. Whether her book should be called a novel is hard to say; it is more a vicarious confession, like most of the best fiction of the time. It is at any rate a unique work of imagination and a consummate achievement of style.

Somewhat apart from the general line which I have attempted to trace through the fiction of the age, there are a number of writers whom I can only mention briefly, though some of them are writers of talent. Walter de la Mare has written some stories which are as unique as his poetry; and *Memoirs of a Midget* is a masterpiece. But what I have said about his poetry in the previous chapter will, in a book of this length, have to stand for his prose as well. Forrest Reid is, in the same province, the province of the strange, the supernatural and the magical, an exquisite and true artist, whose genius has never been adequately recognised, perhaps because of its perfection, which calls no notice to itself. David Garnett's *Lady into Fox* (his first and best story) is strange in a different way, not for its perception of the magical, but for the logical imagination with which it works out a magical occurrence as if it were an ordinary one. It has been dismissed as an artificial trifle, but it is a work of true imagination, a pessimistic comment on life. John Collier's *His Monkey Wife* is somewhat similar in plan, but quite different in treatment, being exuberant and ornate where Mr. Garnett was plain. Both books came out of the time after the War when there was a general feeling that one could do nothing but attend to one's own business. George Beaton's picaresque novel, *Jack Robinson*, came later, but was inspired by somewhat the same spirit. It is a work whose truth is a general or rather a generalised truth, like that of Garnett and Collier, not obviously applicable to the time. The same may be said of Richard Hughes's story, *A High Wind in Jamaica*, and of Christina Stead's *The Salzburg Tales*, both of them works of brilliant literary skill. All these books are evidences of a minor regeneration of the *story*, but none of them shows that the story is a suitable form for the description of contemporary life.

T. F. Powys is perhaps the most remarkable of the storytellers. His books derive their power from an extreme simplification of life which seems to lay bare the forms of good and evil. When this happens life becomes something very like a nightmare filled with simple symbolical figures. The power of Mr. Powys's imagination cannot be denied, nor the lucidity with which he renders it. But the wisdom behind it, which may be reduced to the formula, "Death is best", has, like Hardy's pessimism, a touch of absurd facility which ruins its effect. If life has to be condemned, one feels that this is not the way to condemn it. Mr. Powys gives the impression that he knows a disreputable secret about life, but does not convince us that the real secret of life is disreputable.

There are two other writers, unlike in most ways, but alike in that they are not so much novelists as thinkers who have used the novel to express a semi-philosophical standpoint. Norman Douglas's novel, *South Wind*, was the model of a whole series of novels which have appeared since, ranging in value from the early stories of Aldous Huxley to those of Evelyn Waugh. *South Wind* still remains the best of them. L. H. Myers has embodied his philosophy and his criticism of contemporary life in a long story of ancient India, *The Root and the Flower*. It is a serious comment on the values of civilisation, ingenious, detached, intellectually fascinating, but, I think, a little deficient in imagination.

Contemporary with the work which I have briefly mentioned, there has been an immense output of popular fiction. Here, too, the fashions have changed greatly since the beginning of the century. The ideas of the time have gradually filtered into the best-seller; and what gives the novels of A. S. M. Hutchinson and Warwick Deeping their appeal is a much watered-down and sentimentalised plea for a little more freedom. Novels advocating easier divorce have a wide public. Pleas for international understanding without any over-precise definition of international complications are also pretty sure to be read. Along with this class of popular fiction, there co-exists the ageless kind which is not concerned with ideas at all, but is pure entertainment: it is from almost any point of view a more admirable class, and one also which requires far more ability from the writer. Perhaps its chief ornament is Mr. P. G. Wodehouse, a comic writer of immense talent, whose appeal is not in the least fortuitous, but due to his gifts alone, like the appeal of the old-fashioned music-hall artist. There are also the detective story writers, somewhat class-conscious, and very fond of titles and old school ties, perhaps to excuse their interest in sordid crimes. Their brilliance is the most vulgar thing in contemporary literature; their wit is execrable; but they represent a certain degree of intellectual ability, and they have made a fashion. The detective novel is the extreme logical form of the literature of escape; but it is also harmless and enjoyable, since it pretends to be nothing else.

.   .   .   .

Surveying the fiction of this century as a whole, it may be said that we see in it a breakdown of the novel: the picture

of life cannot be rounded off as it could in times of greater
stability. Yet at the same time one cannot help feeling that
the age of *Ulysses, Sons and Lovers, Tarr, Mrs Dalloway, Men
and Wives,* and *Nightwood,* is a great age of the English novel.
It is at any rate a great age of the English novel in one
province: style. In ages of good order description is comparatively easy, for everything is palpable and in its place.
When good order is failing things become difficult to grasp,
a greater effort is required, and the art of description has
to be developed to keep pace with the changing situation.
The prose of good fiction has become both more elaborate
and more exact since the beginning of the century. By far
the most accurate descriptive writer in the years before the
War was Conrad. To show how prose has changed since
then one need only put one of his best descriptive passages
beside one from a later writer: I shall choose Miss Barnes.
This is from *Nostromo*:

> "A fire of broken furniture out of the Intendencia saloons,
> mostly gilt, was burning in the Plaza, in a high flame
> swaying right up to the statue of Charles IV. The dead body
> of a man was lying on the steps of the pedestal, his arms
> thrown wide open and his sombrero covering his face—the
> attention of some friend, perhaps. The light of the flames
> touched the foliage of the first trees on the Alamada, and
> played on the end of a side street near by, blocked up by a
> jumble of ox-carts and dead bullocks. Sitting on one of the
> carcasses a lepero, muffled up, smoked a cigarette. It was a
> truce, you understand. The only other living being in the
> Plaza besides ourselves was a Cargador, walking to and fro,
> with a long, bare knife in his hand, like a sentry before the
> Arcades, where his friends were sleeping. And the only other
> spot of light in the dark town was the lighted window of
> the club, at the corner of the Calle."

That is a wonderful picture, a masterly composition. But
compare it with this, from *Nightwood*:

> "Against the panels of oak that reared themselves above
> the long table and up to the curving ceiling hung life-sized
> portraits of Guido's claim to father and mother. The lady

153

was a sumptuous Florentine with bright sly eyes and overt mouth. Great puffed pearled sleeves rose to the prick-eared pointings of the stiff lace about the head, conical and braided. The deep accumulation of dress fell about her in groined shadows, the train, rambling through a vista of primitive trees, was carpet thick. She seemed to be expecting a bird. The gentleman was seated precariously on a charger. He seemed not so much to have mounted the animal, as to be about to descend upon him. The blue of the Italian sky lay between the saddle and the buff of the tightened rump of the rider. The charger had been caught by the painter in the execution of a falling arc, the mane lifted away in a dying swell; the tail forward and in, between thin bevelled legs. The gentleman's dress was a baffling mixture of the Romantic and the Religious, and in the cradling crook of his left arm he carried a plumed hat, crown out, The whole conception might have been a Mardi Gras whim. The gentleman's head, stuck on at a three-quarter angle, had a remarkable resemblance to Guido Volkbein, the same sweeping Cabalistic line of the nose, the features seasoned and warm save where the virgin blue of the eyeballs curved out of the lids as if another medium than that of sight had taken its stand beneath the flesh. There was no interval in the speed of the stare, endless and objective."

Something unknown to Conrad has gone into this prose, which has the closeness and precision of poetry and yet is a workable prose medium. It has resources that were not dreamt of thirty years ago. The creation of prose of this quality is one of the achievements of the modern novel; perhaps its greatest achievement.

CHAPTER IV

GENERAL PROSE WRITERS

THE most original prose of this century has been produced by the development of the novel, and in that the age is unlike any of its predecessors. We have no Johnson or de Quincey or Landor or Ruskin, perhaps because we have no general body of accepted belief over which the mind can linger. For prose of the same elaboration we must turn now to fiction; prose of the same temper we do not have at all. The ordinary working prose of the time is plain and without ornament: intended for use.

Yet here too a change has taken place since the years before the War. In these years public debate flourished; the great names were Shaw and Wells on the one side, and Chesterton and Belloc on the other. Chesterton and Belloc stood for Roman Catholicism and Distributivism; Shaw and Wells for Protestantism and Socialism. The two sides were irreconcilable; there is no evidence that one ever convinced the other. But they possessed a common platform; they spoke about the same things and used the same terms. That situation no longer exists: the platform has disappeared along with the debaters. A literary man still utters his thoughts now and then on general questions; Mr. Eliot, Mr. Murry and Mr. Wyndham Lewis have done so. But there is no public answer, at best a semi-private quibbling over abstruse points. Mr. Wyndham Lewis is perhaps the nearest we have to a publicist in the style of Shaw and Chesterton; but he speaks avowedly as an artist, and though his comments cover most of the intellectual and political questions of the day, he deals with them as an artist. If some other specialist,

a theologian or a politician or an economist, were to reply
to him, clearly there could not be a common platform.
Debate can flourish only in a society where the debaters
meet in a fraternal equality of some kind; as mere citizens
if as nothing else. Such a society recognises general principles;
the existence of the Shaw and Chesterton debate rested on
general principles. But when, to quote Hermann Broch
again, philosophy follows a law of its own, science a law of its
own, business a law of its own, economics a law of its own,
poetry a law of its own, painting a law of its own, it must
be extremely difficult, and must become more and more difficult, to find a common platform. Consequently public debate
has virtually disappeared. There is in literature a relatively
large area of Left opinion and a relatively small area of
Right opinion, but nothing that can be called discussion
occurs between the Left and the Right: their opposition to
each other is for all practical purposes dumb. There is a
certain amount of debate among the Left; but it is mainly
semi-private discussion on technical points conducted in a
specialised vocabulary. Generally speaking, discussion has
given way to propaganda. Propaganda states only what
advances its case; it need not mention, and often it does
not see, the objections to its argument. The great virtue of
debate is that it publicly brings up these objections and
makes it necessary that they should be considered and
answered. A feature of contemporary dictatorships is a dislike of all criticism which is not "creative" or "helpful",
that is of all fundamental criticism; and the same attitude
is implied in the Left and the Right groups into which
literature is at present divided. It is a highly unsatisfactory
situation and one of considerable incipient danger; for
when discussion is surrendered the conviction may easily
supervene that the time for discussion is past, that "things
must take their course"; and things are blind and violent.
An undercurrent of violence can actually be felt beneath
this reciprocal silence, which contains the implications of
an ultimatum that has not yet taken effect. It is possible to
show that, the present development of society being what

it is, this was "inevitable"; but it is hard to rest content in that conviction. The development of society determines the forms of our actions; but our actions have also some determining effect on the development of society. It cannot be that debate is impossible, just when it is most necessary and its absence most dangerous. To believe this is, under one disguise or another, to deny the validity of the human reason.

The actors in the great public debate before the War were all reformers. The difference between the Belloc-Chesterton and the Shaw-Wells combination may be conveniently described by saying that the first believed in history and that the second did not. Or rather, the only history in which they believed was unwritten history. Belloc and Chesterton read lessons from the past; Shaw and Wells looked to the future. The ultimate ideal of both sides was an ideal of unity. But Belloc and Chesterton saw it in the past, as the Catholic Church, while Shaw and Wells saw it in the future, as the Socialist State. That is, it was perceived on the one hand as something which was breaking up, and on the other as something which was taking shape. The actual process which both parties were contemplating was the same process, but what the one side called progress the other called disintegration. Shaw and Wells busied themselves in removing obstacles to advance; Belloc and Chesterton insisted that they were destroying landmarks. Again, what Shaw and Wells saw as organisation, Belloc and Chesterton saw as regimentation. And so on. There was occasionally a touch of artificiality in these neat automatic antinomies which appeared so punctually, like rabbits from a hat. But the basis of the debate was solid enough, and it was that Belloc and Chesterton saw life historically and that Shaw and Wells saw it prophetically. The argument that society was really disintegrating when Shaw and Wells thought that it was progressing seemed to be clinched for the time being by the War and the events which followed the War. At any rate it was clear that Belloc and Chesterton had seen the immediate future more truly. The debate has now passed on to a different stage.

Belloc is a fine example of the writer, as distinguished from the imaginative artist; the *clerk* who can turn his pen indifferently to any purpose, history, biography, fiction, theology, politics, controversy, light or serious verse, military science, or the essay. He has written an enormous number of books on a great variety of subjects, and all of them from a consistent standpoint; for though his interests are multifarious, his beliefs always show through them. He has a style of conspicuous, perhaps too conspicuous, nicety, which becomes dry when it is not penetrated by his charm. He is a dogmatic writer, with the suppleness and ingenuity of mind which the defence of a dogma in difficult or unlikely circumstances sometimes produces. He is also a courageous and honourable publicist, and he has never hesitated to speak his mind on any abuse, in the face of unpopularity or the more deadly opposition of official silence. He is most widely known, perhaps, for his essays and his discursive books of travel such as *The Path to Rome* and *The Four Men*, which are delightful but too whimsical for every taste. The constant thing in all his work, apart from his Catholicism, is a clear and consistent idea of civilisation as the creation of the Latin or rather the Mediterranean peoples. There was, it strikes one now, something semi-prophetic in his insistence on this truth; as if he foresaw and were arming against the rise of the Nordic catastrophe.

Chesterton was an original literary character, and a brilliant wit. His youth was passed in the aesthetic 'Nineties; while still young he said something like an Everlasting No to them; but they haunted him all his life. His imagination, and also his humour, easily passed into the monstrous, and the monstrous to him always kept a memory of the green carnation. The gorgeous 'Nineties later became associated in his mind with the gorgeous East; bland, sensual Asiatics abound in his books: projections of Beardsley and Wilde on to a historical stage. With them as an excuse, he rioted in all sorts of sensuous imagery while damning the man who has the keenest delight in the senses: the aesthete that, but for the grace of God, he might himself have become. When he speaks of such things, therefore, when he describes a decadent writer or a splendidly corrupt Asiatic, he is always unconvincing; the recurring antithesis in his books between the good West and the wicked East is the nearest he comes to sham rhetoric.

He was like Belloc a miscellaneous writer in the best sense, rather than an imaginative artist. He had the seriousness of the general writer, of the publicist, and of an honest man, without the disinterested devotion of the poet. Imagination always remained romantic to him, which meant that it was grasped at one remove, as something to be used for effect. On the level of controversy he was sometimes brilliant, though he easily saw himself as a picturesque swordsman; the image of the sword recurs frequently in his books, and it is always an obsolete sword. But in spite of his fantastic approach to every subject, he had a balanced and sure grasp of human nature and also of politics. He saw the unexpected as part of the typical; in his later work he saw it with a surprise which had perhaps grown professional. But it was virtually impossible for him to write without wit; we never feel that his wit is being deliberately whipped up; it is more like an unfortunate habit, a *tic*, against which he fought a losing battle. He had probably more of the quality which we recognise as wisdom than any of his contemporaries; his work is like a rambling building whose walls are shaken by every wind, but which remains standing nevertheless, because the foundations are true.

Shaw's general prose work—and that consists mainly of the prefaces to his plays—strikes one now as the opposite of this: the walls are neatly and efficiently built, with not a brick loose, but their foundations do not seem to go any deeper than the naked eye can follow them. A big wind would not shake this house, for the brick-laying has been too carefully done; but it might easily sweep it away altogether, and deposit it, probably still intact, somewhere else. People have often denied that Shaw's mind is inhuman;

yet that is surely the thing that strikes one first about it.
Yeats tells us that he once dreamt of Shaw as a sewing
machine, new and polished, and was very surprised to notice
that this machine kept perpetually smiling. Shaw's negative
qualities, the talents he does not have, strike one as much
as his positive qualities, the talents he undeniably does have.
He is without imagination and does not seem to know
how ordinary human beings feel; but he makes a virtue of
the fact and his plays are made up of witty improvisation.
As a thinker he is extremely efficient for the same reason,
for it is notorious that in matters of thought men's feelings
can lead them astray. At the same time he supports various
modern creeds to which men of feeling are particularly
attracted. He does not, of course, share their emotion, and
indefatigably pours cold water on it. But the consequence
is that he has to *explain* why he is a Socialist, a vegetarian,
a teetotaller, a non-smoker and more recently a supporter
of dictatorship; and as an explanatory writer he is at his
best. On any specific public question which he takes up
he writes with force and lucidity, in a style stripped of all
excrescences but wit, with the intonation of a brilliant
young man who has just come up from the provinces to put
London in its place. He has always remained that brilliant
young man. When he came to London first he found that
only a few people were right: the Wagnerites, the Ibsenites
and the Fabian Society. Later he discovered that Samuel
Butler had produced the only right theory of evolution;
and from Butler's ideas he himself evolved the only right
gospel, that of the Life Force. But he remained an inveterate
particularist; his philosophy is not an organic whole, but is
made up of a number of peculiar ideas very efficiently
dovetailed together. His prose is direct, concise and vigorous:
an admirable instrument for putting the case *against* anything.

Wells was more concerned with the pro than the contra,
and he had a quicker perception of the possibilities inherent
in the various developments of society. He had also a freer
and more unembarrassed mind, and vastly more imagination; so that he saw the political situation, as it unrolled, as a

series of opportunities to be seized. His prose began by being buoyant and ended by being fretful; for though the possibilities kept punctually arriving, he could discover no man quick or intelligent enough to seize them. He was far more interested in immediate action than Shaw, who was disgusted with human stupidity, like Wells himself, but on the whole content to remain a theorist, since as a theorist he could always be right. What has possessed Wells's mind from the start has been potentiality, not actuality; much of the humour of his early novels, such as *Kipps* and *Mr. Polly*, comes from a comic perception of what might have been. His scientific romances and utopias are pleasurable variations on the same theme; but in his long list of sociological books he had to treat it seriously, and his demand on human alertness and disgust with human stupidity have consequently increased in ratio to each other. Professor Dobrée has dealt in the previous volume with his novels.

The present century, though an age of great advance in historical knowledge, has produced no historian in the grand style, such as Gibbon or even Macaulay. Belloc and Chesterton, being men of tradition, have written a number of interesting historical works, but nothing in the tradition of English literary history, which is a fine combination of the romantic imagination and the social sense. A minor writer of the next generation, Lytton Strachey, did succeed in following that tradition. His style is like a falsetto echo of the eminent historian. It began as a veiled parody of the dignified historical style, employed with deliberate malice, sometimes very effectively; but it ended by getting the better of him, so that he could write in nothing else, whatever his purpose: his last historical work, on Essex and Elizabeth, is a long sequence of carefully polished romantic clichés. In *Eminent Victorians* his social sense, always acute and sometimes deadly, kept his romantic imagination in check. Sentimentality began to creep into his life of Queen Victoria, and everyone knows the concluding paragraph, the famous passage about the pebble: one of the worst falsetto purple patches that he ever wrote. His imagination was essentially schematic; he realised that public men are on one plane of their lives marionettes. His short biographies of Manning and Thomas Arnold are brilliantly successful for this reason. He could sum up wittily an eminent man who was fully conscious of his eminence. But he failed with Gordon of Khartoum, for Gordon had no awareness and no respect for earthly eminence; if comedy of any kind could be made out of him, it was not social comedy. Strachey belonged to the disillusioned generation; but unlike his contemporaries he enjoyed the disillusion. His irony has been condemned as cheap; actually it was tempered by a sense of justice and an attractive humanity. He certainly enjoyed exposing the Victorians, but he enjoyed them as well; in his life of Victoria the enjoyment is tinged with nostalgia.

A number of highly interesting historical and biographical works have appeared in our time: serious works of scholarship and historical imagination, well written and excellent in temper. There have been a succession of works on English history from Mr. G. M. Trevelyan, and on Scottish history from Miss Agnes Mure Mackenzie; also Lord Tweedsmuir's biographies of Cromwell and Montrose, and Mr. Winston Churchill's life of his famous ancestor Marlborough, a fascinating work written in a rhetorical prose which does not reflect the sensibility or the temper of the age, and is conspicuously orotund. Of these writers Lord Tweedsmuir's style is easily the best, being a model of lucidity and grace. But about the historical prose of this century one does not feel, as one feels about that of the eighteenth and nineteenth centuries, that it has helped to form the art of prose in general: this has been left to the novel.

Nor has the voluminous literature of travel added anything important to the development of prose. The most famous travel book of the century is T. E. Lawrence's *The Seven Pillars of Wisdom*, a semi-historical description of his Arabian campaign during the War. Lawrence was a brilliant man of action whose ambition was to be a literary artist. His book is clearly modelled on the greater book of Doughty, and it contains some writing of considerable excellence at one remove, in which the style seems to trammel the expression. It is a remarkable book, not so much as literature, as because it is by and about Lawrence.

The essay has not flourished during our period, though it has been much practised. It has become a profession connected with the newspapers and weekly journals, and is a branch of journalism.

The publicists since Chesterton and Shaw have been chiefly specialists of various kinds who address the general reader in the time they can spare from their own subjects. They may address him on these subjects, like Sir Arthur Eddington and Sir James Jeans, or run their minds over themes of current interest, like Bertrand Russell. Mr. Russell writes an ordered and lucid prose which, when it is touched with emotion, immediately becomes rhetorical. Sir James Jeans makes the astronomical universe extremely interesting; but one feels that he does so by emphasising its adventitious novelty, so that his books read like synthetic fairy tales. Sir Arthur Eddington avoids this temptation and yet makes the most difficult ideas comprehensible to the uninstructed reader. His book, *The Nature of the Physical World*, is a masterpiece of clear exposition, and not a popularisation. The prose of the scientists is a functional prose, without, or with only the most naïve, ornament, lacking in sensitiveness (even Eddington can be painfully facetious), but of admirable lucidity. It is something more and less than good popular prose; more exact and scrupulous on the one hand, and less socially experienced on the other: its attitude to the reader, that distant human object, remains slightly awkward, and this obstacle has to be surmounted by a disarming playfulness. But in spite of this the scientist remains in one world and his reader in another. One has only to compare Berkeley's ease in putting the most subtle propositions before the public with the temper of even a writer like Eddington, to feel the difference between prose perfectly at home with its audience and prose talking across a gulf. Russell has some of Berkeley's ease when he is writing on general questions, but it is marred by the implied

163

superior dogmatism which grows up in narrow, specialised and very intelligent circles. This expository prose of the scientists shows perhaps more clearly than any other kind the truth of Broch's remarks about the specialisation of the mind, and how hard it is, with the best will and the best talents, to overcome that obstacle for a general end.

The prose of the scientists is nevertheless the best expository prose we have at present, far superior to that of the political writers. The late A. R. Orage maintained for a time a tradition of clear and dignified political writing addressed to an educated audience and implying an educated response. R. H. Tawney is in the same tradition. But although there is a greater output of books on politics now than ever before, there is also a definite decline in the art of political writing. This may be due to an uncertainty in the writer about his audience, which he feels he does not know. Or it may be due to the fact that in politics too a specialised vocabulary has become necessary, and the general reader is unacquainted with that vocabulary. Serious work and popular work have in any case become two distinct classes: in the time of Berkeley and Hume, even in that of Carlyle and Ruskin, they were not necessarily so. When our language has digested the numerous specialised terms which have poured into it during the last few decades, or at least such of them as can be digested, we may have a good popular prose again, capable of dealing with every subject. But the present stage is an awkward one.

This century has been pre-eminently an age of ideas at the phase when they have not yet been related to any central conception. In its early years it was influenced by the pseudo-philosophical notions of Ibsen and Nietzsche, Tolstoy and Dostoevsky; notions to be realised, it was thought, in the future. Then came the psychoanalytic phase, pointing inward and backward into the life of the individual, who sought salvation by becoming himself. In imaginative literature this was the period of the private worlds. Finally we have the political phase, once more directed towards the future, in which the individual sees little chance of salvation by becoming himself, if society is left to corrupt or destroy the self he succeeds in becoming. Running across these influences are others: the revival of religion at certain minute points, the appearance of such men as Barth and Maritain, and the indirect effect of abstract science, the faint modifications which the ideas of such men as Einstein, Planck and Eddington have produced upon our thoughts and feelings. Expository prose is the medium of all these ideas; it has to contain and deal with far more material now than it ever knew before. Accordingly its influence has grown while its level has sunk.

A few years ago a proposal was brought forward by writers of several countries for the compilation of an encyclopaedia of modern knowledge. The need for such a systematic summary is obvious and pressing. But the difficulty is how to achieve it in the absence of a generally acceptable interpretive philosophy, or rather in the presence of so many particular ones. The ambition of each separate philosophy and science is to become interpretive in its own right. Taking the two which have influenced literature most obviously in our own time, we have had psychoanalytic interpretations of Marxism, and Marxian interpretations of psychoanalysis. There have also been biological interpretations of theology, and mathematical interpretations of art. The centre, wherever that may be, does not hold. An encyclopaedia might at least formulate this confusion and give some idea of its bounds.

CHAPTER V

CRITICISM

THE criticism of the century has responded to the changing social situation in much the same way as its imaginative literature. The tone of a great deal of it was set by the late T. E. Hulme, a vigorous miscellaneous writer whose scattered notes and papers did not appear until after his death in the War. He was a man of few but decided opinions, who disliked the vague romanticism which still lingered on in literature and particularly in poetry. His case against what he called romanticism was stated decidedly:

> "Put shortly, these are the two views, then. One, that man is intrinsically good, spoilt by circumstance; and the other that he is intrinsically limited, but disciplined by order and tradition to something fairly decent. To the one party man's nature is like a well, to the other like a bucket. The view which regards man as a well, a reservoir full of possibilities, I call the romantic; the one which regards him as a very finite and fixed creature, I call the classical."

The conception of man as a reservoir of possibilities was due, Hulme believed, to a "failure to recognise the *gap* between the regions of vital and human thought and things, and that of the *absolute* values of ethics and religion". To the religious mind man is

> "essentially limited and imperfect. He is endowed with Original Sin. While he can occasionally accomplish acts which partake of perfection, he can never himself *be* perfect. Certain secondary results in regard to ordinary human action in society follow from this. A man is essentially bad,

166

he can only accomplish anything of value by discipline—
ethical and political. Order is thus not merely negative, but
creative and liberating. Institutions are necessary."

Behind all Hulme's literary criticism was the dogma of
Original Sin. Though it was not new, he succeeded in making
a scoop of it and set it out in headlines. He was not quite
disinterested, that is to say, in his employment of it; to him it
was a convenient rejoinder to the romantics. All his public
statements implied an invisible contemporary opponent; and
he had in an exaggerated form the snobbery which consists
in saying to-day what a good number of people will be saying
to-morrow. He insisted therefore on the irreconcilable aspect
of any truth; and to give Original Sin a sensational value, he
calmly ignored the complementary hypothesis of redemption.
He looked on attentively while man fell, and turned his eyes
away while man picked himself up again, or was picked up.
In the passage I have just quoted he says: "A man is
essentially bad, he can only accomplish anything of value by
discipline—ethical and political." This is neither the
religious nor the humanist point of view; in saying that man
can accomplish anything of value *only* by discipline, Hulme
would have had neither Aquinas nor Luther nor Calvin to
support him, for he allowed nothing for Grace. The first part
of his thesis, that man is essentially bad, is religious, though
wrongly stated; the second part, that man can accomplish
anything of value only by discipline is purely secular: it is the
worldly philosophy of the dictator and of the realistic
practical man in general. One cannot help feeling that,
honest as he was, Hulme used religion as a handy bludgeon
in a minor fight which had very little to do with it. He did see
that man was "intrinsically limited" and that he was more
like a bucket than a well; but he sometimes gave the impression that the bucket could never go to the well, and
perhaps was all the better, because the tidier, for it. "Wet"
was a term of abuse to him, and "dry" a term of praise. "I
prophesy that a period of dry, hard classical verse is coming."
And speaking of his contemporaries he says scornfully:

"Poetry that isn't damp isn't poetry at all." These are rhetorical terms; they have been much overworked since his time; and we are not so overjoyed at the thought of dry, hard verse now, having had a good deal of it. All that Hulme meant was that he abominated the feeble romantic verse of his time. His abomination was healthy; but he insisted on formulating it into a general theory of poetry which implicitly excluded most great poetry.

Mr. John Crowe Ransom, the American poet, in a recent volume of criticism, *The World's Body*, says: "The kind of poetry which interests us is not the act of a child, or of that eternal youth which is in some women, but the act of an adult mind; and I will add, the act of a fallen mind, since ours too are fallen." This is the attitude which Hulme was chiefly instrumental in formulating, and it is the attitude of modern criticism. It coincided with the collapse of the "cheerful, optimistic and hopeful" spirit of the first decade of the century. Institutions were necessary; tradition was necessary; and the adult mind was a fallen mind whose fall, providentially for the poet, produced a whole field of experience which had been ignored by the romantic poet, who for the time being was regarded as "innocent", the "child", the "eternal youth". This was obviously a prejudiced view of the romantic poet, if Blake, Wordsworth and Hölderlin are romantic; but a reaction cannot be expected to be objective. There are two kinds of poetry, as Hulme saw: the poetry which regards man as "a reservoir full of possibilities", and the poetry which regards him as "a very finite and fixed creature". To the first kind belongs the poetry of Isaiah, some of Shakespeare's last poetry, some of Milton's, and a great deal of Blake's and Wordsworth's and Hölderlin's. To the second belongs poetic tragedy in general and the greater part of poetry in general. The first kind enjoyed a pre-eminence in the opening years of the century; the general conception of poetry then was romantic. With Hulme came the first vigorous reaction against it, and that reaction, with the encouragement of T. S. Eliot and some other critics, has continued ever since. It was probably

168

inevitable; it was more "adult" than the spirit of the criticism it replaced; but it was not the last word.

Eliot is a far more balanced and substantial critic than Hulme, and far less under the influence of mere reaction. He certainly began with an anti-romantic bias, but it was not caused by exasperation with "damp" poetry or love for "dry" poetry. He had learned a great deal from the scholarly kind of criticism, of which Professor (now Sir Herbert) Grierson's edition of Donne is one of the most brilliant examples. He did not generalise in Hulme's hearty wholesale way; he confined himself as much as possible to precise, minute statement; the generalisation was concealed in the background, where, however, it was quite easy to find. He cast doubt on the current ideas of poetic originality and of "self-expression", by envisaging poetry as a single developing tradition. This tradition was not a fixed thing, like Hulme's "institutions", but was perpetually modified by every new addition that was made to it. He saw originality, therefore, simply as the right thing at the right time, the true development of the tradition. But if poetry is a tradition, that tradition cannot stand by itself; it must be part of a general all-embracing one. Eliot's first criticism is written more or less from the standpoint of a "detached artist" who has an anti-romantic bias. But with the development of his general beliefs it could not remain at that stage. And in one of his later essays he says: "You can never draw the line between aesthetic criticism and moral and social criticism; you cannot draw a line between criticism and metaphysics; you start with literary criticism, and however rigorous an aesthete you may be, you are over the frontier into something else sooner or later." It is almost as hard to stop at tradition without taking the last step to orthodoxy. And in his short book, *After Strange Gods*, Eliot asserts that criticism cannot dispense with theology.

The great advantage of orthodoxy is that it provides that final interpretive philosophy which the mind needs if it is to have a consistent view of life. Eliot asserts that the truth of orthodoxy does not depend on the number of people who support it. But the value of criticism does depend to a great extent on its persuasive power; if it does not convince us it can be of little use to us. And the criticism in *After Strange Gods* is the most unconvincing criticism that Eliot ever wrote, the criticism resting most largely on dogmatic assertion. The connection between literary values and theological truth, in other words, is not clear and unequivocal; it is not demonstrated, but merely asserted. One feels that this is not the way in which theology should modify criticism.

But there is a sense in which all Eliot's criticism from the start has been theological, in that it is the criticism of a mind very definitely aware that it is a "fallen" mind. For a time Eliot seems to have cared for no poetry except the poetry of experience; he was the first to point out clearly that the poets of the Elizabethan and Jacobean ages were capable of "digesting" a far greater variety of experiences than we find in eighteenth century and romantic poetry. In pointing this out he influenced the direction both of criticism and of poetry. This led him also to assert the value of the tough common sense which was called wit in the seventeenth century. These are all adult or "fallen" virtues, and some critics, including F. R. Leavis, have insisted that they must be found in all poetry that will satisfy a mature mind: a claim which is not borne our by the best response to poetry. Leavis is an admirably close and acute writer, in spite of the narrow temper of his criticism; but in insisting on this he excludes one very great kind of poetry, a kind to which in his essay on Dante Eliot gives the title of "the high dream". We do not ask for wit or a tough common sense in the last canto of the *Paradiso*; nor do we look for it in some of Eliot's own poetry, such as *Ash Wednesday*. Eliot's orthodoxy may keep him from seeing in the romantic poetry of Wordsworth and Hölderlin the genuine "high dream"; but it does not keep him from recognising the varieties and ranks of poetry. He sometimes seems a narrow, but he is really, within the framework of "orthodoxy", a comprehensive critic, with a rare apprehension of the qualities which are proper to each kind of poetry. His main influence has nevertheless been on the side of the poetry of experience. To him experience in its fullness is only perceptible by a "fallen" mind; and so there is a theological implication behind his criticism, as there is behind all the criticism which has followed him in this particular, even when the critic was unaware of it.

Herbert Read's criticism has something of the same thorough temper as Eliot's, but is very different in tendency. In Eliot we cannot but be conscious of a deep mistrust of liberty. In *After Strange Gods* he says:

> "The population should be homogeneous; where two or more cultures exist in the same place they are likely either to become fiercely self-conscious or both to become adulterate. What is still more important is unity of religious background; and reasons of race and religion combine to make any large number of free-thinking Jews undesirable. There must be a proper balance between urban and rural, industrial and agricultural development. And a spirit of excessive tolerance is to be deprecated."

These are his requirements for a healthy traditional society; but the tradition is not the English one; there is a touch of the sacerdotal about it. As against this attitude, Read seems to me to stand for the English tradition, especially on its heretical libertarian side. What his attitude to Original Sin is I do not know; but even if one accepts that dogma, there is no compulsion to accept the political and moral conclusions which Hulme drew from it, or even Eliot's more reasonable view. Hulme could see no hope for man but in discipline, because he did not believe in or was not interested in the possibility of salvation. His view of humanity was not unlike that of Hobbes, except for the fact that he insisted on calling it religious. From Original Sin one may draw either the conclusion that man must be supervised into salvation, or the conclusion that man must be given freedom to work out his salvation. The difference is roughly the difference between Catholicism and Protestantism; and on the plane of criticism it is roughly the difference between Eliot and Read. Read has formulated his attitude most clearly in an essay on the man of personality and the man of character; the man who develops "freely" and the man who develops within a fixed plan, to whom "institutions are necessary". (Hulme might as well have said penal institutions, for he certainly did not mean free institutions.) Read's sympathy with liberty is shown in his appreciation of everything which frees man from institutionalised ways of thinking and feeling; it is a consistent attitude, with an efficient reason and a lucid and comprehensive sensibility behind it.

Several years ago a debate was staged by *The Criterion* between the supporters of Classicism and the supporters of Romanticism. A number of writers took part, and the defence of Romanticism was undertaken by Mr. J. Middleton Murry. He is a critic in the true romantic tradition, with a remarkable power of feeling himself intuitively into a poem or a writer, and a tendency to build structures of various degrees of hugeness and vagueness on his intuitions. He combines with his emotional sympathy, which can be profound, an admirably critical treatment of points of detail. His most striking and dangerous gift is the power to identify himself with the writer he is dealing with; and his books on Keats and Shakespeare show close observation and quick and deep insight. But while preaching the virtue of self-obliteration which he practises in his best criticism, Murry cannot keep himself out of his books, and himself not as a man of unquestioned gifts inquiring into literature and life, but as a prophet. Self-obliteration should leave no trace; if the self is gone the obliteration should have gone with it: all that should be left is the new selfless state. Instead of this we have in Murry's later work a more and more picturesque spiritual combat, and a tendency to attribute to every great man the virtue of self-obliteration. In his last book, *Heaven—and Earth*, he luxuriates in vague and exalted ideas with an implied claim to apocalyptic truth which sometimes robs his utterance of credibility.

Somewhat apart from these critics is Mr. I. A. Richards, whose *Principles of Literary Criticism* has been greeted as a revolutionary book, but does not appear to have made a revolution. Mr. Richards is a psychologist, and what he is concerned with is the effect of poetry on the mind. He holds that this approach to poetry is, or can sometime hope to be, scientifically sound. In thinking this he is supported by his faith in the future of neurology. "That the mind," he says, "is the nervous system, or rather a part of its activity, has long been evident, although the prevalence among psychologists of persons with philosophic antecedents has delayed the recognition of the fact in an extraordinary fashion." If the mind is the nervous system, then as soon as we understand everything about the nervous system, we shall have an exact criterion of poetry, for we shall be able to tell what poetry agrees best with the nervous system and does it most good. Yet, regarding our present knowledge of neurology, Mr. Richards has to admit that the account it gives us of the effect of poetry is "only a degree less fictitious than one in terms of spiritual happenings". He then says, however: "It should be borne in mind that the knowledge which the men of A.D. 3,000 will possess, if all goes well, may make all our aesthetics, all our psychology, all our modern theory of value, look pitiful." This is the kind of statement which one almost expects now in any work that sets out to be as scientific as possible.

The mind, Mr. Richards holds, is the nervous system; not, that is to say, primarily a directing intelligence, but a system of multitudinous responses. Mr. Richards pictures it as

"an arrangement of many magnetic needles, large and small, swung so that they influence one another, some able only to swing horizontally, others vertically, others hung freely. As we move, the perturbations in this system will be very complicated. . . . The needles are our interests, varying in their importance, that is, in the degree to which any movement they make involves movement in the other needles. Each new disequilibrium, which a shift of position, a fresh situation, entails, corresponds to a need; and the wagglings which ensue as the system rearranges itself are our responses, the impulses through which we seek to meet the need". Amid all this commotion there is "a final position of rest for all the

173

needles into which they will in the end settle down, a general
poise for the whole system."

Now it is the function of poetry, according to Mr. Richards,
to produce this harmonious though fleeting state; to bring
such order among the needles that they cease from waggling
and are at rest. Any poetry can start them waggling; but only
the best poetry can stop them waggling. This is the neuro-
logical account of the operation of poetry which, Mr.
Richards says, "must frankly be admitted to be only a degree
less fictitious than one in terms of spiritual happenings". But
by A.D. 3000 (if all goes well) the assumption is that it will
be several degrees less fictitious.

The chief anomaly of a theory which conceives poetry as
a means to make the nervous system function properly is that
it ignores or regards as irrelevant the explicit meaning of
poetry, in other words, what the poet says:

> "The joy which is so strangely at the heart of the experience
> is not an indication that 'all's right with the world', or that
> 'somewhere, somehow, there is justice'; it is an indication
> that all is right here and now in the nervous system."

On this line of argument, "I saw eternity the other night"
means that all was right there and then in Vaughan's
nervous system, and that as he saw eternity when in such a
state, and tells us so, it is likely to be good for our nervous
systems too, and stop their waggling. This may be so, but to
insist upon it as the primary fact is to ignore the visionary
quality of Vaughan's statement, in which he speaks of something not felt but seen; his nervous system having been
in the right state for him to see it. For what Vaughan
saw and for what the poet sees in general Mr. Richards has
invented a class of statements which he calls "pseudo-
statements". These are without actual truth, yet without
actual falsehood either, for even the nervous system would
hardly allow itself to be soothed by a lie. In his later book on
Coleridge Mr. Richards seems to modify his attitude on this

point; how far it is difficult to say. If imagination is a general mode of apprehension, and what it apprehends is the world "of whole and indefeasible objects", as Mr. John Crowe Ransom says, then without some truth it can have no serious value, and cannot be very good for the nervous system. The great fault of *Principles of Literary Criticism*, as Mr. D. G. James points out in his excellent book, *Scepticism and Poetry*, is that it ignores the fact that poetry is a way of apprehending the world through imagination. In *Coleridge on Imagination* Mr. Richards tries to supply this omission, but he still clings to his "materialist associationism".

The value of Richards's work does not lie in the principles he lays down, which are derived from a particular conception of science whose validity will not be demonstrable until A.D. 3000 (if all goes well), but in his realisation of the many meanings implicit in poetry, and the closeness with which he pursues these meanings. His chief disciple in this particular line, William Empson, excels him both in fineness and intricacy of perception, and his book, *The Seven Types of Ambiguity*, is almost exasperatingly subtle, like his poetry. Yet it may be claimed that Richards's practice has led to a greater accuracy in criticism, as distinct from theory, and a fuller perception of what may be implied by a poem. The hunting of these implications has sometimes become a game very like the hunting of the Snark, but it is an interesting and often useful one.

The new accuracy of criticism in our time owes, then, something to Mr. Richards on the one hand, and something to such great scholars as Sir Herbert Grierson on the other. The paradox of Richards's denial of truth to poetry is that it makes him see more meanings, or a greater variety of meanings in it. The scholarly critics, on the other hand, have helped to show us how much, in the way of influences, memories and all sorts of remote associations, has gone into certain works of imagination. They have also applied what may be called statistics to criticism, as in Professor Caroline F. E. Spurgeon's book, *Shakespeare's Imagery and What It tells Us*, a masterly piece both of investigation and criticism, with a number of charts showing such things as the "Range and subjects of images in five of Shakespeare's plays", "Range and subject of Marlowe's images", "Dominating images in *Hamlet* and *Troilus and Cressida*", and so on. This century is one of the most brilliant periods of literary scholarship; and that may be partly responsible for the general improvement which has taken place in literary criticism.

During the last five or six years there has been a good deal of theorising about the sociological bases of literary criticism, and an increasing attempt to place the work of art in relation to the society out of which it comes. One of the best statements of the necessity for this is the late Christopher Caudwell's "Illusion and Reality". Stephen Spender's volume, *The Destructive Element*, deals among other things with the distinction between genuine "political" poetry and propaganda. Obviously there is a political or Marxian approach to literature, which is valid so long as it does not claim to be the only one. At present there is an abundance of confusion on this point, which may clear itself up later. What has been written about Marxian criticism in this country has appeared mainly in a few journals. It is often absurd, as when it attributes the faults of Auden's poetry to the fact that he has not yet identified himself sufficiently with the working-class struggle. Its attitude to tradition, on which Lenin insisted, is uncertain, and has never been clearly formulated. Its attitude to aesthetics is equally vague. That being so, I can only mention it here.

CHAPTER VI

DRAMA

THERE was a revival of the drama at the beginning of the century; it has been dealt with by Professor Dobrée in the previous volume. It was a revival mainly of prose drama and drama dealing with social ideas, and its chief names were Shaw, Galsworthy and Granville Barker. But there was also a small amount of poetic drama produced by the repertory theatres, and Professor Dobrée mentions Lascelles Abercrombie and Gordon Bottomley. Then he says: "But the poetic drama movement died; it did not tune in with an age of political excitement and social struggle, and the War interrupted its use as a stage instrument. At the present day there are signs of a new birth, but they do not fall within the scope of this volume."

The poetic drama died because "it did not tune in with an age of political excitement and social struggle". That is a handy measure of the difference between the attitude to poetic drama before the War and the attitude now. There is no obvious inherent reason why poetic drama should not tune in with an age of political excitement and social struggle; there was political excitement enough in the age of Aeschylus and Sophocles, and social struggle enough in the time of Shakespeare. The poetic drama before the War must therefore have been somewhat delicate; and so it was regarded at the time. Political excitement was considered a matter for prose. The social struggle could be presented only in prose. Behind this conviction was the feeling that poetry used one language and that prose used another which was more suitable for "real" things. The return of poetry since then to a variant of the language which people speak has helped to abolish this distinction. It has helped also to make writers realise that political excitement and social struggle are perfectly legitimate themes for the dramatic poet; for as soon as we use the language in which people feel and think a great number of false distinctions fall away and cease to exist. The new political attitude to poetry, in spite of its aberrations, is plainly a more reasonable one than the attitude that poetic drama cannot co-exist with political excitement and social struggle. Actually poetic drama has revived in the last few years under the inspiration of the same thing that made it droop before the War; that is, because it *tunes in* with "an age of political excitement and social struggle".

The first sign of the revival came from T. S. Eliot, who had several times written of poetic drama as a possibility, and perhaps felt tempted to prove his case. His first dramatic work (apart from the fragment *Sweeney Agonistes*) *The Rock*, was written for an occasion, the building of a church, and so, like many beginnings, it was largely fortuitous. *The Rock* is not an impressive dramatic work, and it was not all written by Eliot. *Murder in the Cathedral* is much superior. It deals with two problems concurrently, one of them contemporary (the demarcating line between spiritual and temporal power) the other timeless (the nature of martyrdom and sainthood). The play shows considerable dramatic imagination; it also shows an acute sense of the "stage", as in the plus-fours scene where the murderers excuse themselves to the audience for their action, a scene which is very "effective", apparently, but which I cannot help thinking deplorable. The language of the play is not quite dramatic speech; the choruses are beautiful rather than dramatically relevant; but the play as a whole is finely conceived; and it is not the kind of poetic play which dies because it cannot face the questions of the hour.

Auden is the author of a short, fantastic play, *The Dance of Death*, which has very little literary value, and of two longer plays along with Christopher Isherwood: *The Dog beneath the Skin* and *The Ascent of F6*. All of them are filled with clever stage devices; they have the inevitable choruses;

and they use many of the tricks of the popular revue. They do not show much sustained dramatic power; everything is improvised, more or less cleverly; nothing worked out. There is a theme, but the acts are merely a set of illustrations to it, presented with a businesslike air which conveys the impression that something is being done. *The Ascent of F6* is a clever construction which keeps the reader guessing, and therefore occupied, from scene to scene. The action, that is the ascent of the mountain, is viewed from three angles: that of the leader of the expedition, that of the monied interests who paid him, and that of the ordinary citizen and his wife, who hear of it all through the radio. When Ransom, the leader, reaches the mountain top at last, he finds his mother there. His fine sentiments, his disinterested service of his country, were mere disguises of a mother-fixation, it seems. This may be regarded as tragedy or as comedy, according to the taste of the reader. The outside of the play is hard, the kernel somewhat hollow. Ransom is the hero of a boy's story, grown a little older: the serious English playboy who is good at everything and afraid of nothing. The play is made up of deliberate symbols, and is like a correct dream which an expert psychologist might construct while he is asleep. The parts allotted to the ordinary man and his wife are amusing and bitter. But there is nothing in it, or in any of Auden's other plays, which approaches the quality of his poetry.

Stephen Spender's *Trial of a Judge* is also symbolic, but in a concrete way; the chief figure is not an embodiment of some psychoanalytical formula but of man as a moral being confronted with the main question of the contemporary world: the achievement of social justice. The judge is a man who desires absolute justice and to attain it refuses to commit a single unjust act. On one side of him are the Fascists, with a racial conception of justice; on the other are the Communists, with justice for their final goal, a goal which cannot be reached through justice. The judge is the most impressive figure in the play, and, it seems to me, in contemporary drama. He is an embodiment of the spirit of man

179

at a particular stage of history; he is a representative figure, and that constitutes his value. Every age needs such a figure, as an embodiment of itself and of what it wants to be. Only poetry, and only dramatic poetry, can create such figures, which are not characters but more in the nature of myths. The judge has not the poetic force of Hamlet or Faust; but he is a creation of the same kind. The strength of the play, apart from this, lies in its imaginative grasp of moral realities. The actual struggle is neither between the Fascists and the Communists, nor between the judge and the world he lives in: it takes place within himself. This is perhaps a defect, dramatically; and it is paralleled by a corresponding defect: that the dramatic speech, with its involution, is more suited to monologue than to dialogue. The verse has sometimes great beauty, but it has rarely the direct speaking quality of dramatic utterance. Yet the play is certainly at the centre of the political and social struggle, and it deals with that struggle seriously, in terms of the imagination, and in a poetic way.

It is possible that the importance of this revival of verse drama has been overestimated; for in the way of achievement it can show only one play by Eliot and one play by Spender. But it has demonstrated that verse drama suitable to the time can be written and can be appreciated, which means that it has a function; and that may be a discovery of some importance.

The prose drama since the War has little to show except one playwright of genius, Sean O'Casey, and one playwright of talent, James Bridie. O'Casey's first plays, such as *The Plough and the Stars* and *Juno and the Paycock*, were written in the speech of the Dublin common people, and were masterpieces of style and poetic imagination. In his later plays O'Casey set out to be "literary" and modern; during this severe change his dramatic imagination still remained faithful to him, but his style went to pieces, becoming crude and stilted where it had been sensitive and natural. He is a born dramatist, with the greatest gift for dramatic presentation of any living writer, and he can mingle tragedy and comedy with the most exquisite effect. James Bridie is a playwright of intelligence but not of much imagination: a clear-sighted man with a weakness for clever ideas. He is a trenchant critic of society, the basis of whose criticism one feels to be somewhat inadequate, like Shaw's.

There have been a number of moderately intelligent, quite sincere and extremely competent dramatists since the War; writers such as R. C. Sheriff and John Van Druten, who hardly belong to literary history. There is also Noel Coward, the author of many social comedies and revues, who has perhaps done more than any other writer to popularise post-War disillusionment. There have also been one or two prose plays of genuine imaginative force, perhaps the most striking being J. R. Ackerley's *Prisoners of War* and Turner's *The Man who ate the Popomack*. But the revival of poetic tragedy is the most promising sign.

CHAPTER VII

CONCLUSION

I HAVE tried to trace the development of literature during the thirty-eight years of this century. In doing so I have had to rely on conjecture more than on evidence. This was unavoidable, and for an obvious reason. The periods treated by the other writers in this series are closed periods; we stand outside them, and so we can see them as a whole. The period I have dealt with is still going on; and towards what it is going I can no more tell than anyone else. It is currently thought that the world is dividing into two camps, with Fascists in the one and Communists in the other; but whether this is actually so I should not be prepared to say, even on the evidence of European history during the last decade. If it is so, then before the end of the century there will probably exist a world which is predominantly Fascist or predominantly Communist; and in either case the conditions for the production of literature will have radically changed. It is often said that between the Fascist and the Communist there is no essential difference. This seems to me a shallow generalisation, and I speak neither as the one nor as the other. The ultimate ideal of the Communist is liberty, the ultimate ideal of the Fascist is authority. It may be objected that the ultimate ideal of a political party does not affect its practical policy; but that is not borne out by history. No democracy known to us is a perfect democracy; yet life in a democracy is a different thing from life under a tyranny. Ultimate ideals do have some effect on practical policy.

The period is, in its main outline, a period of disintegration. This can be easily enough seen in literature. The

novelist's picture of life has become incomplete and fragmentary, something which cannot be rounded into a whole.
Poetry, in the time of Pound and Eliot, lost consecutive
meaning and consecutive music. The poetry of the next
generation shows a partial recovery from this state, and
poetic drama is perhaps a sign of further recovery. There
is an obvious reason for this change. The disintegration was
felt as something absolute by the generation of Eliot, for
it was felt as the disintegration of "society" or "civilisation"
regarded as a given pattern. By the younger generation it
is not felt as absolute, but as the falling apart of one kind of
society, which has done its work and must make way for
another. The pattern of society and civilisation, in other
words, is not regarded as a pattern already given, but as
one in process of realisation. Seen in this way, the disintegration, though actual, a general calamity, a general emergency
as palpable as the wrecking of the ship in which we all sail,
is not merely disintegration, but a mode of change, painful,
critical, filled with extreme dangers, but containing also the
possibility of a new organisation of society.

BIBLIOGRAPHY

BIBLIOGRAPHY

BIBLIOGRAPHY

THIS bibliography can make no claim either to completeness or to justice. I do not have an all-round knowledge
of contemporary literature; and there is no general survey of
it to which I can appeal. Also I have had to anticipate the
work of Time, which sorts out writers and their work,
showing us, after they are dead, which were and which were
not important. The critics who have dealt with the previous
periods in this series knew, at least, which writers they had
to write about, for the names of these writers exist in
numerous histories as completely as in a census. As it is,
I may have omitted names out of mere forgetfulness, or
lack of knowledge, or poverty of judgment. This would
have been unpardonable in a survey of the past; but I can
see no remedy for it in dealing with the present.

I have had also another, more specific, difficulty. I could
have included in this bibliography only writers who seemed
to be writers of importance, in which case it would have
been short. But if I had done that, I would not have given
much idea of the present state of literature, and of the period
in which we live. There are a great number of contemporary
writers who, without being first-rate, are "intelligent",
"good" writers. To put them all in would be to compile a
catalogue. Yet it was necessary that some of them should
be put in to complete the picture. Accordingly I have made
a selection, not necessarily the best; but the best I could think
of. I have done the same with the writers of best-sellers,
including fewer specimens of that very large class. This,
I am quite aware, is unsatisfactory.

The various sciences have now become very much more
specialised than they were in the nineteenth century, and
along with them certain other things, such as history, which

is bound up with several ancillary sciences, and theology and philosophy, which are in the same position. The consequence is that we do not have any figures now such as Macaulay, Newman, Darwin, Huxley, Galton, who were general writers and at the same time masters of their specific subjects. I have not the equipment to deal with the immense development of mathematics and physics and psychology during the present century, not to speak of such sciences as chemistry and biochemistry. I am not sufficiently versed in theology or economics to venture any useful remark about them, or indicate where an advance of real importance has been made. Nevertheless certain figures, most of them of foreign birth, have obviously influenced the thought and literature of our age, figures such as Freud, Einstein, Sir James Frazer, Barth, Maritain, Lenin, Sorel, and Marx. Freud's first discoveries about dream symbolism were published in German in 1900, but did not reach England until 1913. Marx has, of course, been known for a long time, but has not been "taken up" by writers until quite recently, for reasons I have already indicated. All these men have influenced modern literature to a greater or less extent; Freud and Marx very greatly; Sorel perceptibly, through the ideas of Hulme; Sir James Frazer perceptibly, through the symbolism of certain poems, and particularly of *The Waste Land*. They stand against the intellectual background of literature. If the reader wants to have some idea of what they stand *for* he should consult a handbook on psychoanalysis (there are many of them), the shorter version of Frazer's *The Golden Bough*, John Strachey's exposition of Marx in *The Theory and Practice of Socialism*, and for the more difficult problems of pure science Sir Arthur Eddington's *The Nature of the Physical World*.

To get an idea of the intellectual background of literature I should therefore recommend some such short course, which can be supplemented at need or according to the reader's line of interest. For the political background of the time there is no objective source of information. There have been numerous books written on the various new political systems which have risen in Europe since the War, in Russia, Italy and Germany. One of the best of these is Sidney and Beatrice Webb's *Soviet Communism: A new Civilisation*. There has been nothing so good on Germany thus far. There is an excellent study of Italian Fascism by Signor Salevemini; adverse, but reasonably objective. But this is a field in which everyone must find his own way. Nobody can avoid making some attempt to do so, and nobody can expect a reliable guide.

On the literature of the period there is no general survey that I know of, but many books on separate aspects. Among the most useful of these are certain anthologies, the best of which, I think, is *The Faber Book of Modern Verse*, edited by Michael Roberts, which has an excellent informative and critical introduction: though *The Modern Poet*, edited by Gwendolen Murphy (1938), also gives an admirably representative and intelligently arranged selection, provided with useful notes. *The Oxford Book of Modern Verse*, edited by W. B. Yeats, is extremely erratic; omitting, among other poets, Wilfred Owen. *Axel's Castle*, by Edmund Wilson, the American critic, is an acute study of modern literature from the political point of view. *Phases of Poetry*, by Herbert Read, and *A Survey of Modernist Poetry*, by Laura Riding and Robert Graves, give in different ways an idea of the problems with which contemporary poetry is concerned or was concerned ten or fifteen years ago. F. R. Leavis's *New Bearings in English Poetry* will be found very useful. The standpoint of the later political poets is best stated, I think, in Stephen Spender's *The Destructive Element*. C. Day Lewis's *A Hope for Poetry* is on the same subject, is lucid, but ignores the complexity of the problem. On the novel there is no general work of the same scope. Wyndham Lewis's *Men Without Art* touches on a number of important points, and the two numbers of *The Enemy* are worth consulting. E. M. Forster's *Aspects of the Novel* describes the difficulties and aims of a modern novelist. G. W. Stonier's *Gog and Magog* contains some intelligent discussion on the same subject. The most intelligent survey of the general state of discursive writing is Bonamy Dobrée's *Modern Prose Style*.

But the best approach to contemporary literature is obviously through its best criticism, such as Hulme's *Speculations*, Eliot's *Collected Essays*, the critical work of Herbert Read, and Pound's *Polite Essays*. By reading these one is plunged at once into the atmosphere of modern literature, and that is the only way to learn anything worth learning about it.

In the list of historical and scientific and philosophical books, I have not attempted to give more than a very brief popular choice. In the poetry and fiction lists there will be found a number of what Mrs. Leavis has called "middle-brows", as well as a few "low-brows". There is no reason why these should be read, if the reader's taste does not lie in that direction; they are included merely for the sake of consistency.

While correcting the final proofs I have received, by the courtesy of the author, a volume which would have helped me greatly if I had known of it before, for it is a thorough general survey of the period, and it contains bibliographies far more detailed than I have been able to provide, but far more detailed also, I think, than is called for by the purpose of the present book. The volume is *Contemporary British Literature*: A Critical Survey and 232 Author-bibliographies. By Fred B. Millett. Third revised and enlarged edition, based on the second revised and enlarged edition by John M. Manly and Edith Rickert. Anyone wanting a more detailed account of the works of contemporary writers and the criticisms that have been applied to them cannot do better than consult this book, which also gives an interesting alternative account of the developments dealt with by me in the present volume.

POETRY

I HAVE divided the poets into the older generation, the middle generation and the younger generation, for convenience purely, except that I have not entirely gone by age.

(A) THE OLDER GENERATION

HOPKINS, GERALD MANLEY (1844–89).

Poems, edited by Robert Bridges, 1918.
Poems, with Additions, edited by Charles Williams, 1930.
Letters, mainly to Robert Bridges and R. W. Dixon, edited by Claude Colleer Abbott, 1935.
Further Letters, edited by Claude Colleer Abbott, 1938.
The Note-Book and Papers of Gerald Manley Hopkins, edited by Humphrey House, 1937.

For critical studies, see Herbert Read's *In Defence of Shelley and other Essays*, F. R. Leavis's *New Bearings in English Poetry*, and a symposium in a special number of *New Verse*, edited by Geoffrey Grigson. The Letters and the Note-Books contain some brilliant criticism of poetry, and are invaluable to the student of Hopkins.

YEATS, WILLIAM BUTLER (1865–1939).

Poetry:
The Wanderings of Oisin, 1889.
The Countess Kathleen, 1890.
The Land of Heart's Desire, 1894.
The Wind among the Reeds, 1899.
The Shadowy Waters, 1900.
Cathleen Ni Houlihan, 1902.

Deirdre, 1903.
Collected Plays and Poems (8 vols.), 1908.
The Wild Swans at Coole, 1917.
Two Plays for Dancers, 1919.
The Tower, 1928.
The Winding Stair, 1933.
Collected Poems, 1933.
Collected Plays, 1934.

Prose:
The Celtic Twilight, 1893.
Ideas of Good and Evil, 1903.
A Vision, 1937.

These three books, and the last particularly, give an idea of the intellectual background of Yeats's poetry. *Autobiographies* (1935) describes Yeats's childhood and youth, and contains some beautiful writing. Criticism of Yeats's poetry may be found in Forrest Reid's *W. B. Yeats: A Critical Study*, Miss Dorothy M. Hoare's *The Works of Morris and of Yeats in Relation to Early Saga Literature*, which is not so strictly specialised as the title sounds, F. R. Leavis's *New Bearings in English Poetry* and Stephen Spender's *The Destructive Element*.

MOORE, THOMAS STURGE (1870–   ).

Poetry:
The Vinedriver and other Poems, 1899.
Aphrodite against Artemis, 1901.
Absalom, 1903.
Danae, 1903.
The Little School, 1905.
Poems, 1906.
Marianne, 1911.
The Sicilian Idyll and Judith, 1911.
The Sea is Kind, 1914.
The Little School (enlarged), 1917.
The Powers of the Air, 1920.
Tragic Mothers, 1920.
Judas, 1923.
Mystery and Tragedy, 1930.

Poems (Collected Edition), 4 vols., 1932–33.
Selected Poems, 1934.

Criticism:
Altdorfer, 1900.
Dürer, 1904.
Correggio, 1906.
Art and Life, 1910.
Hark to These Three, 1915.
Some Soldier Poets, 1919.
Armour for Aphrodite, 1929.
Charles Ricketts, R.A.

Mr. Sturge Moore deals with classical themes in a romantic way, and derives partly from the Nineties, like Yeats. His verse is carefully finished, but somewhat cold.

DE LA MARE, WALTER (1873–   ).

Poetry:
Songs of Childhood, 1902.
The Listeners, 1912.
A Child's Day, 1912
Peacock Pie, 1913.
Motley, 1918.
Flora, 1919.
Collected Poems, 1901–18, 1920.
Down-adown-Derry, 1922.
Poems for Children, 1930.
The Fleeting and other Poems, 1933.
Memory and other Poems, 1938.

Prose:
Henry Brocken, 1904.
The Three Mulla-Mulgars, 1910.
The Return, 1910.
The Veil, 1921.
Crossings, 1921.
Memoirs of a Midget, 1921.
The Riddle, 1923.
Ding Dong Bell, 1924.
Broomsticks, 1925.
The Connoisseur, 1926.

Told Again, 1927.
Desert Islands, 1930.
On the Edge, 1930.
The Lord Fish, 1933.
A Froward Child, 1934.
Early One Morning, 1935.

Perhaps de la Mare's best collection of short stories is *The Return*. *The Lord Fish* is a delightful collection of children's stories. *Early One Morning* is a book on childhood, filled with the most curious knowledge and inference. *Walter de la Mare*, by Forrest Reid, is a critical study.

BOTTOMLEY, GORDON (1874–   ).

The Gate of Smaragdus, 1904.
Chambers of Imagery—two series, 1907, 1912.
A Vision of Giorgione, 1910.
King Lear's Wife and other Plays.
Gruach and Britain's Daughter, 1921.
Poems of Thirty Years, 1925.
Scenes and Plays, 1929.
Lyric Plays, 1932.
The Acts of St. Peter (Exeter Cathedral Festival Play), 1933.

In his short poetic dramas, such as *The Riding to Lithend* (from *King Lear's Wife and Other Plays*) Bottomley conveys a sense of mass and weight of emotion which comes from a grasp of elemental facts. His poetic idiom, on the other hand, is too peculiar to himself to make the utterances of the figures in his plays convincing. But all his poetry has an individual form.

MASEFIELD, JOHN (1878–   ).

Poetry:
Salt-Water Ballads, 1902.
Mainsail Haul, 1905.
The Everlasting Mercy, 1911.
The Widow in the Bye Street, 1912.
The Daffodil Fields, 1913.
Dauber, 1913.

Sonnets and Poems, 1916.
Lollingdon Downs, 1918.
Reynard the Fox, 1922.
King Cole, 1923.
Collected Poems, 1923.

Plays:
   The Tragedy of Nan, 1909.
   Pompey the Great, 1910.
   Philip the King, 1914.
   The Faithful, 1915.
   Good Friday, 1917.
   The Trial of Jesus, 1925.

Novels:
   Captain Margaret, 1908.
   Multitude and Solitude, 1909.
   Sard Harker, 1924.
   Odtaa, 1926.

The Everlasting Mercy and *The Widow in the Bye Street* caused something like a scandal at their appearance, because of their bad language. *The Widow* is a sordid story, told with great vigour, in a loose, somewhat journalistic measure suitable for a popular narrative poem. *Reynard the Fox* has admirable spirit. Among Masefield's stories *Sard Harker* is perhaps the best. Masefield was one of the few writers of his time who had a genuine perception of evil which, though sometimes melodramatic, gives weight to his view of life.

TAYLOR, RACHEL ANNAND (1876–   ).

Poetry:
   Poems, 1904.
   Rose and Vine, 1908.
   Hours of Fiammetta, 1909.

Criticism:
   Aspects of the Italian Renaissance, 1923.
   Leonardo the Florentine, 1927.
   William Dunbar, 1931.

All Mrs. Taylor's work, in prose and verse, is "jewelled"

and skilfully wrought. She is such an extreme romantic that she escapes the sentimentality which so often goes with romanticism as its bad conscience. Her critical studies of the Renaissance are scholarly and Paterian. Her Scottish poems recall the tradition of the Makars rather than that of Burns.

MEW, CHARLOTTE MARY (1870–1928).

> *The Farmer's Bride*, 1915.
> *The Rambling Sailor*, 1929.

A sincere artist who never got the recognition she deserved.

THOMAS, EDWARD (1878–1917).

Poetry:
> *Poems*, 1917.
> *Last Poems*, 1918.
> *Collected Poems*, 1922.

Essays:
> *Cloud Castle and other Papers*, 1922.
> *The Last Sheaf*, 1928.
> *A Literary Pilgrim in England*, 1928, etc.

His life is told by his wife, Helen Thomas, in *World Without End* and *As it Was*. There is a good essay on his poetry in Aldous Huxley's *On the Margin*.

FREEMAN, JOHN (1880–1929).

Poetry:
> *Twenty Poems*, 1909.
> *Fifty Poems, Stone Trees, Presage of Victory*, 1916.
> *Memories of Childhood*, 1918.
> *Memories and other Poems*, 1919.
> *Poems New and Old*, 1920.
> *Music, Two Poems*, 1920.
> *The Grove, Prince Absalom*, 1925.
> *Solomon and Balkis*, 1926.

Collected Poems, 1928.
Last Poems, 1930.

Essays and Criticisms:
The Moderns, 1916.
Portrait of George Moore, 1922.
Punch and Holy Water, 1923.
English Portraits and Essays, 1924.
Hermann Melville, 1926.

Freeman had an acute sense of the cruelty of life. There is a good deal of memory in his poetry. His book on Hermann Melville is an excellent piece of criticism.

MONRO, HAROLD (1879–1932).

Poems, 1906.
Judas, 1908.
Before Dawn, 1911.
Children of Love, 1914.
Trees, 1915.
Strange Meetings, 1917.
Real Property, 1922.
The Earth for Sale, 1928.
Collected Poems, edited by A. Munro, with a biographical sketch, and a critical note by T. S. Eliot, 1933.

Monro was a genuine though somewhat constrained poet with a very high degree of honesty both in what he said and in how he said it. He was known more during his life for his unselfish encouragement of and admiration for other poets than for his own work, which was nevertheless genuine and original.

DRINKWATER, JOHN (1882–1937).

Poetry:
Poems of Men and Hours, 1911.
Poems of Love and Earth, 1912.
Cromwell and other Poems, 1913.
Swords and Ploughshares, 1915.
Olton Pools, 1916.

Tides, 1917.
Seeds of Time, 1921.
Preludes, 1922.
Collected Poems, 1923.

Plays:
Abraham Lincoln, 1918.
Mary Stuart, 1921.
Oliver Cromwell, 1921.
Robert E. Lee, 1923.
Collected Plays, 1925.

Drinkwater was perhaps the most perfect and "finished"
of the Georgians. His work has little intellectual or other vitality.

DAVIES, WILLIAM HENRY (1871–).

Poetry:
The Soul's Destroyer.
Farewell to Poesy.
Songs of Joy.
Foliage.
The Bird of Paradise.
Child Lovers.
Forty New Poems.
A Song of Life.
The Hour of Magic and other Poems, 1922.
Secrets, a Book of Poems, 1924.
A Poet's Alphabet, 1925.
A Song of Love, 1926.
A Poet's Calendar, 1927.
Collected Poems, 1928.
Ambitions and Other Poems, 1929.
Jewels of Song, an anthology, 1930.
Poems, 1930–1, 1932.
My Garden, 1933.
The Poems of W. H. Davies, 1934.
Love Poems, 1935.
The Birth of Song, 1936.

Prose:
The Autobiography of a Super-tramp.

Beggars.
A Weak Woman.
The True Traveller.
Nature.
A Poet's Pilgrimage.
Later Days, 1925.
The Adventures of Johnny Walker, Tramp, 1926.
Dancing Mad, 1927.
My Birds, 1933.

Davies's prose is admirably clear and natural, without a trace of poetic diction.

SQUIRE, SIR JOHN COLLINGS (1884–   ).

Poetry:
Imaginary Speeches, 1912.
Steps to Parnassus, 1913.
The Three Hills and other Poems, 1913.
The Survival of the Fittest, 1916.
Twelve Poems, 1916.
Tricks of the Trade, 1917.
The Lily of Malud, 1917.
The Gold Tree, 1918.
Poems, First Series, 1918.
The Moon, a poem, 1920.
Collected Parodies, 1921.
Poems, Second Series, 1922.

Criticism:
Books in General, 1920.
Life and Letters, 1920.
Books in General, 1921.
Skakespeare as a Dramatist, 1935.

Squire's parodies, which may be found in *Steps to Parnassus* and *Tricks of the Trade,* are brilliant. His criticism is that of a man of wide miscellaneous reading who avoids difficulties.

SHANKS, EDWARD BUXTON (1892–   ).

Poetry:
Songs, 1915.

Poems, 1916.
Queen of China and other Poems, 1919.
The Island of Youth and other Poems, 1921.
Collected Poems, 1926.
Poems, (1912–32), 1933.

Criticism:
First Essays on Literature, 1923.
Bernard Shaw, 1924.
Second Essays on Literature, 1927.

Biography:
Edgar Allan Poe, 1937.

GIBSON, WILFRED (1878–   ).

Poetry:
Stonefolds, 1907.
Daily Bread, 1910.
Fires, 1912.
Thoroughfares, 1914.
Borderlands, 1914.
Battle, 1915.
Friends, 1916.
Livelihood, 1917.
Whin, 1918.
Home, 1920.
Neighbours, 1920.
Krindlesyke, 1922.
Kestrel Edge, and other plays, 1924.
I Heard a Sailor, 1925.
Sixty-three Poems. A Selection, 1926.
Collected Poems, 1905–25, 1926.
The Golden Room, 1928.
Hazards, 1930.
Highland Dawn, 1932.
Islands, 1932.
Fuel, 1934.

A poet of ordinary occurrences.

SACKVILLE-WEST, THE HON. VICTORIA (1892-   ).

Poems:
  The Land, 1926.
  Collected Poems, 1933.

Novels:
  The Edwardians, 1930.
  All Passion Spent, 1931.

Other Prose:
  Knole and the Sackvilles, 1922.
  Passenger to Teheran, 1926.
  Andrew Marvell, 1929.
  Saint Joan of Arc, 1937.
  Pepita, 1937.

WOLFE, HUMBERT (1885-   ).

Poetry:
  London Sonnets.
  Shylock reasons with Mr. Chesterton.
  Circular Saws.
  Kensington Gardens.
  The Unknown Goddess.
  Lampoons.
  News of the Devil.
  Requiem.
  Cursory Rhymes.
  The Silver Cat.
  This Blind Rose.
  Dialogues and Monologues.
  The Wall of Weeping.
  Sonnets for Helen.
  X at Ober-Ammergau.
  Don J. Ewen.

Criticism:
  Notes on English Verse Satire.
  Portrait of Heine.
  Tennyson.

George Moore.
Signpost of Poetry.

A writer of great technical dexterity who does not conceal it. *Requiem*, greeted on its appearance as a great poem, is melodramatic. His satirical poetry is probably his best, and among it *News of the Devil*, *X at Ober-Ammergau*, and *Don. J. Ewen*.

WICKHAM, ANNA (Mrs. Patrick Hepburn) (1883–   ).

Songs of John Oland.
Contemplative Quarry.
The Man with a Hammer.
The Little Old House.

A minor poet of individual talent.

TURNER, WALTER JAMES (1889–   ).

Poetry:
The Hunter, and other Poems, 1916.
The Dark Fire, 1918.
Paris and Helen, 1921.
In Time like Glass, 1921.
Landscape of Cytherea, 1923.
Variations on the Theme of Music, 1924.
Smaragda's Lover, 1924.
The Seven Days of the Sun, 1925.
Marigold, An Idyll of the Sea, 1926.
New Poems, 1928.
Pursuit of Psyche, 1931.
Jack and Jill, 1934.
Songs and Incantations, 1936.

Drama:
The Man who Ate the Popomack, 1922.

Criticism:
Music and Life, 1921.
Beethoven, 1927.
The Aesthetes, 1927.

Music. A Short History, 1932.
Wagner, 1933.
Facing the Music, 1933.
Berlioz, 1934.
Mozart, 1938.

Fiction:
Blow for Balloons, 1935.
Henry Airbubble, 1936.

The Man who Ate the Popomack is an entertaining fantastic comedy of considerable satirical power. *Blow for Balloons* is a fantasy containing scenes of delightful imaginative force and a humorously cantankerous philosophy. Its successor, *Henry Airbubble*, is much inferior. Turner's criticism is animated, frankly prejudiced, extreme, but with abundant vigour.

ABERCROMBIE, LASCELLES (1881–1938).

Poetry:
Interludes and Poems, 1908.
Emblems of Love, 1912.
Deborah, 1912.
Four Short Plays, 1922.
Phoenix, 1923.
Twelve Idylls, 1928.
Collected Poems (in Oxford Poets), 1930.
The Sale of St. Thomas, 1931.

Criticism:
Thomas Hardy, a Critical Study, 1912.
Speculative Dialogues, 1913.
The Epic, 1914.
Theory of Art, 1922.
Principles of English Prosody, 1923.
Theory of Poetry, 1924.
Idea of Great Poetry, 1925.
Romanticism, 1926.
Progress in Literature, 1929.
Liberty of Interpreting (British Academy Shakespeare Lecture), 1930.
Poetry. Its Music and Meaning, 1932.

The Sale of St. Thomas contains poetry of intellectual force and originality. The critical works have the same qualities and show a nice turn for speculation.

SASSOON, SIEGFRIED (1886-   ).

Poetry:
  The Old Huntsman, 1917.
  Counterattack, 1918.
  Satirical Poems, 1926.
  The Heart's Journey, 1928.
  Vigils, 1935.

Fiction:
  Memoirs of a Fox-hunting Man, 1928.
  Memoirs of an Infantry Officer, 1930.
  Sherston's Progress, 1936.

The *Memoirs* are a picture of rural England before the War, describing the ordered life of the big country houses.

BLUNDEN, EDMUND CHARLES (1896-   ).

Poetry:
  Poems, 1914–30.
  Halfway House, 1932.
  Choice or Chance, 1934.
  An Elegy and other Poems, 1937.

Prose:
  The Bonaventure, 1922.
  On the Poems of Henry Vaughan, 1927.
  Leigh Hunt's Examiner, 1928.
  Undertones of War, 1928.
  Nature in English Literature, 1929.
  Life of Leigh Hunt, 1930.
  The Face of England, 1932.
  Charles Lamb and His Contemporaries, 1934.
  The Mind's Eye, 1934.

Blunden's is a "bookman's" criticism. He is a specialist on Leigh Hunt and his circle.

WELLESLEY, DOROTHY (Lady Gerald)

Poems of Ten Years.
Lost Lane.
Matrix.
Deserted House.
Poems, 1920.
Genesis, 1926.
Poems of Ten Years, 1924–34, 1934.

A poet admired by W. B. Yeats.

PALMER, HERBERT (1880–   ).

Poetry:
Two Fishes, 1918.
Two Foemen, 1920.
Two Minstrels, 1921.
The Unknown Warrior, 1924.
Songs of Salvation, Sin, and Satire, 1925.
The Armed Muse, 1930.
Jonah comes to Nineveh, 1930.
Cinder Thursday, 1931.
Collected Poems, 1933.
Summit and Chasm, 1934.
The Vampire, 1936.

Drama:
The Judgement of François Villon, 1927.

Criticism:
The Teaching of English, 1930.

Autobiography:
The Mistletoe Child, 1935.

Palmer has abundant energy, a rhythm and a use of words of his own, and is a singer of public occasions. His reading of life is romantic; he enjoys being in a poetic rage, and sometimes carries it off effectively. There is a great deal of will, and of the will to will, in his poetry, which is full of challenges and defiances designed rather to keep up the reader's heart than to injure the enemy.

205

STITCH, WILHELMINA

Beacons in the Night.
Breath of God.
Brownies and Guides.
Catching the Gleam.
Fragrant Minute for Every Day.
Friendly Things.
Garnered Gleanings.
Golden Web.
Heap o' Folk.
Homespun.
Joy's Loom.
Lasting Fragrance.
Little Book of Singing Rhymes.
Little People.
Mingled Yarn.
Morning Glory.
New Trail.
Out of Doors.
Short and Sweet.
Silken Threads.
Silver Linings.
Simple Life.
Tapestries.
Through Sunny Windows.
Triple Stitch.
Where Comfort Is.
Where Sunlight Falls.

Wilhelmina Stitch is too well-known for me to say anything about her: incomparably the most widely known poet in this book. I have given a fairly complete list of her works, for I could not resist the titles.

Rupert Brooke, James Elroy Flecker and Ralph Hodgson have been dealt with in the previous volume.

(B) THE MIDDLE GENERATION

POUND, EZRA LOOMIS (1885–   ).

Poetry:
Personae, 1909.
Exultations, 1909.
Provençal, 1910.
Canzoni, 1911.
Ripostes, 1921.
Cathay, 1915.
Lustra, 1916.
Lustra and Other Poems, 1917.
Quia Pauper Amavi, 1919.
Umbra (collected early poems), 1920.
Hugh Selwyn Mauberley, 1920.
Cantos I–XVI, 1925.
Personae (collected poems), 1926.
Cantos XVII–XXVII, 1928. *XXX*, 1930.
Cantos, XXXI–XLI, 1934.
Fifth Decad of Cantos, 1937.

Prose:
The Spirit of Romance, 1910.
Gaudier Brzeska, 1916.
Pavannes and Divisions, 1918.
Instigations, 1920.
Indiscretions, 1923.
Antheil and the Treatise on Harmony, 1924.
Imaginary Letters, 1930.
How to Read, 1931.
Prolegomena, Vol. I, 1932.
A. B. C. of Economics, 1933.
A. B. C. of Reading, 1934.
Make it New, 1934.
Social Credit and Impact, 1935.
Jefferson and/or Mussolini, 1935.
· *Polite Essays*, 1936.
Digest of the Analects, 1937.

Translations and Anthologies:

The Sonnets and Ballate of Guido Cavalcanti, 1912 and 1913.
Certain Noble Plays of Japan, from the Fenollosa MSS., with Introd. by W. B. Yeats, 1916.
Noh, or Accomplishment, 1917.
12 Dialogues of Fontenelle, 1917.
Gourmont's Physique de l'Amour.
The Ta Hio (American version), 1928.
Cavalcanti, Complete Definitive Text, 1932.
Catholic Anthology, editor of, 1915.
Letters of John Butler Yeats, editor of, 1917.
Active Anthology, 1933.
The Chinese Written Character, by Ernest Fenollosa, edited with notes, 1936, etc.

On points of technique Pound is an admirable critic. *How to Read* is an odd handbook, maddening but educative. The style is dislocated, like the thought, except when it is dealing with some specific passage, when it is pointed and exact.

ELIOT, THOMAS STEARNS (1888–   ).

Poetry:

Prufrock and other Observations, 1917.
Ara Vos Prec, 1920.
Poems, 1920.
The Waste Land, 1923.
Ash Wednesday, 1930.
Sweeney Agonistes. Fragment of an Aristophanic drama, 1932.
The Rock, a Pageant Play, 1934.
Murder in the Cathedral, 1935.
Collected Poems, 1907–35, 1936.

Criticism:

The Sacred Wood, 1920.
Homage to John Dryden, 1924.
For Lancelot Andrewes. Essays on Style and Order, 1928 (issued in a revised form in 1936 as Essays, Ancient and Modern).
Thoughts after Lambeth, 1931.
Dante, 1931.
The Use of Poetry and the Use of Criticism, 1933.
After Strange Gods, 1933.
Collected Essays.

Translation:
A rendering of the *Anabasis* of St. J. Perse.

Critical studies of Eliot include *Thomas Stearns Eliot*, by Thomas MacGreevy and *The Achievement of T. S. Eliot* by F. O. Matthiessen. There are numberless references to him in periodicals and books of criticism; perhaps the most cogent of these are to be found in F. R. Leavis's *New Bearings in English Poetry* and Edmund Wilson's *Axel's Castle*.

READ, HERBERT (1893–   ).

Poetry:
Naked Warriors, 1919.
Eclogues, 1919.
Mutations of the Phoenix, 1923.
The End of a War, 1933.
Poems, 1915–35.

Criticism:
Reason and Romanticism.
English Prose Style, 1928.
Phases of English Poetry, 1928.
The Sense of Glory, 1929.
Wordsworth (Clark Lectures), 1930.
The Meaning of Art, 1931.
Form in Modern Poetry, 1932.
Art Now, 1933.
Art and Industry, 1934.
In Defence of Shelley, 1935.
Art and Society, 1936.
Poetry and Anarchism, 1938.
Surrealism, edited by H.R., 1938.

Fiction:
The Green Child.

Autobiography:
In Retreat, 1925.
The Innocent Eye, 1933.

In Retreat, a short narrative, is one of the most striking documents produced by the War.

OWEN, WILFRED (1893–1918).

> *Poems, with an introd. by Siegfried Sassoon*, 1930.
> *Poems, with an Essay by Edmund Blunden and several unpublished poems*, 1931.

ROSENBERG, ISAAC (1890–1918).

> *Night and Day*, 1912.
> *Youth*, 1915.
> *Moses, a Play*, 1916.
> *Poems, selected and edited by Gordon Bottomley, with an introductory memoir by Lawrence Binyon*, 1922.
> *The Collected Works of Isaac Rosenberg*, edited by Gordon Bottomley and Denys Harding, with a foreword by Siegfried Sassoon, 1937.

GRAVES, ROBERT RANKE (1895–   ).

Poetry:
> *Poems*, 1914–26.
> *Poems*, 1926–30.
> *Poems*, 1930–3.
> *Collected Poems*, 1938.

Criticism:
> *The Meaning of Dreams.*
> *Poetic Unreason*, 1925.
> *On English Poetry.*

Fiction:
> *I, Claudius*, 1934.
> *Claudius the God*, 1934.
> *Antigua Penny Puce*, 1936.

Autobiography:
> *Goodbye to all That, an autobiography*, 1929.
> *But It Still Goes On, a Miscellany*, 1930.
> *T. E. Lawrence to his Biographer*, 1937.

I, Claudius and *Claudius the God* are remarkable for the intimate portrait of the chief figure, who is a first-rate character.

RIDING, LAURA (1901–).

Poetry:
A Joking Word.
A Lying Word.
The Life of the Dead.
Collected Poems, 1938.

Criticism:
Anarchism Is Not Enough.
Experts Are Puzzled.
Everybody's Letters.
A Survey of Modernist Poetry (with Robert Graves).

Fiction:
Progress of Stories.

Miss Riding's critical work contains acute thought, expressed in terms so personal to herself that it is sometimes difficult to grasp, but often illuminating.

SITWELL, EDITH (1887–).

Poetry:
The Mother and other Poems, 1915.
Clowns House. ⎫
Bucolic Comedies. ⎬ 1916, 17, 18.
Sleeping Beauty. ⎭
Elegy on Dead Fashion, 1926.
Gold Coast Customs, 1929.
Collected Poems, 1930.

Criticism:
Aspects of Modern Poetry, 1934.

Biography:
Alexander Pope, 1930.
The English Eccentrics, 1933.
Victoria of England, 1936.

History:
Bath, 1932.

Fiction:
I Live Under a Black Sun, 1937.

Anthology:
The Pleasures of Poetry, An Anthology.

SITWELL, SACHEVERELL (1900-   ).

Poetry:
Doctor Donne and Gargantua, 1930.
Canons of Giant Art, 1933.
Dance of the Quick and the Dead, 1936.
and others.

Criticism:
Southern Baroque Art, 1924.
German Baroque Art, 1927.
The Visit of the Gypsies, 1929.
These Sad Ruins, 1929.
The Fair-haired Victory, 1930.
Spanish Baroque Art, 1931.
Mozart, 1932.

Fiction:
All Summer in a Day, 1926.

Biography:
Life of Liszt, 1934.

All Summer in a Day contains some beautiful imaginative prose. Of the half-pictorial, half-fanciful books on art, *Southern Baroque Art* still remains the best.

SITWELL, OSBERT (1892-   ).

Poetry:
Twentieth Century Harlequinade and other Poems, 1916.
Argonaut and Juggernaut, 1919.
Who Killed Cock Robin?, 1931.
Out of the Flame, 1923.
Collected Poems and Satires, 1931.

Fiction:
Triple Fugue, and other Stories, 1924.
Before the Bombardment, 1926.
Dumb Animal and other Stories, 1930.
Miracle on Sinai, 1933.
Penny Foolish, 1935.

Criticism:
Portrait of Michael Arlen, 1931.

Essays:
Discursions on Travel, Art and Life, 1925.

The novels, mainly satirical, with a fine sense of period, are the best of Osbert Sitwell's work.

YOUNG, ANDREW (1885–).

Winter Harvest.
The White Blackbird.
Collected Poems.
Nicodemus (a religious play).

Young's poetry, mainly about natural scenes, has a metaphysical turn, and a mastery of delicate detail. He is never trivial and never commonplace.

MUIR, EDWIN (1887–).

Poetry:
First Poems, 1925.
Chorus of the Newly Dead, 1928.
Six Poems, 1932.
Variations on a Time Theme, 1934.
Journeys and Places, 1937.

Criticism:
Latitudes.
Transition.
The Structure of the Novel.

Biography:
John Knox.

Fiction:
The Marionette.

Philosophic poetry, with moving rhythms and effective imagery. [B.D.]

CAMPBELL, IGNATIUS ROY DUNNACHIE (1902-).

Poetry:
The Flaming Terrapin.
The Wayzgoose.
Adamastor.
The Georgiad.

Prose:
Taurine Provence.

MACDIARMID, HUGH

Poetry:
Sangschaw.
Penny Wheep.
A Drunk Man Looks at Thistle.
To Circumjack Cencrastus.
First Hymn to Lenin.
Scots Unbound and Other Poems.
Stony Limits and Other Poems.

Prose:
Scottish Eccentrics.

BRANFORD, FREDERICK VICTOR

The White Stallion, 1924.
Titans and Gods.
Five Poems.

Mr. Branford is a Promethean, with rhetorical rather than poetic power. Influenced by Francis Thompson.

PITTER, RUTH

Mad Lady's Garland.
Trophy of Arms.

Miss Pitter's work is closely related to dream, original in imagination, and beautifully wrought.

CHURCH, RICHARD (1893-   ).

Poetry:
Flood of Life, 1917.
Hurricane, 1919.
Philip, 1923.
Portrait of the Abbot, 1926.
The Dream, 1927.
Theme and Variations, 1928.
Mood without Measure, 1928.
The Glance Backward, 1930.
News from the Mountain, 1932.
Twelve Noon, 1936.

Fiction:
Oliver's Daughter, 1930.
High Summer, 1931.
The Prodigal Father, 1933.
Apple of Concord, 1935.
The Porch, 1937.

Biography:
Mary Shelley, 1928.

Church's poetry is mainly poetry of personal experience, sensitively felt, and judged by a reflective mind. It has considerable compass; it is never false; and at its best is moving as emotion twice felt, by the senses and the mind. Perhaps the best of the novels is *The Porch*, the first volume of what is intended to be a long work.

(C) THE YOUNGER GENERATION

AUDEN, WYSTAN HUGH (1907–   ).

Poetry:
Poems, 1930.
Look Stranger, 1936.

Drama:
The Dance of Death, 1933.
The Dog Beneath the Skin, 1935. With Christopher Isherwood.
The Ascent of F. 6, 1936. With Christopher Isherwood.

Fiction:
The Orators, 1932.

Travel:
Letters from Iceland, 1937. With Louis MacNeice.

Anthology:
The Poet's Tongue, 1935. With John Garrett.
The Oxford Book of Light Verse, 1938.

The Orators is written in a prose which recalls Nietzsche and Rimbaud, and embodies the attitude which, in Auden's opinion, is demanded from the revolutionary younger generation: an ascetic, martial, up-and-doing attitude.
New Verse produced a special Auden number in 1938. There is also criticism of Auden in Stephen Spender's *The Destructive Element*, and he has been much written about in various periodicals.

SPENDER, STEPHEN (1909–   ).

Poetry:
Twenty Poems, 1930.
Poems, 1933.
Vienna, 1936.

Criticism:
The Destructive Element, 1935.

216

Drama:
Trial of a Judge, 1938.

Fiction:
The Burning Cactus, 1936.

Politics:
Forward from Liberalism, 1937.

The Burning Cactus is a volume of short stories, somewhat immature, but showing a remarkable sensibility. *Forward from Liberalism* is an attempt to prove that the aims of Liberalism, as men like John Stuart Mill conceived them, can be achieved only through Communism.

LEWIS, CECIL DAY (1904–   ).

Poetry:
Country Comets.
Transitional Poem.
From Feathers to Iron.
The Magnetic Mountain.
A Time to Dance.
Collected Poems, 1929–33.
Noah and the Waters.

Criticism:
A Hope for Poetry.

Fiction:
The Friendly Tree.

A Hope for Poetry is a defence of political poetry.

MACNEICE, LOUIS (1907–   ).

Poetry:
Blind Fireworks, 1929.
Poems, 1935.
The Agamemnon of Aeschylus, a translation, 1936.

Prose:
Letters from Iceland (with W. H. Auden), 1937.
I Crossed the Minch, 1938.
Modern Poetry, 1938.

217

EMPSON, WILLIAM (1907–   ).

Poetry:
Poems, 1935.

Criticism:
Seven Types of Ambiguity, 1930.
Some Versions of Pastoral, 1935.

Mr. Empson's poetry is obscure, intelligent and intricate, and contains some beautiful lines and various kinds of ambiguity.

BOTTRALL, FRANCIS JAMES RONALD (1906–   ).

The Loosening and Other Poems, 1931.
Festivals of Fire, 1934.

Influenced heavily by Eliot, *The Golden Bough*, post-War disillusion, and the modern "poetic idiom".

TESSIMOND, A. S. J. (1902–   ).

Walls of Glass.

A poet of the younger generation, without its political optimism.

MADGE, CHARLES (1912–   ).

Disappearing Castle, 1937.

Partly "political" and partly "surrealist".

CAMERON, NORMAN (1905–   ).

Winter House and Other Poems.

A neat, semi-epigrammatic poet.

BOWES-LYON, LILIAN

Bright Feather Fading.
Poems.
White Hare.
Poems.

A poet very much under the influence of Hopkins, but with a genuine verbal gift.

SOUTAR, WILLIAM (1898–   ).

Conflict, 1931.
Seeds in the Wind, 1933.
The Solitary Way, 1934.
Brief Words, 1935.
Poems in Scots, 1935.
A Handful of Earth, 1936.

Soutar's poems in Scots are his best, and closest to natural feeling. In English he tends to become rhetorical. His poems for children are charming.

HEPPENSTALL, RAYNER

Poetry:
First Poems, 1935.
Sebastian, 1937.

Prose:
Middleton Murry: A Study in Excellent Normality, 1934.
Apology for Dancing, 1936.

Heppenstall's poetry is emotionally confused, and gives the impression of something fighting with great energy and some enjoyment against its own realisation. *Sebastian* is mostly religious poetry, and describes an experience of some kind, not very clearly. *Apology for Dancing* is about the Ballet.

PROKOSCH, FREDERIC (1908-   ).

Poetry:
The Assassins, 1936.
The Carnival, 1938.

Fiction:
The Asiatics, 1935.
The Seven who Fled, 1937.

Both Prokosch's poetry and prose are strongly inspired by a sense of huge spaces and of death. In the first quality he resembles the German poet Hölderlin. He is a writer of imaginative force weakened by facile emotion. The poems in *The Assassins* are filled with vivid images of a dying world. In *The Carnival* there is an inordinate expression of pity, but also some poetry of great beauty. The two novels are well worth reading.

BARKER, GEORGE (1913-   ).

Poetry:
Thirty Preliminary Poems, 1933.
Poems, 1935.
Calamiterror, 1937.

Prose:
Alanna Autumnal, 1933.
Janus, 1935.

Barker seems to me to be a poet of genius still at the unformed stage, but with astonishing flashes. *Calamiterror* is a pouring out of all sorts of material, good and bad, deep and shallow, all of it touched with horror. The two prose works, the first half of *Janus* in particular, are more clearly realised and more technically finished.

THOMAS, DYLAN (1914-   ).

Eighteen Poems, 1934.
Twenty-five Poems, 1936.

A poet with a very remarkable verbal gift and a fine sense of form. His poetry has in a high degree the "natural magic" which Arnold attributed to the Celtic genius. It is filled, like Barker's, with images of parturition and death. It contains lines of extraordinary beauty and imaginative force, but the meaning is so obscure, perhaps because of an excessive allusiveness, that I find it difficult to understand.

MONTGOMERIE, WILLIAM

Via.
Squared Circle.

A young poet of unusual intellectual power, whose imagery, though too diffuse, has sometimes a fine intensity.

GASCOYNE, DAVID (1916–   ).

Poetry:
Man's Life is this Meat.

Prose:
Opening Day (a novel).
A Short Survey of surrealism.

Gascoyne's poetry is surrealist, like some of Barker's and Thomas's. It is vivid, but unformed.

See also under Fiction: Joyce, Lawrence, Lewis, Benson, Huxley, Aldington, Madox Ford, Collier, Coppard, Townsend Warner, Quennell, Hughes, Plomer. Under General Prose, see Chesterton, Belloc. Under Criticism, see Murry, Lucas, de Sola Pinto, Roberts.

FICTION

(1) THE OLDER GENERATION

BARRIE, SIR JAMES (1860–1935).

Novels:
Better Dead, 1881.
Auld Licht Idylls, 1883.
When a Man's Single, 1888.
A Window in Thrums, 1889.
My Lady Nicotine, 1890.
The Little Minister, 1891.
Sentimental Tommy, 1896.
Tommy and Grizel, 1900.
The Little White Bird, 1902.
Peter Pan in Kensington Gardens, 1906.
Peter and Wendy, 1911.

Plays:
The Professor's Love Story, 1895.
The Little Minister, 1897.
The Admirable Crichton, 1903.
Little Mary, 1903.
Peter Pan, 1904.
What Every Woman Knows, 1908.
A Kiss for Cinderella, 1916.
The Old Lady Shows her Medals, 1917.
Dear Brutus, 1917.
Mary Rose, 1920.
Shall we Join the Ladies?, 1922.

WELLS, HERBERT GEORGE (1866–   ).

Novels and Tales:
The Time Machine, 1895.

FICTION

The Stolen Bacillus, 1895.
The Wonderful Visit, 1895.
The Island of Dr. Moreau, 1896.
The Wheels of Chance, 1896.
The Plattner Story, 1897.
The Invisible Man, 1897.
The War of the Worlds, 1898.
When the Sleeper Wakes, 1899.
Tales of Space and Time, 1899.
Love and Mr. Lewisham, 1900.
The First Men in the Moon, 1901.
The Sea Lady, 1902.
Twelve Stories and a Dream, 1903.
The Food of the Gods, 1904.
Kipps, 1905.
In the Days of the Comet, 1906.
The War in the Air, 1908.
Tono-Bungay, 1909.
Ann Veronica, 1909.
The History of Mr. Polly, 1910.
The New Machiavelli, 1911.
Marriage, 1912.
The Passionate Friends, 1913.
The Wife of Sir Isaac Harman, 1914.
Mr. Britling Sees it Through, 1916.
The Soul of a Bishop, 1917.
Joan and Peter, 1918.
Christina Alberta's Father, 1925.
The World of William Clissold, 1926.
Mr. Blettsworthy on Rampole Island, 1928.
The Bulpington of Blup, 1933.
The Croquet Player, 1936.
The Brothers, 1937.
and others.

Other Works:
Anticipations, 1901.
Mankind in the Making, 1903.
A Modern Utopia, 1905.
New Worlds for Old, 1908.
First and Last Things, 1908 (revised, 1917).
An Englishman looks at the World, 1914.

The World Set Free, 1914.
The Outline of History, 1920.
The Open Conspiracy, 1928.
The Book of Catherine Wells, 1928.
The Science of Life (with Julian Huxley and G. P. Wells), 1929.
The Work, Wealth and Happiness of Mankind, 1932.
The Shape of Things to Come, 1933.
Experiment in Autobiography, 1934.
The Anatomy of Frustration, 1936.
and others.

The World of William Clissold is more a sociological treatise than a novel, and contains a convenient summary of Wells's ideas.

GALSWORTHY, JOHN (1867–1933).

Novels and Tales:
    Jocelyn, 1898.
    The Island Pharisees, 1904.
    The Man of Property, 1906.
    The Country House, 1907.
    Fraternity, 1909.
    The Patrician, 1911.
    The Dark Flower, 1913.
    Five Tales, 1918.
    The Forsyte Saga, 1922.
    The White Monkey, 1924.
    Swan Song, 1928.
    A Modern Comedy, 1929.
    Flowering Wilderness, 1934.

Plays:
    The Silver Box, 1906.
    Strife, 1909.
    Justice, 1910.
    The Skin Game, 1920.
    Loyalties, 1922.
    Old English, 1924.
    Collected Plays, 1930.
    Letters, edited by E. Garnett, 1934.
    Life and Letters, by H. V. Marrot, 1935.

BENNETT, ENOCH ARNOLD (1867–1931).

Novels:
A Man from the North, 1898.
The Grand Babylon Hotel, 1902.
Anna of the Five Towns, 1902.
The Grim Smile of the Five Towns, 1907.
Buried Alive, 1908.
The Old Wives' Tale, 1908.
Clayhanger, 1910.
Hilda Lessways, 1911.
The Card, 1911.
The Matador of the Five Towns, 1912.
The Pretty Lady, 1918.
Riceyman Steps, 1923.
Elsie and the Child, 1925.
Imperial Palace, 1930.

Play:
The Great Adventure, 1913.

Miscellaneous:
Things that have Interested Me, 1921, 1923, 1925.
Journals, 1896–1928.   Edited by Newman Flower.
Arnold Bennett, by Dorothy Cheston Bennett, 1935.
Letters to His Nephew, 1936.
"A.B.", a minor marginal note, by Pauline Smith, 1933.

ONIONS, OLIVER (1873-   ).

Widdershins.
In Accordance with the Evidence.
The Debit Account.
The Story of Louie.
The Two Kisses.
A Crooked Mill.
Mushroom Town.
The New Moon, 1918.
A Case in Camera, 1920.
The Tower of Oblivion, 1921.
Peace in Our Time, 1923.

Ghosts in Daytime, 1924.
The Spite of Heaven, 1925.
Whom God Hath Sundered, 1926.
Cut Flowers, 1927.
The Painted Face, 1929.
The Open Street, 1930.
A Certain Man, 1931.
Catalan Circus, 1934.
The Collected Ghost Stories of Oliver Onions, 1935.
A Penny for the Harp, 1938.

Mr. Onions is a conscientious artist in the realistic style, in many ways superior to Bennett, but without the surface vitality which leads to popularity. *Widdershins*, a collection of eerie stories, is very good indeed.

HOLME, CONSTANCE

Crump Folk Going Home, 1913.
The Lonely Plough, 1914.
The Old Road from Spain.
Beautiful End.
The Splendid Fairing.
The Trumpet in the Dust.
The Things which Belong.
He Who Came.

BARING, MAURICE (1874-).

Fiction:
  "C".
  Cat's Cradle.
  In My End in my Beginning. (The story of Mary, Queen of
    Scots.)
and others.

Other prose:
  Puppet Show of Memory.
  Diminutive Dramas.
  Sarah Bernhardt.

A writer of traditional grace.

MAUGHAM, WILLIAM SOMERSET (1874-   ).

Fiction:
   Liza of Lambeth, 1897.
   The Making of a Saint, 1898.
   Orientations, 1899.
   Mrs. Craddock, 1902.
   The Bishop's Apron, 1906.
   The Explorer, 1907.
   Of Human Bondage, 1915.
   The Moon and Sixpence, 1919.
   The Trembling of a Leaf, 1921.
   On a Chinese Screen, 1922.
   The Painted Veil, 1925.
   The Casuarina Tree, 1926.
   Ashenden, 1928.
   The Gentleman in the Parlour, 1930.
   Ah King, 1933.
   Altogether, 1934.
   Cosmopolitans, 1936.
and others.

Drama:
   Schiffbruchig (at Berlin, in German), 1902.
   A Man of Honour, 1903.
   Penelope.
   Smith, 1909.
   Grace, 1910.
   The Land of Promise, 1914.
   Caroline, 1916.
   Love in a Cottage, 1918.
   Caesar's Wife: Home and Beauty, 1919.
   The Unknown, 1920.
   The Circle, 1921.
   East of Suez, 1922.
   Our Betters, 1923.
   The Camel's Back, 1924.
   The Letter, 1927.
   The Constant Wife, 1927.
   The Sacred Flame, 1929.

Autobiography:
   The Summing Up, 1938.

REID, FORREST (1876–   ).

> *The Bracknels*, 1912.
> *The Spring Song.*
> *Uncle Stephen.*
> *Apostate.*
> *Brian Westby*, 1934.
> *The Retreat*, 1936.

and others.

RICHARDSON, HENRY HANDEL

> *Maurice Guest*, 1908.
> *The Getting of Wisdom*, 1910.
> *The Fortunes of Richard Mahoney*, 1930.
> *Two Studies*, 1931.
> *The End of a Childhood*, 1934.

MAYNE, ETHEL COLBURN

Fiction:
> *The Clearer Vision*, 1898.
> *Jessie Vandeleur.*
> *The Fourth Ship.*
> *Gold Lace.*
> *One of Our Grandmothers.*
> *Blindman.*
> *Nine of Hearts*, 1923.
> *Inner Circle*, 1925.

Biography:
> *Byron* (2 vols.).
> *The Life and Letters of Anne Isabella, Lady Noel Byron*, 1929.

Criticism:
> *Browning's Heroines.*

Miss Colburn Mayne is chiefly known as a short-story writer. *Inner Circle* contains some of the best of her work.

CARSWELL, CATHERINE

Novels:
Open the Door.
The Camomile.

Biography:
Robert Burns.
The Savage Pilgrimage (on D. H. Lawrence).
and others.

Open the Door is one of the best Scottish novels which have appeared during the present century. The Life of Burns is both a work of scholarship and a new interpretation of Burns the man.

MCKENNA, STEPHEN (1888–   ).

The Reluctant Lover, 1912.
Sonia, 1917.
Ninety-six Hours' Leave, 1917.
Sonia Married, 1919.
Lady Lilith, 1920.
An Affair of Honour, 1925.
Saviours of Society, 1926.
The Secretary of State, 1927.
Lady Cynthia Clandon's Husband, 1936.
and many others.

A popular novelist whose success began with *Sonia* in 1917. His subject is "society", which he views with a noble shake of the head.

WODEHOUSE, PELHAM GREVILLE (1881–   ).

The Pothunters, 1902.
A Prefect's Uncle.
Tales of St. Austin's, 1903.
The Gold Bat, 1904.
The Head of Kay's, 1905.
The White Feather, 1907.

Love Among the Chickens, 1906.
The Swoop, 1909.
Mike, 1909.
A Gentleman of Leisure, 1910.
The Prince and Betty, 1911.
The Little Nugget, 1912.
Psmith in the City, 1910.
Psmith, Journalist, 1915.
Something Fresh, 1915.
Uneasy Money, 1917.
Piccadilly Jim, 1918.
A Damsel in Distress, 1919.
Jill the Reckless, 1920.
The Coming of Bill, 1920.
Indiscretions of Archie, 1921.
The Clicking of Cuthbert, 1922.
The Girl on the Boat, 1922.
Leave it to Psmith, 1923.
The Inimitable Jeeves, 1924.
Ukridge, 1924.
Bill the Conqueror, 1924.
Carry on, Jeeves, 1925.
Sam the Sudden, 1925.
The Heart of a Goof, 1926.
The Small Bachelor, 1927.
Meet Mr. Mulliner, 1927.
Money for Nothing, 1928.
Mr. Mulliner Speaking, 1929.
Summer Lightning, 1929.
Very Good, Jeeves, 1930.
Louder and Funnier, 1932.
Doctor Sally, 1932.
Hot Water, 1932.
Mulliner Nights, 1933.
Heavy Watcher, 1933.
Thank you, Jeeves, 1934.
Right Ho, Jeeves, 1934.
Blandings Castle, 1935.
The Luck of the Bodkins, 1935.
Mulliner Omnibus, 1935.

Young Men in Spats, 1936.
Laughing Gas, 1936.
Lord Emsworth and Others, 1937.

HUTCHINSON, ARTHUR STUART-MENTEITH (1879–).

Once Aboard the Lugger, 1908.
The Happy Warrior, 1912.
The Clean Heart, 1914.
If Winter Comes, 1921.
This Freedom, 1922.
The Eighth Wonder, 1923.
One Increasing Purpose, 1925.
The Uncertain Trumpet, 1929.
The Golden Pound, 1930.
The Book of Simon, 1930.
Big Business, 1932.
The Soft Spot, 1933.
A Year that the Locust, 1935.

If Winter Comes and *This Freedom*, both of them spectacular successes, owed their popularity to their broad-minded acceptance of ideas which had shocked people twenty years before. All Mr. Hutchinson's stories are concerned in some form with "this freedom". Mr. Warwick Deeping's *Sorrel and Son* belongs to the same class, by now a well-known type of best-seller.

DEEPING, GEORGE WARWICK

Unrest, 1916.
Martin Valliant, 1917.
Valour, 1918.
Second Youth, 1919.
The Prophetic Marriage, 1920.
Lantern Lane.
The House of Adventure, 1921.
Orchards, 1922.
The Secret Sanctuary, 1923.

Apples of Gold, 1923.
Three Rooms, 1924.
Suvla John, 1924.
Sorrel and Son, 1925.
Doomsday, 1927.
Kitty, 1928.
Old Pybus, 1928.
Roper's Row, 1929.
The Road, 1931.
Old Wine and New, 1932.
Smith, 1932.
Two Black Sheep, 1933.
Seven Men Came Back, 1934.
The Man on the White Horse, 1934.
Sackcloth into Silk, 1935.
No Hero—This, 1936.

See the note on A. S. M. Hutchinson.

(B) THE MIDDLE GENERATION

JOYCE, JAMES AUGUSTINE ALOYSIUS (1882–   ).

Fiction:
Dubliners, 1914.
A Portrait of the Artist as a Young Man, 1916.
Ulysses, 1920.
Anna Livia Plurabella, 1930.
Tales Told of Shaun and Shem, 1932.
Haveth Childer Everywhere, 1931.
The Mime of Mick, Nick and the Maggies, 1933.
Storiella as she is Fyung, 1934.

Drama:
Exiles, 1918.

232

Poetry:
  Chamber Music, 1907.
  Pomes Penyeach, 1927.
  James Joyce's Ulysses, by Stuart Gilbert, is an analysis of the
    structure and meaning of that novel.

LAWRENCE, DAVID HERBERT (1884–1930).

Novels and short stories:
  The White Peacock, 1911.
  The Trespasser, 1912.
  Sons and Lovers, 1913.
  The Prussian Officer, 1914.
  The Rainbow, 1915 (banned). New edition in 1929.
  Women in Love, 1919.
  The Lost Girl, 1920.
  Aaron's Rod, 1922.
  Kangaroo, 1923.
  St. Mawr, 1923.
  The Ladybird, 1923.
  England, my England, 1924.
  The Boy in the Bush (with M. L. Skinner), 1924.
  The Plumed Serpent, 1926.
  The Woman who Rode Away, 1928.
  The Virgin and the Gypsy, 1930.
  Love Among the Haystacks, 1930.
  The Man Who Died, 1931.
  Lady Chatterley's Lover, 1931.
  The Lovely Lady, 1932.
  A Modern Lover, 1934.
  Tales of D. H. Lawrence, 1934.

Poetry:
  Love Poems and Others, 1913.
  Amores, 1916.
  Look! We have come Through, 1917.
  New Poems, 1918.
  Birds, Beasts and Flowers, 1923.
  Pansies, 1929.
  Nettles, 1930.
  Collected Poems, 1932.

The Ship of Death and Other Poems, 1933.
Last Poems, edited by Richard Aldington, 1933.

Plays:
The Widowing of Mrs. Holroyd, 1914.
David, 1926.
A Collier's Friday Night, 1934.
Plays, 1933.

Other Prose:
Twilight in Italy, 1916.
Sea and Sardinia, 1923.
Fantasia of the Unconscious, 1923.
Psychoanalysis and the Unconscious, 1923.
Studies of Classic American Literature, 1924.
Movements in European History, 1925. '
Mornings in Mexico, 1927.
Etruscan Places, 1932.
Apocalypse, 1932.
Apropos of Lady Chatterley's Lover, 1930.
Pornography and Obscenity, 1929.
Assorted Articles, 1932.

Much has been written on Lawrence since his death, most of it biographical. The following is a short list:

Son of Woman, by J. Middleton Murry, 1931.
The Savage Pilgrimage, by Catherine Carswell, 1932.
Lawrence and Brett, by the Hon. Dorothy E. Brett, 1935.
Lorenzo in Taos, by Mabel D. Luhan, 1932.
"Not I, but the Wind," by Frieda Lawrence, 1934.
D. H. Lawrence, A Personal Record, by E.T., 1935.
A Poet and Two Painters, by Knud Merrild, 1938.

We are given an intimate picture of Lawrence in his *Letters*, edited by Aldous Huxley, 1932. Some of the letters deserve to stand with his best work.

LEWIS, WYNDHAM (1886-   ).

Fiction:
Tarr, 1918.
The Wild Body, 1927.

The Childermass, 1928.
The Apes of God, 1930.
Filibusters in Barbary, 1932.
Snooty Baronet, 1932.
The Revenge for Love, 1937.

Criticism:
Time and the Western Man, 1927.
The Lion and the Fox, 1927.
The Art of Being Ruled, 1926.
Paleface, 1929.
Hitler, 1931.
The Diabolical Principle and the Dithyrambic Spectator, 1931.
Doom of Youth, 1932.
Men without Art, 1934.
Left Wings over Europe, 1936.

Poetry:
One Way Song, 1933.

Autobiography:
Blasting and Bombardiering, 1937.
Wyndham Lewis, by H. C. Porteous, 1932, is a critical study.

MANSFIELD, KATHERINE (1888–1923).

Fiction:
Bliss, and Other Stories.
The Doves' Nest, and Other Stories.
The Garden Party, and Other Stories.
In a German Pension.
Something Childish, and Other Stories.
Journal. Edited by J. Middleton Murry.
Letters. Edited by J. Middleton Murry.
The Life of Katherine Mansfield. By J. Middleton Murry.

BENSON, STELLA (1892–1933).

Fiction:
Christmas Formulas, 1932.
Collected Short Stories.

Good-bye, Stranger.
I Pose.
Little World.
Living Alone.
Mundos.
Pipers and a Dancer.
Poor Man.
This is the End.
Tobit Transplanted.
Worlds within Worlds.

Poetry:
Poems.

HUDSON, STEPHEN

Richard Kurt, 1919.
Elinor Colhouse, 1921.
Prince Hempseed, 1922.
Tony, 1924.
Myrtle, 1925.
Richard Myrtle and I, 1926.
A True Story, 1930.
Celeste and Other Sketches, 1930.
The Other Side, 1937.

MACKENZIE, COMPTON (1883-   ).

Fiction:
The Passionate Elopement, 1911.
Carnival, 1912.
Sinister Street, 1913, 1914.
Guy and Pauline, 1915.
Sylvia Scarlett, 1918.
Sylvia and Michael, 1919.
Poor Relations, 1919.
The Vanity Girl, 1920.
Rich Relatives, 1921.
The Altar Steps, 1922.
The Parson's Progress, 1923.
The Heavenly Ladder, 1924.

Santa Claus in Summer, 1924.
The Old Men of the Sea, 1924.
Coral, 1925.
Fairy Gold, 1926.
Rogues and Vagabonds, 1927.
Vestal Fire, 1927.
Extremes Meet, 1928.
Extraordinary Women, 1928.
The Three Couriers, 1929.
The Four Winds of Love:—
The East Wind, 1937.
The South Wind, 1937.

Poetry:
Poems, 1907.
Kensington Rhymes, 1912.

Memoirs:
Gallipoli Memories, 1929.
First Athenian Memories, 1931.
Greek Memories, 1932. (Withdrawn.)

Biography:
Prince Charlie, 1932.

Criticism:
Literature in My Time, 1933.

History:
Marathon and Salamis, 1934.
Prince Charlie and His Ladies, 1934.
Catholicism and Scotland, 1936.

Local:
The Book of Barra (with J. L. Campbell), 1936.

WALPOLE, SIR HUGH SEYMOUR (1884–   ).

Fiction:
The Wooden House, 1909.
Maradick at Forty, 1910.
Mr. Perrin and Mr. Trail, 1911.
The Prelude to Adventure, 1912.

Fortitude, 1913.
The Duchess of Wrexe, 1914.
The Golden Scarecrow, 1915.
The Dark Forest, 1916.
The Green Mirror, 1918.
The Secret City, 1919.
Jeremy, 1919.
The Captives, 1920.
The Thirteen Travellers, 1921.
The Young Enchanted, 1922.
The Cathedral, 1922.
Jeremy and Hamlet, 1923.
The Old Ladies, 1924.
Portrait of a Man with Red Hair, 1925.
Harmer John, 1926.
Jeremy at Crale, 1927.
Wintersmoon, 1928.
The Silver Thorn, 1928.
Hans Frost, 1929.
Rogue Herries, 1930.
Above the Dark Circus, 1931.
Judith Paris, 1931.
The Fortress, 1932.
All Souls' Night, 1933.
Vanessa, 1933.
Captain Nicholas, 1934.
The Inquisitor, 1935.
John Cornelius, 1937.

Criticism:
Joseph Conrad, 1916.
Anthony Trollope (English Men of Letters), 1928.
The Waverley Pageant, 1932.

RICHARDSON, DOROTHY M. (Mrs. Alan Odle)

Fiction:
Pointed Roofs, 1915.
Backwater, 1916.
Honeycomb, 1917.
The Tunnel, Interim, 1919.

Deadlock, 1921.
Revolving Light, 1923.
The Trap, 1925.
Oberland, 1927.
Dawn's Left Hand, 1931.
Clear Horizon, 1935.
Dimple Hill, 1937.

History:
The Quakers—Past and Present, 1914.

Dorothy Richardson was one of the first to exploit the technique of minute observation of fleeting mental states which later went into the art of *Ulysses* and *Mrs. Dalloway.* Her work sometimes drags, but *Oberland* is a delightful book and has considerable poetic power.

WOOLF, VIRGINIA (1882-   ).

Fiction:
The Voyage Out, 1915.
Night and Day, 1919.
Monday or Tuesday, 1921.
Jacob's Room, 1922.
Mrs. Dalloway, 1925.
To the Lighthouse, 1927.
Orlando, 1928.
The Waves, 1931.
The Years, 1937.

Criticism:
The Common Reader, 1925.
A Room of One's Own, 1929.
The Common Reader, Second Series, 1932.

Biography:
Flush, 1933.

HUXLEY, ALDOUS LEONARD (1894-   ).

Fiction:
Limbo, 1920.

Crome Yellow, 1921.
Mortal Coils, 1922.
Antic Hay, 1923.
Little Mexican, 1924.
Those Barren Leaves, 1925.
Two or Three Graces, 1926.
Point Counter Point, 1928.
Brief Candles, 1930.
Brave New World, 1932.
Eyeless in Gaza, 1936.

Criticism:
On the Margin, 1923.
Along the Road, 1925.
Jesting Pilate, 1926.
Proper Studies, 1927.
Music at Night, 1931.
Texts and Pretexts.
The Olive Tree and Other Essays, 1936.

Poetry:
The Burning Wheel, 1916.
The Defeat of Youth, 1918.
Leda, 1920.
The Cicadas, 1931.

Drama:
The World of Light, 1931.

MYERS, LEO HAMILTON (1881–   ).

The Orissers, 1923.
The Clio, 1925.
The Near and the Far, 1927.
Prince Jali, 1930.
The Root and the Flower, 1935.
Strange Glory, 1936.

GARNETT, DAVID (1892–   ).
Lady into Fox.
A Man in the Zoo.

The Sailor's Return.
Go She Must.
The Old Dovecote, 1928.
No Love, 1929.
The Grasshoppers Come, 1931.
A Rabbit in the Air, 1932.
Pocahontas, 1933.
Bean-eye, 1935.

ALDINGTON, RICHARD (1892–   ).

Fiction:
Death of a Hero, 1929.
The Colonel's Daughter, 1931.
Soft Answers, 1932.
All Men are Enemies, 1933.
Women must Work, 1934.
Very Heaven, 1937.

Poetry:
Images, Old and New, 1915.
War and Love, 1918.
Images of Desire, 1919.
Exile, and Other Poems, 1923.
A Fool i' the Forest, 1925.
Collected Poems, 1928.
A Dream in the Luxembourg, 1930.

Criticism:
Literary Studies, 1924.
French Studies, 1925.
Voltaire, 1926.

Mr. Aldington's poetry is imagistic. *Death of a Hero* is one of the best and bitterest of the war novels.

FORD, FORD MADOX (1873–   ).

Fiction:
Romance (with Joseph Conrad).
No More Parades, 1925.
A Man Could Stand Up, 1926.

The Last Post, 1927.
No Enemy, 1929.
Vive Le Roy, 1937.

Poetry:
Poems for Pictures.
Songs from London, 1910.
Collected Poems, 1914.

Criticism:
Rosetti, A Critical Monograph.
The Critical Attitude, 1911.
Henry James, A Critical Study, 1914.
Joseph Conrad, 1924.
The English Novel, 1930.

Biography:
Life of Madox Brown.
Thus to Revisit, 1921.

Discursive:
The Great Trade Route, 1937.
Provence, 1938.

His four war novels, beginning with *No More Parades*, are among the best that have been written.

POWYS, THEODORE FRANCIS (1875–   ).

Fiction:
Fables.
The Left Leg.
Black Bryony.
Mark Only, 1924.
Mockery Gap, 1925.
Mr. Tasker's Gods.
Innocent Birds, 1926.
Mr. Weston's Good Wine, 1928.
The Dew-pond.
The House with the Echo, 1929.
Kindness in a Corner, 1930.
The White Paternoster, 1930.
The Only Penitent, 1931.

When Thou Wast Naked, 1931.
The Two Thieves, 1932.
Captain Patch, 1935.
Make Thyself Many, 1935.

Speculation:
Soliloquies of a Hermit, 1926.

POWYS, JOHN COWPER (1872–   ).

Fiction:
Wolf Solent, 1929.
A Glastonbury Romance, 1933.
Jobbir Skald, 1935.
Maiden Castle, 1937.
Morwen or Vengeance of God, 1937.

Criticism:
The Religion of a Sceptic.
The Meaning of Culture, 1930.
In Defence of Sensuality.
Dorothy M. Richardson, 1931.
Philosophy of Solitude, 1933.
Art of Happiness, 1935.

Autobiography:
Autobiography, 1934.

Wolf Solent and *A Glastonbury Romance* are strongly flavoured "mystical" novels, in which a few admirable scenes are lost amid a waste of bombastic "evil". The *Autobiography* is interesting.

POWYS, LLEWELYN (1884–   ).

Fiction:
Ebony and Ivory, 1922.
Black Laughter, 1924.
Apples be Ripe, 1930.

Essays:
Thirteen Worthies, 1923.
The Verdict of Bridlegoose, 1926.

The Pathetic Fallacy.
Earth Memories, 1933.
Glory of Life, 1934.
Damnable Opinions, 1935.
Dorset Essays, 1936.
Twelve Months.
Rats in the Sacristy, Somerset Essays, 1937.

Memoirs:
Confessions of Two Brothers, 1916.

A pessimistic Pantheist, but a charming writer with an exquisite visual talent.

MACAULAY, ROSE

Fiction:
What Not, 1919.
Potterism, 1920.
Dangerous Ages, 1921.
Mystery of Geneva, 1922.
Told by an Idiot, 1923.
Orphan Island, 1924.
Crewe Train, 1926.

Criticism:
A Casual Commentary: Essays, 1925.
Some Religious Elements in English Literature, 1931.
John Milton, 1933.

A satirical novelist.

DELAFIELD, E. M. (1890–   ).

Fiction:
Zella sees Herself.
The War-workers.
The Pelicans.
Consequences.
Tension.
The Heel of Achilles.

Humbug.
The Optimist.
A Reversion to Type
Messalina of the Suburbs, 1924.
Mrs. Harter, 1924.
The Chips and the Block, 1925.
Jill, 1926.
The Entertainment, 1927.
The Way Things Are, 1928.
What is Love?, 1928.
Women are Like That, 1929.
Turn Back the Leaves, 1930.
Diary of a Provincial Lady, 1931.
Challenge to Clarissa, 1931.
Thank Heaven Fasting, 1932.
The Provincial Lady Goes Further, 1932.
General Impressions, 1933.
The Provincial Lady in America, 1934.
Faster! Faster!, 1936.
Nothing is Safe, 1937.

Criticism:
Ladies and Gentlemen in Victorian Fiction, 1937.

General:
Straw Without Bricks: I Visit Soviet Russia, 1937.

A satirical novelist.

JONES, E. B. C. (1893–   ).

Quiet Interior.
Singing Captives.
Wedgwood Medallion.
Helen and Felicia.
Morning and Cloud.

A writer of distinction, with a delicate appreciation of shades of feeling, and a grasp of underlying character.

MUIR, WILLA (1890–   ).

Novels:
Imagined Corners.
Mrs. Ritchie.

Criticism:
Mrs. Grundy in Scotland.

JAMESON, MARGARET STORM (1897–   ).

Fiction:
The Lovely Ship, 1927.
The Voyage Home, 1930. ⎫
A Richer Dust, 1931.   ⎬ Trilogy.
Farewell to Youth, 1928. ⎭
The Triumph of Time, 1932.
No Time like the Present, 1930.
Company Parade, 1934.
Love in Winter, 1935.
In the Second Year, 1936.
None Turn Back, 1936.
The Moon is Making, 1937.
Here Comes a Cradle, 1938.

Good example of the long-short story.
A Day Off, 1933.
Delicate Monster, 1937.

History:
The Decline of Merry England (An Historical Essay).

Criticism:
Modern Europe in Europe, 1920.
The Georgian Novel and Mr. Robinson, 1929.

O'BRIEN, KATE

Fiction:
Without My Cloak, 1931.
The Ante-Room, 1934.
Mary Lavelle, 1936.

Drama:
Distinguished Villa, 1927.

246

WEST, REBECCA (1892–).

Fiction:
The Return of the Soldier, 1918.
The Judge, 1922.
Harriet Hume, 1929.
The Thinking Reed, 1936.

Criticism:
Henry James, 1916.
The Strange Necessity, 1928.
D. H. Lawrence: An Elegy, 1930.

Biography:
St. Augustine, 1933.

An independent mind, witty and vigorous, enlivens everything that Rebecca West writes, whether fiction or criticism. *The Thinking Reed* is probably the best novel.

DOBRÉE, VALENTINE (1894–).

Your Cuckoo Sings by Kind.
A sensitive description of childhood and adolescence.
The Emperor's Tigers, 1929.
To Blush Unseen, 1935.

COLLIER, JOHN

Fiction:
Devil and All.
Easy Go Grange.
Green Thoughts.
His Monkey Wife.
Tom's A-Cold.
Defy the Foul Fiend.

COPPARD, ALFRED EDGAR (1878–).

Fiction:
Adam and Eve and Pinch Me, 1921.

Clorinda Walks in Heaven, 1922.
The Black Dog, 1923.
Fishmonger's Fiddle, 1925.
The Field of Mustard, 1926.
Yokohama Garland, 1926.
Silver Circus, 1928.
Count Stefan, 1928.
Pink Furniture, 1930.
My Hundredth Story, 1931.
Mixey's Harlequin, 1931.
Easter Day, 1931.
Crotty Shinkwin, 1932.
Rummy, 1932.
Dunky Fitlow, 1933.
Ring the Bells of Heaven, 1934.
Emergency Exit, 1934.
Polly Oliver, 1935.

Poetry:
Pelagea and Other Poems, 1926.
Collected Poems, 1928.
Cherry Ripe (poems), 1935.

A well-known short-story writer, to whose work may be compared that of

BEACHCROFT, THOMAS O.

A Young Man in a Hurry, 1934.
You Must Break Out Sometimes, 1936.
The Man who Started Clean (novel), 1938.

KINGSMILL, HUGH (1889–   ).

Fiction:
The Will to Love.
The Dawn's Delay.

Criticism:
Matthew Arnold.
The Return of William Shakespeare.
After Puritanism.

Biography:
  Frank Harris.
  Samuel Johnson.
  The Sentimental Journey. (A biography of Dickens.)

Anthologies:
  What They Said at the Time.
  Wholly Matrimony.

The Dawn's Delay contains three brilliant comic stories. The Life of Johnson is the best of the biographies. *The Return of William Shakespeare*, a farce, contains some first-rate criticism in dialogue form.

WARNER, SYLVIA TOWNSEND

Poetry:
  The Espalier, 1925.
  Time Importuned.
  Opus 7.
  Whether a Dove or Seagull (with Valentine Ackland).

Fiction:
  Lolly Willowes, 1926.
  Mr. Fortune's Maggot.
  The True Heart.
  The Salutation, 1932.

Lolly Willowes is a story of a witch: the rural setting is finely described. The poetry has a fresh rustic flavour, without being pretty.

EDWARDS, DOROTHY

Rhapsody.

DENNIS, GEOFFREY POMEROY

Fiction:
  Mary Lee, 1922.
  Harvest in Poland, 1925.
  Declaration of Love, 1927.
  The End of the World, 1930.

Sale by Auction, 1932.
Bloody Mary's, 1934.

General:
Coronation Commentary, 1936.

Mary Lee describes a narrow Nonconformist upbringing with striking power: a remarkable book. *Harvest in Poland* is melodramatic. *Bloody Mary's* is a good school story.

JESSE, F. TENNYSON

Fiction:
The Milky Way.
Secret Bread.
The White Riband.
The Happy Bride.
Anyhouse.
Tom Fool.
Moonraker.
Many Latitudes.
The Lacquer Lady.
Solange Stories.
A Pin to See the Peep-Show.

Plays:
The Mask.
Billeted.
The Pelican.

A novelist of imagination with a weakness for "strong" situations.

DOUGLAS, NORMAN (1868–   ).

Novels:
South Wind, 1917.
They Went, 1921.

Other Prose:
Siren Land, 1911.
Together, 1923.

Fountain in the Sand, 1923.
Old Cambria, 1928.
London Street Games, 1931.
Looking Back, 1933.

GERHARDI, WILLIAM ALEXANDER (1895-   ).

Fiction:
  Futility, 1922.
  The Polyglots, 1925.
  A Bad End, 1926.
  The Vanity Bag.
  Pretty Creatures.
  Short Stories, 1927.
  Jazz and Jasper, 1928.
  Pending Heaven, 1930.
  Resurrection, 1934.
  Of Mortal Love, 1936.
  Coronation Club, 1937.

Criticism:
  Anton Chehov. A Critical Study, 1923.

Autobiography:
  Memoirs of a Polyglot, 1931.

A brilliant comic writer without any reforming purpose, except possibly in his early works *Futility* and *The Polyglots,* which show the influence of Wells. *Resurrection,* which contains a justification of belief in personal immortality, is probably his best work.

BUTTS, MARY (1892-1935).

  Ashes of Rings.
  Imaginary Letters.
  Armed with Madness.
  Death of Felicity Taverner.
  The Macedonian.
  Crystal Cabinet.
  Scenes from the Life of Cleopatra.

Her stories show a concern with "mystical" evil which often declines into melodrama.

EVANS, CARADOC

Fiction:
My People, 1915.
Capel Sion, 1916.
My Neighbours, 1920.
Nothing to Pay, 1930.
Wasps.
This Way to Heaven, 1934.

Drama:
Taffy, 1924.

A satirist of Welsh life.

GUNN, NEIL M. (1891–   ).

Fiction:
The Grey Coast.
Hidden Doors.
Morning Tide.
The Lost Glen.
Sun Circle.

Plays:
The Ancient Fire.
Back Home.

A sensitive delineator of Highland life.

STRONG, LEONARD ALFRED GEORGE (1896–   ).

Fiction:
Dewar Rides.
The English Captain.
The Jealous Ghost.
The Garden.
The Brothers.
Don Juan and the Wheelbarrow.
Sea Wall.
Corporal Tune.
The Seven Arms.

Mr. Sheridan's Embrella.
Tuesday Afternoon.
The Last Enemy.
The Swift Shadow, with others.

Poetry:
   Dublin Days.
   The Lowery Road.
   Difficult Love.
   Northern Light.
   Call to the Swan.

Criticism:
   Common Sense about Poetry.
   A Letter to W. B. Yeats.
   Life in English Literature (with M. Redlich).
   The Hansom Cab and the Pigeons.
   The Minstrel Boy.
   The Man Who Asked Questions.

An excellent story-teller, with a partiality for primitive situations, preferably in Celtic surroundings. *The Garden* is a story of childhood and probably his best.

O'FLAHERTY, LIAM (1897–   ).

Fiction:
   Thy Neighbour's Wife.
   The Black Soul.
   Spring Sowing.
   The Informer.
   The Tent, and other stories, 1926.
   Mr. Gilhooly, 1926.
   The Assassin, 1928.
   The Mountain Tavern, and other stories, 1929.
   The House of Gold, 1929.
   The Puritan, 1932.
   Sherrett, 1932.
   Shame and the Devil, 1934.
   Famine, 1937.

Biography:
The Life of Tim Healy, 1927.

Autobiography:
Two Years, 1930.

Travel:
I Went to Russia, 1931.
A Tourist's Guide to Ireland, 1929.

A powerful realistic writer, excellent when he is dealing with "the root facts of life", but with very little sensibility and no style.

MITCHISON, NAOMI MARGARET (1897–   ).

Fiction:
The Conquered, 1923.
When the Bough Breaks, 1924.
Cloud Cuckoo Land, 1925.
The Laburnum Branch, 1926.
Black Sparta, 1928.
Barbarian Stories, 1929.
The Hostages, 1930.
The Corn King and the Spring Queen, 1931.
The Delicate Fire, 1933.
We Have Been Warned, 1935.
The Fourth Pig, 1936.

Travel:
Vienna Diary, 1934.

Most of the early novels are about ancient Greece and most of the later ones about modern life from a Socialist's point of view.

MOTTRAM, RALPH HALE (1883–   ).

Fiction:
The Spanish Farm.
Sixty-four, Ninety-four.
The Crime of Vanderlynden's.
Our Mr. Dormer.
The English Miss.

The Boroughmonger.
Castle Island, 1931.
The Headless Hound, 1931.
Home for the Holidays, 1932.
Dazzle, 1932.
The Lame Dog, 1933.
Early Morning, 1935.
Flower Pot End, 1935.
Time to be Going, 1937.

Biography:
John Crome of Norwich, 1932.
Portrait of an Unknown Victorian, 1936.

History:
A History of Financial Speculation.
Success to the Mayor, 1937.

Poetry:
Poems Old and New, 1930.

The first three novels in this list, which make up a trilogy
called *The Spanish Farm,* are among the best of the War novels.

SWINNERTON, FRANK ARTHUR (1884-   ).

Fiction:
The Merry Heart, 1909.
The Young Idea, 1910.
The Casement, 1911.
The Happy Family, 1912.
The Chaste Wife, 1916.
Nocturne, 1917.
Coquette, 1921.
The Three Lovers, 1922.
Young Felix, 1923.
The Elder Sister, 1925.
Summer Storm, 1926.
A Brood of Ducklings, 1928.
Sketch of a Sinner, 1929.
Elizabeth, 1934.
Harvest Comedy, 1937.

Criticism:
George Gissing, a Critical Study, 1912.
R. L. Stevenson, a Critical Study, 1914.
Tokefield Papers, 1927.
A London Bookman, 1928.
Authors and the Book Trade, 1932.
The Georgian Literary Scene, 1935.

Autobiography:
Swinnerton, an Autobiography, 1937.

A "middle-brow" novelist.

BLAKE, GEORGE (1893–   ).

Fiction:
Mince Collop Close, 1923.
The Wild Men, 1925.
Young Malcolm, 1926.
Paper Money, 1928.
The Path to Glory, 1929.
The Seas Between, 1930.
Returned Empty, 1931.
Sea Tangle, 1932.
Rest and Be Thankful, 1934.
The Shipbuilders, 1935.
David and Joanna, 1936.
Down to the Sea, 1937.

General:
The Heart of Scotland, 1934.

An excellent Scottish satirist.

KENNEDY, MARGARET (1896–   ).

The Ladies of Lyndon, 1923.
The Constant Nymph, 1924.
Red Sky at Morning, 1927.
The Fool of the Family, 1930.
Return I dare not, 1931.

A Long Time Ago, 1932.
Together and Apart, 1936.

Most of Miss Kennedy's novels, like *The Constant Nymph*, which was a popular success, are about artists, whom she treats with professional efficiency.

SAYERS, DOROTHY LEIGH (1893–   ).

Fiction:
Whose Body?, 1923.
Clouds of Witnesses, 1926.
Unnatural Death, 1927.
The Unpleasantness at the Bellona Club, 1928.
Lord Peter Views the Body, 1928.
The Documents in the Case (with Robert Eustace), 1930.
Strong Poison, 1930.
The Five Red Herrings, 1931.
Have His Carcase, 1932.
Hangman's Holiday, 1933.
Murder Must Advertise, 1933.
The Nine Tailors, 1934.
Gaudy Night, 1935.
Busman's Honeymoon, 1937.
Ask a Policeman, 1933.

Poetry:
Op. 1, 1916.
Catholic Tales, 1919.

The most "brilliant" of the detective-story writers. Brilliant in a different way is

INNES, MICHAEL (pseudonym).

Murder in the President's Lodging.
Hamlet Revenge.
Lament for a Makar, 1938.

HERBERT, ALAN PATRICK (1890–   ).

Fiction:
The Secret Battle.

The Water Gipsies.
Holy Deadlock, 1936.

Poetry:
Ballads for Broadbrows.

A popular humorist, and a well-known libertarian. *The Secret Battle* is a very good War novel.

MACKAIL, DENIS GEORGE (1892–   ).

Romance to the Rescue, 1921.
Bill the Bachelor, 1922.
According to Gibson, 1923.
Summertime, 1923.
Greenery Street, 1925.
The Fortunes of Hugo, 1926.
The Flower Show, 1927.
Tales from Greenery Street, 1928.
Another Part of the Wood, 1929.
The Young Livingstones, 1930.
The Square Circle, 1930.
Ian and Felicity, 1932.
Having Fun, 1933.
Summer Leaves, 1934.
The Wedding, 1935.
Back Again, 1936.
Jacinth, 1937.

A popular retailer of the simple humours of the upper middle classes. A mild enemy of the high-brows.

MORGAN, CHARLES LANGRIDGE (1894–   ).

Fiction:
The Gunroom, 1919.
My name is Legion, 1925.
Portrait in a Mirror, 1929.
The Fountain, 1932.
Sparkenbroke, 1936.

Criticism:
>*Epitaph on George Moore*, 1935.

The Fountain became a best-seller by demonstrating that mysticism was compatible with good form.

NICHOLS, BEVERLEY

Fiction:
>*Patchwork*, 1921.
>*Self*, 1922.
>*Crazy Pavements*, 1927.
>*Prelude*, 1920.

Autobiography:
>*Twenty-five*, 1926.

Political:
>*The Star Spangled Manner*, 1928.
>*When the Crash Comes*, 1933.

Rustic:
>*Down the Garden Path*, 1932.

Religious:
>*The Fool Hath Said*, 1936.

Travel:
>*No Place Like Home*, 1936.

A sophisticated writer who lost his style in a garden and has since been a moral inspiration to thousands.

ARLEN, MICHAEL (1895–   ).

>*The London Venture.*
>*The Romantic Lady.*
>*Piracy.*
>*These Charming People.*
>*The Green Hat.*
>*May Fair.*
>*Young Men in Love.*
>*Lily Christine.*
>*Babes in the Wood.*

259

Men Dislike Women, 1931.
Man's Mortality, 1933.
Hell! said the Duchess, 1934.
The Crooked Coronet, 1937.

The Green Hat is, or was, a famous best-seller. *These Charming People* may stand as a description of most of the characters in Mr. Arlen's novels, who come from Mayfair, a romantic quarter of London.

(C) THE YOUNGER GENERATION

COMPTON-BURNETT, IVY

Pastors and Masters, 1925.
Brothers and Sisters, 1929.
Men and Wives, 1931.
More Women than Men, 1933.
A House and its Head, 1935.
Daughters and Sons, 1937.

BOWEN, ELIZABETH DOROTHEA COLE (1899–).

The Hotel, 1927.
The Last September, 1929.
Joining Charles, 1929.
Friends and Relations, 1931.
To the North, 1932.
The Cat Jumps, 1934.
The House in Paris, 1935.
The Death of the Heart, 1938.

A sensitive and intelligent writer, with a sense of form. *The Death of the Heart* is a remarkable novel.

O'FAOLAIN, SEAN (1900–).

Fiction:
Midsummer Night Madness, 1932.
A Nest of Simple Folk, 1933.

There's a-Birdie in the Cage, 1935.
A Born Genius, 1936.
Bird Alone, 1936.
A Purse of Coppers, 1937.

Poetry:
Lyrics and Satires from Tom Moore, 1929.

Biography:
Life Story of De Valera, 1933.
Constance Markievicz, 1934.
King of the Beggars, 1937.

O'Faoláin's work has a union of sensibility and intelligence which makes him one of the most brilliant novelists of his generation. *Bird Alone* is perhaps his best novel.

SACKVILLE-WEST, HON. EDWARD (1901–).

Fiction:
Piano Quintet, 1925.
The Ruin, 1926.
Simpson, 1931.
The Sun in Capricorn, 1934.

Biography:
A Flame in Sunlight, 1936.

A strange, sometimes morbid, but powerful imagination, with a touch of "Gothic" in it, runs through the novels. *A Flame of Sunlight* is a life of de Quincey.

BATES, HERBERT ERNEST (1905–).

Novels:
The Two Sisters.
Catherine Foster.
Charlotte's Row.
The Fallow Land.
The Poacher.
A House of Women, 1936.

Stories:
> *Day's End.*
> *Seven Tales and Alexander.*
> *The Black Boxer.*
> *The Woman who had Imagination.*
> *Cut and Come Again.*
> *Something Short and Sweet.*

Miscellaneous:
> *Flowers and Faces.*
> *Through the Woods.*
> *Down the River.*
> *The Last Bread.*

One of our best short-story writers. He is most at home in country scenes.

QUENNELL, PETER (1905–).

Fiction:
> *The Phoenix Kind.*
> *Sympathy, and Other Stories.*

Poetry:
> *Poems.*

Criticism:
> *Baudelaire and the Symbolists.*
> *Aspects of 17th Century Verse.*

Biography:
> *Byron, The Years of Fame.*

Sympathy, and Other Stories contains Quennell's best imaginative prose work, which is ironical and intelligent. *Baudelaire and the Symbolists* is a volume of good criticism. Some of the poems have an exquisite lucent quality.

CALDER-MARSHALL, ARTHUR (1908–).
> *Two of a Kind,* 1933.
> *About Levy.*
> *Crime against Cania.*

Dead Centre.
The Pink Doll.
At Sea, 1934.
Pie in the Sky, 1937.

Clarity and objectivity are Mr. Calder-Marshall's main virtues. *At Sea* is perhaps his best novel.

GREENE, GRAHAM (1904–   ).

The Man Within.
Rumour at Nightfall.
Stamboul Train.
It's a Battlefield.
The Bear Fell Free.
Brighton Rock, 1938.

HANLEY, JAMES (1901–   ).

Fiction:
    Drift, 1930.
    The Last Voyage, 1931.
    The German Prisoner, 1930.
    A Passion before Death, 1930.
    Boy, 1931.
    Ebb and Flood, 1931.
    Aria and Finale, 1932.
    Captain Bottell, 1933.
    The Furys, 1934.
    Men in Darkness, 1931.
    The Maelstrom, 1935.
    Stoker Bush, 1935.
    The Secret Journey, 1936.
    The Wall, 1936.
    Half-an-Eye, 1937.
    Hollow Sen, 1938.

Sociology:
    Grey Children, 1937.

Autobiography:
    Broken Water, 1937.

HUGHES, RICHARD ARTHUR WARREN (1900-).

Fiction:
A High Wind in Jamaica, 1929.
The Spider's Palace, 1931.
In Hazard, 1938.

Drama:
The Sister's Tragedy, and Other Plays, 1924.
Plays, 1928.

Poetry:
Gipsy-Night and Other Poems, 1922.
The Sister's Tragedy, 1922.
Confessio Juvenis, 1926.

LINKLATER, ERIC (1899-).

Fiction:
Whiteman's Saga, 1929.
Poet's Pub, 1929.
A Dragon Laughed, 1930.
Juan in America, 1931.
The Men of Ness, 1932.
The Crusader's Key, 1933.
Magnus Merriman, 1934.
Ripeness is All, 1935.
God Likes Them Plain, 1935.
Juan in China, 1937.
The Impregnable Women, 1938.

Drama:
The Devil's in the News, 1934.

Biography:
Ben Jonson and King James, 1931.
Mary Queen of Scots, 1933.
Robert the Bruce, 1934.

Mr. Linklater has an exuberant comic gift, seen at its best in *Juan in America* and *The Impregnable Women.* In the latter it is used for a serious satirical purpose. He is the most genuinely Rabelaisian writer of his time.

ISHERWOOD, CHRISTOPHER

Fiction:
   The Memorial.
   Mr. Norris Changes Trains.
   Sally Bowles.

Drama:
   The Ascent of F. 6 (with W. H. Auden).
   The Dog Beneath the Skin (with W. H. Auden).

Autobiography:
   Lions and Shadows, 1938.

PLOMER, WILLIAM CHARLES FRANKLYN (1903-   ).

Fiction:
   Turbott Wolfe, 1926.
   I Speak of Africa, 1927.
   Paper Houses, 1929.
   The Family Tree, 1929.
   The Case is Altered, 1932.
   The Child of Queen Victoria, 1933.
   The Invaders, 1934.

Poetry:
   Notes for Poems, 1928.

Biography:
   Cecil Rhodes, 1933.

EVANS, MARGIAD

   The Wooden Doctor.
   Turf or Stone.
   Creed.

The Wooden Doctor contains several scenes of intense imagination, but ends sentimentally. Miss Evans is one of the most gifted novelists of the younger generation, though her work thus far has been erratic.

MORRISON, N. BRYSSON

Breakers.
Solitaire.
The Gowk Storm.
The Strangers.
When the Wind Blows, 1937.

Also a writer of intense imagination. *The Gowk Storm* is the best of her novels.

BATES, RALPH

Lean Men.
The Olive Field.

MILLER, HENRY

Tropic of Cancer, 1934.
Black Spring, 1936.

BARNES, DJUNA

Nightwood, 1936.

UPWARD, EDWARD

Journey to the Border, 1938.

BEATON, GEORGE

Jack Robinson, 1933.

STEAD, CHRISTINA

The Salzburg Tales, 1934.
Seven Poor Men of Sydney, 1934.
Beauties and Furies, 1936.

WAUGH, EVELYN ARTHUR ST. JOHN (1903-   ).

Fiction:
Decline and Fall, 1928.
Vile Bodies, 1930.
Black Mischief, 1932.
Handful of Dust, 1934.

266

Biography:
Rossetti, 1928.
Edmund Campion, 1935.

Travel:
Waugh in Abyssinia, 1936.

ALLAN, JOHN R. (1906–).

Fiction:
Farmer's Boy.
Down at the Farm.

Political:
A New Song to the Lord.

Farmer's Boy is a local classic, perfect of its kind.

Among historical novelists may be included

IRWIN, MARGARET

Royal Flush, 1932.

See also under Poetry: de la Mare, Masefield, Davies, Turner, Sassoon, Read, Graves, Riding, Sitwell, Church, Auden, Spender, Day Lewis, Prokosch, Barker, Gascoyne. Under Drama, see Ervine, van Druten, Sherriff. Under General Prose, see Chesterton, Belloc, Tomlinson, Leonard Woolf. Under Criticism, see Dobrée, Lubbock, Waddell, Lucas, Priestley.

DRAMA

FOR Shaw, see General Literature. For Yeats, Bottomley, Abercrombie, Turner, Eliot, Auden and Spender, see Poetry. Under Fiction, see Galsworthy, Barrie, Somerset Maugham, Joyce, Lawrence, Huxley, O'Brien, Tennyson Jesse, Gunn, Hughes, Linklater, Isherwood. Under Criticism, see Lucas and Priestley.

O'CASEY, SEAN (1884–   ).

Drama:
The Shadow of a Gunman.
Juno and the Paycock.
The Plough and the Stars.
The Silver Tassie, 1928.
Within the Gates, 1933.

Criticism:
The Flying Wasp, Essays on the Theatre, 1937.

JOHNSTON, DENNIS WILLIAM (1901–   ).

The Moon on the Yellow River, 1932.
The Old Lady Says "No!", 1932.

His work may be taken as succeeding that of O'Casey. *The Old Lady Says "No!"* has a surrealist technique.

BRIDIE, JAMES (1888–   ).

The Switchback and Other Plays.
The Anatomist, 1931.
Tobias and the Angel, 1931.
Jonah and the Whale, 1932.

A Sleeping Clergyman, 1933.
Marriage is No Joke, 1934.
Mary Read, 1934.
The Black Eye, 1935.

ERVINE, ST. JOHN GREER (1883-   ).

Drama:
  Mixed Marriage, 1910.
  Jane Clegg, 1911.
  John Ferguson, 1914.
  The First Mrs. Fraser, 1928.
  People of Our Class, 1934.
  Boyd's Shop, 1935.

Fiction:
  Mrs. Martin's Man.
  Alice and a Family.
  Changing Winds.
  The Foolish Lovers.
  The Wayward Man.

Politics:
  Sir Edward Carson and the Ulster Movement.
  Parnell.
  If I Were Dictator.

Criticism:
  The Organised Theatre.
  How to Write a Play.
  The Theatre in My Time.

General:
  Some Impressions of my Elders, 1923.
  A Journey to Jerusalem, 1936.

A popular dramatist.

VAN DRUTEN, JOHN WILLIAM (1901-   ).

Drama:
  Chance Acquaintance, 1927.
  Young Woodley, 1928.

Diversion, 1928.
After All, 1929.
London Wall, 1931.
There's Always Juliet, 1931.
Somebody Knows, 1932.
Behold We Live, 1932.
The Distaff Side, 1933.
Flowers of the Forest, 1934.
Most of the Game, 1935.
Gertie Maude, 1937.

Fiction:
Young Woodley, 1929.
A Woman on Her Way, 1930.
And Then You Wish, 1936.

Young Woodley is the best known of the plays.

SHERRIFF, ROBERT CEDRIC (1896–   ).

Drama:
Journey's End, 1929.
Badger's Green, 1930.
Windfall, 1933.

Fiction:
The Fortnight in September, 1931.
Green Gates, 1936.

Journey's End is a War play.

COWARD, NOEL (1899–   ).

Plays:
The Vortex.
Easy Virtue.
Fallen Angels.
Hay Fever.
The Queen was in the Parlour, 1926.
This was a Man.
The Marquise, 1927.
On with the Dance.

Home Chat.
Sirocco.
This Year of Grace.
Bitter Sweet, 1929.
Private Lives, 1930.
Cavalcade, 1931.
Conversation Piece, 1934.
Point Valdine, 1935.
To-night at Eight-thirty, 1936.

Poetry:
Collected Sketches and Lyrics, 1931.

Autobiography:
Present Indicative, 1937.

MUNRO, C. K. (pseudonym) (1889–   ).

At Mrs. Beams, 1921.
Progress, 1923.
The Rumour, 1922.
Storm, 1924.
Cocks and Hens, 1927.
Veronica, 1929.
The Birth, Death and Life of Mr. Ene, 1930.
Bluestone Quarry, 1931.

Criticism:
Watching a Play, 1932.

GRANVILLE-BARKER, HARLEY (1877–   ).

Plays:
Waste.
The Madras House, 1910.
and others.

Criticism:
On Dramatic Method, 1931 (Clark Lectures).
Prefaces to Shakespeare's Plays (a brilliant feat of criticism).

GENERAL PROSE

IN this division only the most rough and ready classification is possible. I have begun with the Controversialists, a rapidly diminishing class, and gone on to the historians and biographers (a *non sequitur* which I do not justify), the travellers, the scientists, and the political writers. Most of these classes overlap.

(1) THE CONTROVERSIALISTS

SHAW, GEORGE BERNARD (1856–).

Plays:
  Plays, Pleasant and Unpleasant, 1898.
  Three Plays for Puritans, 1900.
  Man and Superman, 1903.
  John Bull's Other Island, 1904.
  Major Barbara, 1905.
  The Doctor's Dilemma, 1906.
  Getting Married, 1908.
  Fanny's First Play, 1911.
  Pygmalion, 1912.
  Heartbreak House, 1917.
  Back to Methuselah, 1921.
  Saint Joan, 1923.
  The Apple Cart, 1929.
  Too True to be Good, 1932.
  On the Rocks, 1933.
and others.

Other Writings:
  The Quintessence of Ibsenism, 1891 and 1913.

272

The Perfect Wagnerite, 1898.
Our Theatres in the Nineties, 1931. (Coll. articles.)
Music in London, 1890–4. (Coll. articles.) 1931.
The Intelligent Woman's Guide to Socialism and Capitalism, 1928.
Major Critical Essays, 1932.
Prefaces, 1934,
and others.

CHESTERTON, GILBERT KEITH (1874–1936).

Verse:
The Wild Knight.
Ballad of the White Horse, 1913.
Poems, 1915.

Essays and Criticism:
The Defendant, 1902.
Browning, 1903.
G. F. Watts, 1904.
Heretics, 1905.
Dickens, 1906.
Orthodoxy, 1908.
Tremendous Trifles, 1909.
George Bernard Shaw, 1909.
What's Wrong with the World, 1910.
The Victorian Age of Literature, 1913.
The Everlasting Man, 1925.
Chaucer, 1932.
St. Thomas Aquinas, 1933.
Avowals and Denials, 1934.
The Well and the Shallows (Catholic Essays), 1935

History:
A Short History of England, 1917.

Autobiography:
Autobiography, 1936.
and others.

Fiction:
The Napoleon of Notting Hill, 1904.
The Man Who was Thursday, 1907.

The Innocence of Father Brown, 1911.
The Flying Inn, 1914.
The Wisdom of Father Brown, 1914.
The Incredulity of Father Brown, 1926.
The Secret of Father Brown, 1927.
The Scandal of Father Brown, 1935.

and others.

BELLOC, HILAIRE (1870–   ).

Verse:
Verses and Sonnets, 1895.
The Bad Child's Book of Beasts, 1896.
More Beasts for Worse Children, 1897.
Cautionary Tales, 1907.
Verses and Sonnets, 1924.
New Cautionary Tales, 1930.

Essays, etc.:
The Path to Rome, 1902.
Caliban's Guide to Letters, 1903.
Hills and the Sea, 1906.
On Nothing, 1908.
On Everything, 1909.
On Anything, 1910.
On Something, 1911.
The Four Men, 1912.

History and Biography:
Danton, 1899.
Robespierre, 1901.
Marie Antoinette, 1910.
The Girondians, 1911.
A Continuation of Lingard's History to the Death of Edward VII, 1914.
History of England (4 vols.), 1925, 1928, 1931.
Richelieu, 1930.
Wolsey, 1930.
Cromwell, 1933.
Milton, 1935.

and others.

Politics:
The Servile State, 1912.
The Free Press, 1917.
The House of Commons and the Monarchy, 1920.

Fiction:
Mr. Emanuel Burden, 1904.
Mr. Clutterbuck's Election, 1908.
and others.

(B) HISTORY AND BIOGRAPHY

TREVELYAN, GEORGE MACAULAY (1876–   ).

History:
England in the Age of Wycliffe.
England under the Stuarts.
Garibaldi and the Making of Italy, 1911.
The Life of John Bright, 1913.
Recreations of an Historian, 1919.
Scenes from Italy's War, 1919.
Lord Grey of the Reform Bill, 1920.
British History in the Nineteenth Century (1782–1901), 1922.
Manin and the Venetian Revolution of 1848, 1923.
History of England, 1926.
England under Queen Anne, 1928.
Blenheim, 1930.
Ramillies and the Union with Scotland, 1932.
The Peace and the Protestant Succession, 1934.
Sir George Otto Trevelyan: A Memoir, 1932.
Grey of Fallodon, 1937.

Criticism:
The Poetry and Philosophy of George Meredith.

Trevelyan's most important work deals with the age of Queen Anne. His style is pleasantly readable, but rarely achieves dramatic intensity.

HAMMOND, JOHN LAWRENCE LE BRETON (1872–).

Charles James Fox, 1903.
Joint author with his wife of *The Village Labourer, 1760–1832*, 1911.
The Town Labourer, 1760–1832, 1917.
The Skilled Labourer, 1760–1832, 1919.
Lord Shaftesbury, 1923.
The Rise of Modern Industry, 1925.
The Age of Chartists, 1930.
James Stansfield, 1932.
The Bleak Age, 1934.
Life of C. P. Scott, 1934.

The Village Labourer and *The Town Labourer* are standard works.

TAWNEY, RICHARD HENRY (1880–).

The Agrarian Problem in the Sixteenth Century.
The Acquisitive Society, 1921.
Education: The Socialist Policy.
Thomas Wilson: A Discourse of Usury.
Religion and the Rise of Capitalism, 1926.
Equality, 1931.
Land and Labour in China, 1932.

In *Religion and the Rise of Capitalism* Tawney traces the effect of Calvinism on the economic development of England. A brilliant book.

STRACHEY, GILES LYTTON (1880–1932).

Biography:
Eminent Victorians, 1918.
Queen Victoria, 1921.
Essex and Elizabeth, 1928.
Portraits in Miniature, 1931.

Criticism:
Landmarks in French Literature, 1911.
Books and Characters, 1922.

NICOLSON, HON. HAROLD (1886–   ).

Paul Verlaine, 1921.
Tennyson, 1923.
Byron, The Last Journey, 1924.
Swinburne, 1926.
Some People, 1927.
The Development of English Biography, 1928.
Lord Carnock, 1930.
People and Things, 1931.
Public Faces, 1932.
Curzon, The Last Phase, 1934.
Small Talk, 1937.

All these books, except the last, are biographical or about biography. Mr. Nicholson was influenced by Strachey at the beginning, but not very deeply. *Some People*, with its comic glimpse of Curzon, is one of his most delightful books.

MACKENZIE, AGNES MURE

History:
An Historical Survey of Scottish Literature to 1714 (1933).
Robert Bruce, King of Scots, 1934.
The Rise of the Stewarts, 1935.
The Scotland of Mary and the Religious Wars, 1936.
The Passing of the Stewarts, 1937.
The Foundations of Scotland, 1938.

Criticism:
The Women in Shakespeare's Plays, 1924.
The Process of Literature, 1929.

Fiction:
The Half Loaf, 1925.
The Quiet Lady, 1926.
Lost Kinnellan, 1927.
Keith of Kinnellan, 1930.
Cypress in Moonlight, 1931.
Between Sun and Moon, 1932.

Miss Mure Mackenzie's volumes on the history of Scotland are brilliant, both in historical interpretation and in historical imagination. They are also a counterblast to the Whig reading of history, and are infused throughout with a feeling for the international life of the times which they cover.

GUEDALLA, PHILIP (1889–   ).

The Partition of Europe, 1715–1815, 1914.
Supers and Supermen, 1920.
The Industrial Future, 1921.
The Second Empire, 1922.
Masters and Men, 1923.
A Gallery, 1924.
A Council of Industry, 1925.
Napoleon and Palestine (Davis Lecture), *1925.*
Independence Day, 1926.
Palmerston, 1926.
Conquistador, 1927.
Gladstone and Palmerston, 1928.
Bonnet and Shawl, 1928.
The Duke (Wellington), *1931.*
The Queen and Mr. Gladstone, 1933.
The Hundred Days, 1934.
The Hundred Years, 1936.

A picturesque historian with an amusing but sometimes exasperating wit.

LIDDEL-HART, BASIL HENRY (1895–).

New Methods of Infantry Training, 1918.
Science of Infantry Tactics, 1921; 3rd edition, 1926.
Paris, or The Future of War, 1925.
A Greater than Napoleon—Scipio Africanus, 1926.
The Remaking of Modern Armies, 1927.
Great Captains Unveiled (Jenghiz Khan, Sabutai, Gustavus, Wallenstein, Saxe, Wolfe), *1927.*
Reputations—Ten Years After (historical studies of Joffre, Foch, Haig, Petain, Ludendorf, Falkenhayn, Galliéni, Pershing, Allenby, Liggett), *1928.*
The Decisive Wars of History, 1929.
Sherman, 1930.

The Real War, 1914–1918, 1930.
Foch—The Man of Orleans, 1931.
The British Way in Warfare, 1932.
The Future of Infantry, 1933.
The Ghost of Napoleon, 1933.
T. E. Lawrence—in Arabia and After, 1934; new edition, 1935.
A History of the World (enlarged from *The Real War*), 1934.
When Britain Goes to War (enlarged from *The British Way in Warfare*),* 1935.
The War in Outline, 1936.
Europe in Arms, 1937.
Captain Liddell-Hart is an expert on military history and military science, and has a lucid expository style.

BRYANT, ARTHUR

Charles II.
Samuel Pepys, 3rd vol., 1938.
Stanley Baldwin, 1937.
Macaulay, 1932.

BUCHAN, JOHN (LORD TWEEDSMUIR) (1875–   ).

Biography and History:
A History of the Great War, 1921–22.
Montrose, 1928.
Julius Caesar, 1932.
Oliver Cromwell, 1934.
Augustus, 1937.
and others.

Of Lord Tweedsmuir's many historical novels and tales of adventure, perhaps *Witchwood* is the best.

Poetry:
Poems, Scots and English, 1917.

Certain historians have produced valuable, more specialised studies, of which a small selection is given.

OLIVER, F. S.

Alexander Hamilton.
The Endless Adventure, 3rd vol., 1938.

LODGE, SIR RICHARD

Studies in Eighteenth Century Diplomacy, 1740–9, 1930.

WILLIAMS, BASIL

Stanhope. A Study of Eighteenth Century War and Diplomacy, 1932.

HORN, D. B.

Sir Charles Hankey Williams and European Diplomacy, 1747-68, 1930.

NAMIER, L. B.

England at the Time of the American Revolution.

SIMPSON, F. A.

Louis Napoleon and the Recovery of France.
The Rise of Louis Napoleon, 1909, revised, 1924.

There have also been general histories, at once learned and popular, one of the best being

FISHER, RT. HON. HUGH A. L. (1865–   ).

A History of Europe,

while specialised studies have been written on various countries, of which one might note

ELGOOD, P. G.

The Transit of Egypt, 1928.
Bonaparte's Adventure in Egypt, 1931,
and

LLOYD, GEORGE, LORD

Egypt since Cromer, Vol. 2, 1934.

An interesting development in form is provided by

TURBERVILLE, ARTHUR STANLEY (1888–   ).

Welbeck Abbey, Vol. I, 1938.
The History of the House of Lords in the Eighteenth Century.

TOYNBEE, ARNOLD JOSEPH (1889-).

Nationality and the War, 1915.
Chapters on Greece in the Balkans: A History, 1916.
The Western Question in Greece and Turkey, 1922.
Chapter on History in the Legacy of Greece, 1921.
*Chapter on the Non-Arab Territories of the Ottoman Empire in the
History of the Peace Conference of Paris*, Vol. VI, 1923.
Greek Historical Thought, 1924.
Greek Civilisation and Character, 1924.
The World after the Peace Conference, 1925.
A Survey of International Affairs for 1920–23; 1924 1925; (Vol. I;
The Islamic World since the Peace Settlement), 1926, 27, 28, 29,
30, 31, 32, etc.)
Turkey in the Nations of the Modern World Series, 1926 (with
K. P. Kirkwood).
A Journey to China, 1931.
Editor of British Commonwealth Relations, 1934.

Among the best biographies of the period are Lord Tweeds-
muir's (John Buchan's) *Cromwell* and *Montrose*, Catherine
Carswell's *Robert Burns*, J. M. Hone's *George Moore*, the Right
Hon. Winston S. Churchill's *Marlborough*, and Professor
R. W. Chambers's *Thomas More*.

(C) TRAVEL

LAWRENCE, THOMAS EDWARD (1888–1935).

Seven Pillars of Wisdom, a Triumph, 1926 and 1935.
Revolt in the Desert (an abridgement of the above), 1927.
The Odyssey of Homer (a translation), 1932.
The Letters of T. E. Lawrence of Arabia. Edited by David
Garnett, 1938.

BELL, GERTRUDE

Letters, 1927.

STORRS, SIR RONALD

Orientations, 1937.

TOMLINSON, H. M. (1873-   ).

Travel:
The Sea and the Jungle, 1912.
Old Junk, 1918.
London River, 1921.
Waiting for Daylight, 1922.
Tidemarks, 1924.
South to Cadiz, 1934.
Below London Bridge (with H. Chas. Tomlinson), 1934.

Fiction:
Gallion's Reach, 1927.
All our Yesterdays, 1930.

Memoirs:
Norman Douglas, 1931.
There is some fine imaginative prose in the travel books.

Among books which must be included in this section are J. R. Ackerley's *Hindu Holiday*, an exquisite picture of Indian life, witty and sensitive.

In a different style Malcolm Muggeridge's *Winter in Moscow*, a vivid adverse picture, should also be mentioned. *Old Calabria*, by Norman Douglas, is a fascinating book.

(D) SCIENCE

RUSSELL, BERTRAND WILLIAM, EARL (1872-   ).

German Social Democracy, 1896.
Essay on the Foundation of Geometry, 1897.
Philosophy of Leibniz, 1900.
Principles of Mathematics, 1903.
Philosophical Essays, 1910.
Problems of Philosophy, 1911.
Principia Mathematica (with A. N. Whitehead), 1910.
Our Knowledge of the External World as a Field for Scientific Method in Philosophy, 1914.
Principles of Social Reconstruction, 1917.

Mysticism and Logic, 1918.
Roads to Freedom, 1918.
Introd. to Mathematical Philosophy, 1919.
The Practice and Theory of Bolshevism, 1920.
The Analysis of Mind, 1921.
The Problem of China, 1922.
The A.B.C. of Atoms, 1923.
The Prospects of Industrial Civilization (with Dora Russell), 1923.
The A.B.C. of Relativity, 1925.
On Education, 1926.
The Analysis of Matter, 1927.
An Outline of Philosophy, 1927.
Sceptical Essays, 1928.
Marriage and Morals, 1929.
The Conquest of Happiness, 1930.
The Scientific Outlook, 1931.
Education and the Social Order, 1932.
Freedom and Organisation, 1814–1914, 1934.
In Praise of Idleness, 1935.
Which Way to Peace?, 1936.
The Amberley Papers (with Patricia Russell), 1937.

Mysticism and Logic is one of the best of the general volumes.

EDDINGTON, SIR ARTHUR STANLEY (1882–   ).

Stellar Movements and the Structure of the Universe, 1914.
Report on the Relativity Theory of Gravitation, 1918.
Space, Time and Gravitation, 1920.
The Mathematical Theory of Relativity, 1923.
The Internal Constitution of the Stars, 1926.
Stars and Atoms, 1927.
The Nature of the Physical World, 1928.
Science and the Unseen World, 1929.
The Expanding Universe, 1933.
New Pathways in Science, 1935.
Relativity Theory of Protons and Electrons, 1936.

The Nature of the Physical World and *Science and the Unseen World* are understandable, up to a point at least, by the general reader. The first is a masterpiece of exposition.

JEANS, SIR JAMES HOPWOOD (1877–   ).

    The Dynamical Theory of Gases, 1904.
    Theoretical Mechanics, 1906.
    The Mathematical Theory of Electricity and Magnetism, 1908.
    Radiation and the Quantum-Theory, 1914.
    Problems of Cosmogony and Stellar Dynamics, 1919.
    Atomicity and Quanta, 1926.
    Astronomy and Cosmogony, 1928.
    Eos, or the Wider Aspects of Cosmogony, 1928.
    The Universe Around Us, 1929.
    The Mysterious Universe, 1930.
    The Stars in their Courses, 1931.
    The New Background of Science, 1933.
    Through Space and Time, 1934.
    Science and Music, 1937.

The Mysterious Universe and *The Universe Around Us* are excellent popular expositions.

WHITEHEAD, ALFRED NORTH (1861–   ).

    A Treatise on Universal Algebra, 1898.
    Principia Mathematica (with Bertrand Russell), 1910–12.
    Science and the Modern World, 1926.

The last mentioned is a consideration of the philosophical questions raised by the modern non-materialist conception of science.

All these writers have had some effect on popular thought, and indirectly on literature. To estimate the effect of psychology in the same sphere, the reader should go to such books as Freud's *Interpretation of Dreams* and *Totem and Tabu*, and Jung's *Psychology of the Unconscious* and *Psychological Types*. Behaviourist and *Gestalt* psychology have not had much effect on literature.

A book which has had some influence is J. W. Dunne's *An Experiment with Time*, which outlines a new and suggestive conception of Time, and tries to formulate a proof of personal immortality. *The Serial Universe*, its successor, is somewhat

284

disappointing. The ideas canvassed in these books have already been assimilated into fiction and the drama.

Some of the best writing of the period has appeared in works which are not "popular", though of great scientific importance, notably in the books of

BRAGG, SIR WILLIAM, O.M. (1862–   ).

> *Crystals.*
> *Concerning the Nature of Things.*

(E) POLITICS

BARKER, ERNEST (1874–   ).

> *The Political Thought of Plato and Aristotle,* 1906. Revised edition under the title of *Greek Political Theory,* 1918.
> *The Dominican Order and Convocation,* 1913.
> *Political Thought in England from Herbert Spencer to To-Day,* 1915.
> *The Crusades,* 1923.
> *National Character,* 1927.
> *Church, State and Study* (Essays), 1930.
> *Burke and Bristol,* 1931.
> *Universities in Great Britain,* 1931.
> *Translation with Introduction of Gierke's National Law and the Theory of Society,* 1934.
> *Oliver Cromwell and the English People,* 1937.

Particularly valuable for the period we have been studying is *Political Thought in England from Herbert Spencer to To-Day.*

ANGELL, SIR NORMAN (1874–   ).

> *Patriotism Under Three Flags,* 1903.
> *Europe's Optical Illusion,* 1910.
> *Peace Theories, and the Balkan War,* 1912.
> *The Foundations of International Polity,* 1914.
> *Prussianism and its Destruction,* 1914.
> *Why Freedom Matters,* 1916.
> *War Aims,* 1917.

The Political Conditions of Allied Success, 1918.
The Economic Chaos and the Peace Treaty, 1919.
The Fruits of Victory, 1921.
If Britain is to Live, 1923.
Must Britain Travel the Moscow Road?, 1926.
The Public Mind, Its Disorders, Its Exploitation, 1926.
The Story of Money, 1930.
Can Governments Cure Unemployment? (with Harold Wright), 1931.
The Unseen Assassins, 1932.
The Press and the Organisation of Society, 1933.
The Great Illusion, 1933.
From Chaos to Control, 1933.
The Menace to our National Defence, 1934.
Preface to Peace, 1935.
The Money Mystery, 1936.
The Money Game, 1936.
This Have and Have-not Business, 1936.
The Defence of the Empire, 1937.
Is Pacifism the Road to Peace?, 1937.

The Great Illusion has appeared in England, America, France, Germany, Holland, Denmark, Sweden, Spain, Italy, Russia, Japan, and China, as well as in Hindi, Bengali, Urdu, Marathi and Tamail.

Norman Angell is an economic pacifist with a lucid style. A first rate expositor.

ROWNTREE, R. SEEBOHM (1871–   ).

Poverty, a Study of Town Life.
Betting and Gambling, a National Evil.
Land and Labour, 1910.
Unemployment (with B. Lasker).
A Social Study, 1911.
How the Labourer Lives (with May Kendall), 1913.
The Way to Industrial Peace, 1914.
The Human Needs of Labour, 1918.
The Human Factor in Business, 1921.

The titles describe the subject-matter of these volumes, which are liberal and humanitarian in spirit.

KEYNES, JOHN MAYNARD (1883–   ).

Indian Currency and Finance, 1913.
The Economic Consequences of the Peace, 1919.
A Treatise on Probability, 1921.
A Revision of the Treaty, 1922.
A Tract on Monetary Reform, 1923.
A Short View of Russia, 1925.
The End of Laissez-Faire, 1926.
A Treatise on Money, 2 vols., 1930.
Essays in Persuasion, 1931.
Essays in Biography, 1933.
The General Theory of Employment, Interest and Money, 1936.

The Economic Consequences of the Peace is an admirable book, still worth reading, though written to elucidate the European problem after the War.

WOOLF, LEONARD SIDNEY (1880–   ).

Politics:
International Government, 1916.
Co-operation and the Future of Industry, 1918.
The Future of Constantinople, 1917.
Empire and Commerce in Africa, 1920.
Socialism and Co-operation, 1921.
Hunting the Highbrow.
Essays, 1927.
Imperialism and Civilisation, 1928.
After the Deluge, 1931.

Fiction:
The Village in the Jungle, 1913.
The Wise Virgins, 1914.

Empire and Commerce in Africa is a devastating analysis of England's exploitation of the black races. The *Essays* are of popular interest. *The Village in the Jungle* is a brilliant novel.

LASKI, HAROLD J. (1893–   ).

The Problem of Sovereignty, 1917.
Authority in the Modern State, 1919.
Political Thought, from Locke to Bentham, 1920.

Foundations of Sovereignty, 1921.
A Grammar of Politics, 1925.
Communism, 1927.
Liberty in the Modern State, 1930.
The Dangers of Obedience, 1930.
An Introduction to Politics, 1931.
The Crisis and the Constitution, 1932.
Democracy in Crisis, 1933.
The State in Theory and Practice, 1935.
The Rise of European Liberalism, 1936.

Perhaps the most brilliant Left wing theorist.

STRACHEY, EVELYN JOHN ST. LOE (1901–).

Revolution By Reason, 1925.
Workers' Control in the Russian Mining Industry, 1928.
The Coming Struggle for Power, 1932.
The Menace of Fascism, 1933.
The Nature of the Capitalist Crisis, 1935.
The Theory and Practice of Socialism, 1936.

An effective Left Wing propagandist, with a clear style.

COLE, GEORGE DOUGLAS HOWARD (1889–).

The World of Labour, 1913.
Self-Government in Industry, 1917.
The Intelligent Man's Guide Through World Chaos,
and others.

Cole has a methodical statistical mind, which makes him an excellent guide to the reader who wants to know something about the contemporary confusion.

Other books on politics which have had some influence are *National Guilds*, edited by A. R. Orage, 1914, and various books by C. H. Douglas outlining the theory of Social Credit. The best of these are probably *Economic Democracy* and *Social Credit. Forward from Liberalism*, by Stephen Spender, is one of the most sympathetic arguments for Communism.

See also, under Poetry: Yeats, Pound, Eliot, Sitwell, Church, Auden, Spender, MacNeice. Under Fiction, see Wells, Bennett, Somerset Maughan, Colburn Mayne, Lawrence, Wyndham Lewis, Mackenzie, Huxley, Kingsmill, Dennis, O'Flaherty, Mitchison, Mottram, Blake, Nicholas, O'Faoláin, Sackville-West, Bates, Quennell, Hanley, Linklater, Plomer, Waugh, Allan. Under Drama, see Ervine, Coward.

CRITICISM

GRIERSON, SIR HERBERT JOHN (1866–   ).

The First Half of the Seventeenth Century (periods of European Literature), 1906.
The Poems of John Donne, edited with Introduction and Commentary, 1912.
Metaphysical Poets, Donne to Butler, 1921.
Blake's Illustrations to Gray's Poems, 1922.
The Background of English Literature and other Collected Essays, 1925.
The Poems of John Milton, 1925.
Lyrical Poetry from Blake to Hardy, 1928.
Cross-current in the Literature of the Seventeenth Century, 1929.
Letters of Sir Walter Scott, twelve Vols., issued 1937.
Carlyle and Hitler, 1933.
Milton and Wordsworth, Prophets and Poets, 1937.

The edition of Donne's poems is a great achievement of literary scholarship, and has considerably influenced the course of modern poetry. *Cross-Currents in the Literature of the Seventeenth Century* is indispensable to students of that period.

de SELINCOURT, ERNEST (1870–   ).
Editor of:
Hyperion, a facsimile of Keats's autograph MS. Edited with critical introduction and notes, 1905.
The Poems of Keats, a critical edition, 1905. Fifth edition, revised, 1926.

Poems of Keats (text), 1906.

Wordsworth's Guide to the Lakes, critical edition, 1906.

The Minor Poems of Spenser, with introduction and textual notes, 1910.

The Poems of Spenser, with biographical critical introduction, 1912.

Introduction to Landor's Imaginary Conversations. World's Classics, 1915.

Wordsworth's Prelude, edited from the MSS., 1926, 2nd edition revised, 1928.

Letters of William and Dorothy Wordsworth (1787–1805), 1935. *(1806–20)*, 2 vols., 1936.

Biography:
Dorothy Wordsworth, 1933.

Criticism:
Oxford Lectures on Poetry, 1934.
Wordsworth's Prelude is one of the great modern feats of editing.

SPURGEON, CAROLINE F. E. (1869–   ).

Mysticism in English Literature, 1913.
Five Hundred Years of Chaucer Criticism and Allusion, 1925.
Keats's Shakespeare, 1928.
Shakespeare's Imagery and What It Tells Us, 1935.

CHAMBERS, RAYMOND WILSON (1874–   ).

Widsith, a Study in Old English Heroic Legend, 1912.
England Before the Norman Conquest, 1926.
Thomas More, 1935.

He edited, along with W. P. Ker, *The Chronicle of Froissart* and many other books. The life of More is one of the best biographies which have appeared in recent years. The Introduction to his edition of *The Continuity of English Prose*, is a brilliant piece of historical criticism.

TILLYARD, EUSTACE MANDEVILLE WETENHALL (1889–   ).

The Hope Vases, a catalogue and discussion of the Greek Vases formerly in the Deepdene collection.

Lamb's Criticism.
The Poetry of Sir Thomas Wyatt, a Selection and a Study.
Milton, 1930.
Milton's Correspondence and Academic Exercises (with introduction and notes).
Poetry Direct and Oblique, 1937.
Shakespeare's Last Plays, 1938.

Milton is an admirable piece of independent criticism, both scholarly and vivacious. It may be regarded in part as a reply to Eliot's adverse comments on Milton. *Poetry Direct and Oblique* is a consideration of "obscurity" in poetry.

DOBRÉE, BONAMY (1891–   ).

Criticism and Biography:
Restoration Comedy, 1924.
Essays in Biography, 1925.
Histriophone.
Timotheus, 1925.
Sarah Churchill, 1927.
Restoration Tragedy, 1930.
The Lamp and the Lute, 1929.
Variety of Ways, 1932.
William Penn, 1932.
Letters of Lord Chesterfield, with Life, 1932.
John Wesley, 1933.
Giacomo Casanova, 1933.
As Their Friends Saw Them, 1933.
Modern Prose Style, 1934.

Historical:
The Floating Republic (with G. E. Manwaring), 1935.
English Revolts, 1938.

Fiction:
St. Martin's Summer.

Restoration Comedy and *Restoration Tragedy* are standard works on their subject, and are delightfully written. *Modern Prose Style* is indispensable to any student of contemporary literature. *The Lamp and the Lute* is a volume of criticism. Dobrée's criticism has a delightful lightness and balance.

291

FRY, ROGER (1866–1934).

> *Architectural Heresies of Painter*, 1921.
> *Characteristics of French Art*, 1932.
> *Henri Matisse*, 1935.
> *Reflections on British Painting.*
> *Ten Original Architectural Lithographs.*
> *Transformations.* Essays, 1926.
> *Vision and Design.* Essays, 1937.

An art critic. In *Vision and Design* he tentatively outlines a theory of art suited to the time.

MACARTHY, DESMOND (1878–   ).

> *Portraits.*
> *Criticism.*
> *Experience*, 1935.
> *Leslie Stephen*, 1937.

By far the most humane, open-minded and interesting of the traditional critics, with an urbane temper, a conversational style, and an absence of prejudice. The volumes of portraits and criticism are delightful reading.

MURRY, JOHN MIDDLETON (1889–   ).

> Criticism:
> *Fyodor Dostoevsky*, 1917.
> *The Evolution of an Intellectual*, 1920.
> *Aspects of Literature*, 1920.
> *The Things We Are*, 1922.
> *The Problem of Style*, 1922.
> *Pencillings*, 1923.
> *Discoveries*, 1924.
> *To The Unknown God*, 1924.
> *Keats and Shakespeare*, 1925.
> *Life of Jesus*, 1926.
> *Things to Come*, 1928.
> *God*, 1929.
> *Studies in Keats*, 1930.
> *Son of Woman*, 1931.

Countries of the Mind, 1931.
William Blake, 1933.
Between Two Worlds, 1934.
Shakespeare, 1936.
Heaven—and Earth, 1938.

Politics:
　The Necessity of Communism, 1932.
　The Necessity of Pacifism, 1937.

Biography:
　The Life of Katherine Mansfield (with Ruth E. Mantz), 1933.

Fiction:
　Still Life, 1917.
　The Voyage, 1924.

Poetry:
　Poems, 1919.

LUBBOCK, PERCY (1879–　　).

Criticism:
　The Craft of Fiction, 1921.

Fiction:
　Earlham, 1922.
　Roman Pictures, 1923.
　The Region Cloud, 1925.
　Shades of Eton, 1929.

The Craft of Fiction, though written in a somewhat cushioned style, contains some penetrating criticism of the novel.

WADDELL, HELEN (1889–　　).

Criticism:
　The Wandering Scholars, 1927.
　John of Salisbury in Essays and Studies, 1928.
　Beasts and Saints, 1934.
　The Desert Fathers, 1936.

Fiction:
　Peter Abelard, 1933.

Translation:
Mediaeval Latin Lyrics, 1929.
Lyrics from the Chinese, 1913.

LUCAS, FRANK LAURENCE (1894–   ).

Criticism:
Seneca and Elizabethan Tragedy.
Euripides and his Influence.
Authors Dead and Living.
Tragedy.
Eight Victorian Poets.
Studies, French and English.
The Decline and Fall of the Romantic Ideal.

Poetry:
Time and Money.
Marionettes.
Ariadne.
Poems, 1935.

Fiction:
Cecile.
The Woman Clothed With the Sun, and other Stories.

Drama:
Four Plays.
Editor of *The Complete Works of J. Webster.*
The Decline and Fall of the Romantic Ideal puts the case against
the current Eliotian trend of criticism.

PINTO, VIVIAN DE SOLA (1895–   ).

Criticism:
Sir Charles Sedley. A Study in the Life and Literature of
the Restoration, 1927.
Peter Sterry, Platonist and Puritan, a critical and biographical
study, with a selection from his writings, 1934.
Rochester. Portrait of a Restoration Poet, 1935.

Poetry:
Duality, 1919.
The Invisible Sun, 1934.

Editor of:

The Poetical and Dramatic Works of Sir Charles Sedley, edited with Prefaces, Commentary, etc., 1928.
The Tree of Life, an Anthology (with G. G. Neill Wright), 1929.
Selections from Shelley, edited with Introd. and Notes, 1931.
Lord Berners, a Selection from his Works, 1937.

RICHARDS, IVOR ARMSTRONG (1893–   ).

Foundations of Aesthetics (with C. K. Ogden and James Wood), 1921.
The Meaning of Meaning (with C. K. Ogden), 1923.
Principles of Literary Criticism, 1924.
Science and Poetry, 1925.
Practical Criticism, 1929.
Mencius on the Mind, 1931.
Basic Rules of Reason, 1933.
Coleridge on Imagination, 1934.

ROBERTS, MICHAEL

Poetry:
Poems, 1936.

Criticism:
Critique of Poetry, 1934.
The Modern Mind, 1937.
T. E. Hulme, 1938.

The Modern Mind contains some fine observations on the development of the English language and its connection with the change in our beliefs. It is a work of original thought and great interest.

STONIER, G. W.

Gog Magog.
Shadow Across Page, 1937.
Gog Magog is a study of modern literature.

LEAVIS, FRANK RAYMOND (1895–   ).
New Bearings in English Poetry.
For Continuity.
Mass Civilization and Minority Culture.
Culture and Enviroment (with Denys Thompson).

JAMES, D. G.
Scepticism and Poetry: An Essay on the Poetic Imagination, 1937.
A defence of the imagination as a genuine means of appre-
hending the world. Contains an incisive criticism of I. A.
Richard's theories.

HOARE, DOROTHY M.
*The Works of Morris and of Yeats in Relation to Early Saga
Literature,* 1937.

LEWIS, C. S.
The Allegory of Love, 1937.
An original and suggestive study of medieval tradition.

CAUDWELL, CHRISTOPHER (1907–37).
Illusion and Reality, 1937.
An extremely able piece of interpretative criticism from the
Marxian point of view.
Caudwell's real name was Christopher St. John Sprigge, under
which he wrote eight detective stories.

LYND, ROBERT (1879–   ).
Irish and English.
Portraits and Impressions, 1908.
Home Life in Ireland, 1909.
Rambles in Ireland, 1912.
The Book of This and That, 1915.
If the Germans Conquered England, and other Essays, 1917.
Old and New Masters.
Ireland a Nation, 1919.

The Passion of Labour, 1920.
The Art of Letters, 1921.
The Pleasure of Ignorance, 1921.
The Sporting Life, 1922.
Books and Authors, 1922.
Solomon in all his Glory, 1922.
The Blue Lion, 1923.
The Peal of Bells, 1924.
The Money-Box, 1925.
The Orange Tree, 1926.
The Little Angel, 1926.
The Goldfish, 1927.
Dr. Johnson and Company, 1928.
The Green Man, 1928.
It's a Fine World, 1930.
Rain, Rain, Go to Spain, 1901.
The Cockleshell, 1933.
Both Sides of the Road, 1934.
I Tremble to Think, 1936.
In Defence of Pink, 1937.

The most voluminous and probably the best of contemporary occasional essayists, whose criticism is always humane and always against ignorance, intolerance and humbug.

PRIESTLEY, JOHN BOYNTON (1894–   ).

Essays:
  Brief Diversions, 1922.
  Papers from Liliput, 1922.
  I for One, 1923.
  Talking, 1926.
  Self-selected Essays, 1932.

Criticism:
  Figures in Modern Literature, 1924.
  The English Comic Characters, 1925.
  George Meredith (English Men of Letters), 1926.
  Peacock (English Men of Letters), 1927.
  The English Novel, 1927.
  English Humour, 1928.

Travel:
  English Journey, 1934.
  Midnight on the Desert, 1937.

Fiction:
  Adam in Moonshine, 1927.
  The Good Companions, 1929.
  Angel Pavements, 1930.
  Doomsday Men, 1938.

Drama:
  Dangerous Corner, 1932.
  The Roundabout, 1933.
  Laburnam Grove, 1935.
  Duet in Floodlight, 1935.
  I Have Been Here Before, 1937.
  I'm a Stranger Here, 1937.

English Journey is an excellent survey of industrial England.

YOUNG, G. M.

  Gibbon.
  Charles I and Cromwell.
  Portrait of an Age (the Victorian).
  Daylight and Champaign, 1937.

STOKES, ADRIAN

  Stones of Rimini.

SCOTT, GEOFFREY

  The Architecture of Humanism (2nd ed. revised, 1924).
  Portrait of Zelide.

WILLIAMS, CHARLES

  Poetry at Present, 1930.
  The English Poetic Mind, 1932.
  Reason and Beauty in the Poetic Mind, 1933.

Play:
  Thomas Cranmer, 1936.

POTTER, STEPHEN

> *D. H. Lawrence.*
> *Coleridge and S.T.C.,* 1935.
> *The Muse in Chains,* 1937.

BARFIELD, OWEN

> *Poetic Diction,* 1928.

Shakespearian Studies have been abundant. Amongst these already noted under Middleton Murry and Caroline Spurgeon (together with Wyndham Lewis's *The Lion and the Fox*) may be placed

DOVER WILSON, JOHN (1881–   ).

> *The Essential Shakespeare,* 1932.
> and the Prefaces to the *New Cambridge Shakespeare.*

CHAMBERS, SIR EDMUND KERCHEVER (1866–   ).

> *William Shakespeare,* 1930.
> *The Elizabethan Stage,* 1923.

WILSON KNIGHT, G.

> *Myth and Miracle.*
> *The Wheel of Fire,* 1930.
> *The Imperial Theme,* 1931.
> *The Shakesperian Tempest,* 1932.
> *Principles of Shakespearian Production,* 1936.

CHARLTON, H. B.

> *Shakespearian Comedy,* 1938.

All these are of major importance. All more technical studies have been omitted; but the *Companion to Shakespeare Studies* provides the information leading to such studies.

Cognate studies are

BOAS, FREDERICK S.

Marlowe and his Circle, 1929.
Tudor Drama, 1933.

KNIGHTS, L. C.

Ben Jonson, 1937.
How Many Children had Lady Macbeth?, 1933.

WELSFORD, ENID

The Court Masque, 1927.
The Fool, His Social and Literary History, 1935.

ELLIS-FERMOR, U. M.

The Jacobean Drama, 1936.

WAR BOOKS

The following is a short selective list of war books, some of which have been mentioned under their authors. War reading is, for obvious reasons, an important element in the history of the period, and much of it can be ranked as literature.

Poetry:
  Wilfred Owen: *Poems*, 1921.
  Siegfried Sassoon: *Counter Attack*, 1918.
  Herbert Read: *Naked Warriors*, 1919.
  　　　　　　　The End of a War, 1933.
  David Jones: *In Parenthesis*, 1937.

The last is not only one of the best War books, but an extremely interesting literary experiment, partly in prose, partly in free verse, with considerable imaginative power.

Prose:

A very good and sufficiently comprehensive idea of the War literature of all nations on all fronts (including some poetry) is to be obtained in the anthology *Vain Glory*, edited by Guy Chapman, 1937.

  Edmund Blunden: *Undertones of War*, 1928.
  Robert Graves: *Goodbye to All That*, 1929.
  Herbert Read: *In Retreat*, 1925.
  Frederic Manning: *Her Privates We*, 1930.
  Siegfried Sassoon: *Memoirs of a Fox Hunting Man*, 1928.
  　　　　　　　　Memoirs of an Infantry Officer, 1930.
  The Master of Belhaven: *War Diaries*, 1924.
  R. H. Mottram: *Spanish Farm*, etc.
  Brigadier-General Spears: *Liaison*, 1914.
  V. M. Yeats: *Winged Victory*, 1934. A first-rate airman's book.
  Private Frank Richards: *Old Soldiers Never Die*, 1933. One of the best books by a non-commissioned man.

All the above deal with the Western Front. The best work on the feeling of the period is F. M. Ford's tetralogy (see under Ford).

An admirable view of naval activities is given by a collection of accounts under the title of *The Fighting at Jutland*, edited by H. W. Fawcett and G. W. W. Hooper. Compton Mackenzie: *Gallipoli Memories*, 1929, offers an interesting view, mainly from behind the front, of the Turkish adventure. T. E. Lawrence: *The Seven Pillars of Wisdom*, embodies the finest account of the Arab portion of the War.

The best short history of the War for popular reading is C. R. M. F. Caldwell's *A History of the Great War*, 1914–18, 1934.

INDEX OF NAMES

Numbers in Roman type refer to the Introduction, in *italics* to the Bibliography, and in heavy type to the Lists of Authors' works.

S

T

U

V

W